Fondazione Valore Italia

1961 / 2011

ITALIAN UNIQUENESS

THE MAKING
OF A NATIONAL IDENTITY

Marsilio

ITALIAN UNIQUENESS
THE MAKING OF A NATIONAL IDENTITY
1961/2011 Fifty years of *Italian know-how* through the Premio Compasso d'Oro ADI

With the High Patronage of the President of the Italian Republic, Giorgio Napolitano

1861 > 2011 > >
150° anniversario Unità d'Italia

Promoted by

Ministero
dello Sviluppo
Economico
Direzione Generale
per la Lotta alla Contraffazione -
Ufficio Italiano Brevetti e Marchi

Realized by

Fondazione Valore Italia

In collaboration with

ADI ASSOCIAZIONE
PER IL DISEGNO
INDUSTRIALE

FONDAZIONE ADI

ROMA CAPITALE
Assessorato alle Politiche Culturali e Centro Storico

Giovanni Alemanno
Mayor

Dino Gasperini
*Councillor for Cultural Policies
and the Historic Centre*

ESPOSIZIONE
PERMANENTE
DEL MADE IN ITALY
E DEL DESIGN
ITALIANO

Fondazione Valore Italia

Massimo Arlechino, *President*
Umberto Croppi, *Director*

Board of directors
Davide Viziano
Francesco Caroleo Grimaldi
Alberto di Luca
Ruben Razzante
Ignazio Abrignani

Auditing board
Renzo Bellora
Fabrizio Pescatori
Guido Perfetti

The Fondazione Valore Italia is the institution that
the Ministry of Economic Development has entrusted
with the *Esposizione Permanente del Made in Italy
e del Design Italiano* (The permanent exhibition
of Italian-made design and production). It is a body
directly responsible to the Ministry for planning the
economics of creativity and culture. Its main aim is
to capitalize on Italian productive excellence and the
heritage of knowledge that created it. In the context
of national policies for countering counterfeiting,
it backs up governmental activities with initiatives
to educate consumers in order to reinforce ideas about
the protection of intellectual and industrial property;
it does this by highlighting the creative and industrial
work that characterizes the excellence of Italian-made
products.

ITALIAN UNIQUENESS
THE MAKING OF A NATIONAL IDENTITY
1961/2011 Fifty years of *Italian know-how* through the Premio Compasso d'Oro ADI

Palazzo delle Esposizioni
MACRO Testaccio La Pelanda
Rome, 31 May - 25 September 2011

Show curated by
Enrico Morteo

Art Direction
Enzo Eusebi

Supervisory Committee
Antonio Marzano
Paolo Mieli
Giuseppe Roma

Steering Committee
Massimo Arlechino
Luisa Bocchietto
Umberto Croppi
Giovanni Cutolo
Enzo Eusebi
Luca Milan
Enrico Morteo
Claudio Maria Pascoli
Guido Maria Razzano
Alessandra Maria Sette
Giovanna Talocci

Organizational secretarial office
for the Fondazione Valore Italia
Assunta Di Giura
Valeria Di Marzo
Giuseppina Del Re
Alessandro Moresi
Claudio Papetti
Martina Teodori
Elisa Cecchi
Alessandro Ferrante
for ADI
Alessandra Fontaneto
in collaboration with
Giacomo Cesaro
Michele D'Innella

General coordination
Umberto Croppi
Coordination assistant
Alessandra Maria Sette

The Fondazione Valore Italia technical office
Luca Milan

Institutional Relations
Federica Alatri
Silvia Libianchi
Guido Maria Razzano

Communications and editorial coordination
Claudio Maria Pascoli

Press Office
Paolo Mazzanti
Laura Tecce

Legal consultancy
Roberto Pecorario

Installation design
Technical office, Fondazione Valore Italia
Enzo Eusebi

Logo and coordinated image
Humus Design srl

Installation
Cavir srl

Graphics realized by
Artiser srl

Transport
Montenovi srl

Videos realized by
Pixel srl

Catalogue edited by
Enrico Morteo
Alessandra Maria Sette

Photos by
Mimmo Capurso

Photographic references
Archivio Collezione Storica Compasso d'Oro (cscdo)
Archivio Storico della Presidenza della Repubblica
(ASPR), Archivio Fotografico, autorizzazione n. 5
Ugo Mulas © Ugo Mulas Heirs. All rights reserved

Translations
Isobel Butters (micro-stories)
Francesca Clementina Immirzi (micro-stories)
Michael Haggerty

The show has been realized in collaboration with

DIPARTIMENTO DESIGN
TECNOLOGIA DELL'ARCHITETTURA
TERRITORIO E AMBIENTE DATA

SAPIENZA
UNIVERSITÀ DI ROMA

The short films of the *Pre-visioni* series are by
Tommaso Agnese
Nicolò Lombardi
Alberto Scapin

The pieces of music for *Italian Uniqueness*
were specifically composed and played
by Maurizio Giammarco

Videos realized by
Show Biz Visual Communications Srl
Author and art direction
Enrico Morteo
Production, Ranuccio Sodi
Director, Daniele Zanzari
General organization and editorial coordination
Alessandra Messori
Shooting and photographs, Maurizio Romanelli
Cutting and editing, Grazia Licari, Maria Grazia
D'Andrea
Images and repertoire research
Mietta Albertini
Editing consultant, Alberto Saibene
Technical coordination and editorial office
Matteo Simone
Graphics and authoring, Lorenzo Todeschini
Stage, Mario Cavallini

Lenders
Archivio Bianchetti
Maurizio Cattelan Archive
Archivio Storico Fiat
Archivio Ugo Mulas
Archivio Storico Piaggio "Antonella Bechi Piaggio"
Archivio Storico Presidenza della Repubblica
Archivio Albe and Lica Steiner - DPA - Politecnico di Milano
Massimo and Sonia Cirulli Archive
Fondazione Marisa Bellisario
Fondazione Cittadellarte
Museo Piaggio
Brancolini Grimaldi
Enrico Morteo
Massimo Vitali
Centro Studi Teatro Stabile Torino
Istituto Nazionale Fisica Nucleare di Roma

MASSIMO & SONIA CIRULLI
ITALIAN VISUAL, DECORATIVE AND
ADVERTISING ART OF XX CENTURY **ARCHIVE**
WWW.CIRULLIARCHIVE.ORG

The cataloguing of the Massimo & Sonia Cirulli
Archive was developed together with the Agenzia
nazionale per le nuove tecnologie, l'energia
e lo sviluppo economico sostenibile - ENEA, Italy

Acknowledgements
The curator, Enrico Morteo, and the Fondazione
Valore Italia would like to thank all those who have
willingly offered their help:
Mario Bellini, Cini Boeri, Alberto Bombassei,
Franco Cardini, Piero Castiglioni, Giovanni F. Casucci,
Aldo Cibic, Philippe Daverio, Michele De Lucchi,
Piero Derossi, Maurizio Ferraris, Beppe Finessi,
Elio Fiorucci, Roberto Gavazzi, Giorgetto Giugiaro,
Aldo Grasso, Giulio Iacchetti, Antonia Jannone,
Franco La Cecla, Italo Lupi, Massimo Marchiori,
Vittorio Marchis, Alessandro Mendini, Cristina Morozzi,
Giampiero Mughini, Gaetano Pesce, Stefano Pistolini,
Franco Raggi, Paolo Rizzatto, Patricia Urquiola.

We also thank
Stefania Bruni, Vincenzo Chianese, Yuri Consorti,
Michela Corrado, Riccardo D'Orazi, Pierpaolo Filipponi,
Lara Gabriele, Rosario Mastrobattista, Lorenzo
Moretti, Luigi Pecorario, Laura Pellegrini, Fabio
Varese, Marco Vecchiattini: with their professionalism
they have all helped towards the realization of the
event.

Our particular thanks to
Mario De Simoni and to all the staff
of the Palazzo delle Esposizioni.

The President of the Fondazione Valore Italia thanks
Luigi Mastrobuono, the Head of the Department
of the Ministry of Economic Development; Giuseppe
Tripoli, the Head of the Department for Business and
Internationalization; and Loredana Gulino, the General
Director of the UIBM Department for the Fight against
Counterfeiting.

Gianni Letta, under-secretary to the Presidency
of the Council of Ministers, has supported *Italian
Uniqueness* from the very first.

Index

Italian Uniqueness 1961/2011

The Compasso d'Oro Collection and Show

Stories

GIOVANNI ALEMANNO

The Mayor of Roma Capitale

In 1954, the premio Compasso d'Oro prize was established in Italy: one of the most prestigious design awards in the world. In 2004, with an initiative that had no precedents in the field of international design, the Ministry of Cultural Heritage and Activities announced that the premio Compasso d'Oro - ADI collection with its more than 300 projects was "of exceptional artistic and historical interest" and, as a result, would become part of the national heritage.

Today the *Italian Uniqueness. 1961/2011 The Making of a National Identity* exhibition in Rome, which is part of the official programme of the celebrations for the 150th anniversary of Italian unity, will have as its protagonists the historical collection of the Compasso d'Oro, the 22nd edition of the prize, and the three young winners of a competition organised together with Rome's Centro Sperimentale di Cinematografia.

We must thank the Fondazione Valore Italia for having promoted and advanced Italian products – design in particular – in two of the city's most important exhibition centres. In the rooms of the Palazzo delle Esposizioni, in fact, the public will be able to see the historical collection of the Compasso d'Oro prize and so follow the past fifty years of high quality Italian creativity. In the rooms of MACRO Testaccio and La Pelanda, recently converted into exhibition areas, some four hundred objects competing for the 22nd edition of the prize will be on view.

So, for this cultural event offered by the City of Rome, an art venue has become complementary to a place that once manufactured industrial products. It is part of an ideal itinerary that starts from the city centre, passes by the Pyramid, and leads towards the Eur and the historic Palazzo della Civiltà Italiana, the future headquarters of the Fondazione Valore Italia and of the *Esposizione Permanente del Made in Italy e del Design Italiano*. This is the most recent event in a series of exhibitions that began two years ago with a show in the Ara Pacis called *Disegno e Design. Brevetti e creatività italiana*.

It is a journey that explores and highlights numerous examples of Italian creativity united with industrial production, of beauty united with function: a union the has generated a heritage of images that are by now part of our daily life, though we are often unaware of their origins.

PAOLO ROMANI
Minister of Economic Development

With *Italian Uniqueness* the Italian productive system makes a fully justified entry into the festivities for the hundred and fiftieth anniversary of Italian unity. This is a concrete way of making sure that these celebrations become a part of real, everyday life by reminding us just what an important element our know-how has contributed to our national identity

It is also a way for laying a basis for the commitment that the country/system (excuse the use of a rather overused term) has to face up to in the world's new economic context: today products made in Italy need to maintain their connotations of *uniqueness* while bringing them into line with new market conditions.

The event organised by the Fondazione Valore Italia has the merit of not simply dwelling on the recent past but also of underlining those high-quality characteristics that have allowed our country to become one of the top ten of the world's most highly industrialized nations; a further merit of both the show and the present catalogue is to ask questions about the future.

What must Italian production do in order to better face up to the challenge of globalization? Apart from increasing our efforts in sectors with a higher degree of innovation, does it still make sense to involve ourselves in more traditional manufacturing sectors, thanks to which we have become famous throughout the world? And if yes, on what terms?

The Ministry of Economic Development has for some time been active in the task of removing all those obstacles to development that our businesses might come up against in both domestic and foreign markets. In the past few years we have undertaken a progressive simplification of many rules regarding business; the system for public incentives has been reviewed, and now we are working on the application of an efficient policy for the protection of intellectual and industrial property.

Our Fondazione Valore Italia, which for the ministry plays an important role as a planning laboratory in the field of creative and cultural economy, is giving important backup to the application of these policies. On this occasion *Italian Uniqueness* has had the merit of having pinpointed the historical collection of the Compasso d'Oro - ADI as a qualified means for this journey through our productive system.

I must compliment the Fondazione Valore Italia for the work it has undertaken so far and for having given us, with this show, an important foretaste of what will be seen in the forthcoming *Esposizione Permanente del Made in Italy e del Design Italiano*.

I would like to finish by giving my deepest thanks to the protagonists of this great history: the businessmen and all those others whose work has allowed the birth and development of Italian production. I hope that *Italian Uniqueness* might be a festival for them above all, one from which to draw energy in order to continue the fascinating journey of quality and excellence.

GIANCARLO GALAN
Minister of Cultural Heritage and Activities

The important event of the celebrations of the hundred and fiftieth anniversary of Italian unification has meant a notable commitment, both organisationally and economically, for the Ministry of Cultural Heritage and Activities, together with the departments of the Prime Minister's office.

This has been an occasion for launching important works for a reappraisal our cultural heritage and also a way for being able to organise events throughout Italy, events through which to discover, each time from a different viewpoint, the roots of our sense of identity which are constantly reinforced by the confluence in Italian culture of many local traditions and cultures. But I am particularly happy that the *Italian Uniqueness* event has allowed me to celebrate a particular aspect that has contributed to the unification of our nation: the culture of a well-made enterprise.

A mixture between our cultural heritage and industrial production should certainly not be a surprise. The same habit of collaboration which has been established with the Fondazione Valore Italia and the various departments of the ministry I have the honour to direct, allows an understanding of the increasingly close identification between "know-how" and the "cultural system". And in fact this is how it is: our high-quality production stands on a firm cultural basis that considers beauty and well-made objects as cardinal elements and, in its turn, the progress of Italian-made production leads to a reinforcement of this cultural tradition of ours.

The *Italian Uniqueness* show, together with the essays in this catalogue, will help the visitor/reader to pinpoint the various areas of contact between culture and industry, and to understand how this reciprocal contamination has been almost exclusive to Italian production. It is this Italian uniqueness that I would like to underline in this brief note.

I must thank the Fondazione Valore Italia for the great work it has been carrying out for years with regard to this particular aspect of the cultural development of our high-quality production: it has been able to find an interpretative key that could be of great help to our economic system and maintain its particular competitiveness on the world markets. And I must express a particular pleasure in knowing that the future *Esposizione Permanente del Made in Italy e del Design Italiano*, the realisation and management of which are the main mission of the Fondazione, will begin with an important contribution from the departments of my ministry in close collaboration with our Beni Sonori ed Audiovisivi central institute for sound and audiovisual projects. It will be housed in a building (the Palazzo della Civiltà Italiana in Rome) which is a masterpiece of Italian rationalist architecture. I am convinced that our reciprocal collaboration will give rise to a situation that, thanks to Italian-made production, will contribute to reinforcing the links that identify us.

DINO GASPERINI

Councillor for Cultural Policies and the Historic Centre of Roma Capitale

"An artist's dream is in any case to find a place in a museum, while the designer's dream is to find a place in the local market." Bruno Munari, a versatile man concerned with the art of design of art and the art of design, highlights the categories of the "final destination" – museums or markets – and of the "public" – observers or potential clients – as the basic difference between art and design. On the one hand the artist seeks admiration. On the other, the designer seeks usefulness. So on the one hand there is an awareness of the extraordinariness and thus the undoubted, or almost undoubted, unrepeatability of the piece – leaving aside the need to discuss the importance of copies and multiples – and on the other the search for the greatest efficiency and popularity produced by multiplication and repeatability themselves. Again: on the one hand there is the success surrounding the name of the artist. On the other the success that, perhaps, is only really such when the artist's name is forgotten and attention is given only to the product. It is sufficient to think of anonymous design, a neglected but not negligible presence in all our homes. Today more than ever art is design and for many it represents their most accessible – though at certain levels not always accessible to everyone – contact with beauty. A democratic beauty, to be contemplated and experienced. An everyday beauty to be consumed and studied.

In museums design is part of the marvels of forms and history chronicling consumption, and also chronicling customs. Year after year, object after object. And so design, a term which in its widest sense involves disciplines and sectors deeply different from each other, is the witness to whole epochs: it is a record, icon and muse in an interplay of quotations and evolutions that the market passes down to our storehouse of images, and vice-versa. The shows concentrates on fifty years of "Italian know-how", as the title suggests: a half century of Italian production on a journey through national excellence documented and underpinned by the selection of the Compasso d'Oro which shows us production and taste, the imagination and rules of creativity, from the project to the product, from an individual's idea to a fashion followed by many.

And at its heart is the history of our country, seen in films, advertising, the market and marketing: consumption in its being as an object and a subject, between tradition and innovation, history and its communications, economy and geography. In other words, identity.

MASSIMO ARLECHINO
President of the Fondazione Valore Italia

With *Italian Uniqueness* we wish to celebrate the one hundred and fiftieth anniversary of our nation in a way that is quite different from the other major festivities which, quite rightly, are centred on the rediscovery of our Risorgimento fathers and their relevance today. However, we of the Fondazione Valore Italia have another task: to favour and promote Italian know-how: in other words, our high-quality production.

Because what else has made us proud of being Italian over the past fifty years? This is why our event focuses on the role that products made in Italy have had in reinforcing our feelings of national identity in the years from 1961, the last celebration of Italian unity, until today: a period that almost perfectly coincides with the development and affirmation of our products throughout the markets of the world.

The similarity between the words uniqueness and unity is quite clear: the uniqueness of our know-how is a factor of our unity and, at the same time, it is our unity that allows us to maintain and develop uniqueness. And that "our" in these two phrases means "us": the human factor, the adhesive that binds together unity and uniqueness!

Of course *Italian Uniqueness* is an exhibition, but it is not just that. It aims to give its own contribution to a new way of thinking, a new way of consuming, a new way of producing.

Over the past fifty years Italy has undergone hardships from an economic and social point of view. It has had, however, protagonists – businessmen and workers – able to originate and produce small masterpieces, objects of everyday or exclusive use, but objects which are always characterized by the highest quality and the capacity to transmit emotions.

Today our designers, businessmen and workers realize that they are having to undergo a new and difficult period, an economic difficulty that is prevalent throughout the whole world and which risks undermining our productive identity: with *Italian Uniqueness* we hope to rediscover the treasures we can offer. We want to make consumers understand why Italian products have an extra gear with respect to other foreign competitors; but we also want to initiate a serious mutual discussion on which to base our future and to make sure that in 2061, for the two hundredth anniversary of Italian unity, there will still be a frontline "uniqueness" to celebrate.

We must offer our heartfelt thanks to Giorgio Napolitano, the President of the Republic, who, with his activity over the past years, has helped us to understand the importance of the celebrations for our hundred and fiftieth years' anniversary; to Silvio Berlusconi, our Prime Minister who, during his period as interim Minister for Economic Development, entrusted the Fondazione with the task of constructing an event which has allowed us to celebrate Italy's birthday by giving an overview of the development of our high-quality production. And we must also thank Minister Romani for having backed this initiative throughout its realization.

In order to accomplish all this we have had the precious collaboration of the Fondazione ADI which put at our disposal the collection of the Compasso d'Oro prize in order to construct the various stages of a development which, we hope, might continue and be part of the celebrations for the two hundredth anniversary of Italian unity.

LUISA BOCCHIETTO *President of* ADI
GIOVANNI CUTOLO *President of the Fondazione* ADI

Thanks to the sensitivity, backing and commitment of the Fondazione Valore Italia, and of the Ministry of Economic Development and of the other institutions in general, design has finally been recognised as an identity mark of the new Italy and as such placed at the heart of the Roman festivities for the hundred and fiftieth anniversary of the unity of our country.

The evident proof of this is to be seen in the two large shows in the Palazzo delle Esposizioni and in MACRO Testaccio, installed thanks to the essential collaboration of ADI and the Fondazione ADI.

After over fifty years of backing and promoting the economic, social and cultural values of design, we can now say that we are greatly satisfied.

Design today, however much it is considered a strongpoint of the economy if not of culture, has grown and consolidated itself outside the important cultural institutions of our country.

Confident of its own autonomy and its disruptive energetic drive, design in fact has allowed itself to be promoted through the pages of magazines, posters for fairs and the thousands of shop widows in which its products have been advertised.

It is not out of place to note that even today Italy still does not have a national museum that systematically and exhaustively collects the most significant design objects and investigates the various areas of design activity. If we make an exception for the occasional help given by public institutions when design has been an excuse for demonstrating the quality of our exports, only the universities have attempted to keep track of design's history and culture. Of course this has not stopped many archives of project-makers and designers from finishing up in France, Switzerland, America, Canada and Germany.

All told, we can unhesitatingly state that until now design has been an activity sustained by private businesses; there is, of course, no doubting their ability to produce, but they have not always been interested in evaluating and historicizing design for the future.

But on the other hand, ADI and the Fondazione ADI are bodies that were founded on the autonomous decision of professionals and entrepreneurs.

LOREDANA GULINO

General Director of the Department for the Fight against Counterfeiting - UIBM
The Ministry of Economic Development

Whoever passes by the Palazzo della Civiltà Italiana in Rome, the venue for the forthcoming permanent exhibition of products made in Italy, will find it difficult to ignore the inscription that decorates this characteristic building, known as the square Coliseum: "A POPULATION OF POETS OF ARTISTS OF HEROES / OF SAINTS OF THINKERS OF SCIENTISTS / OF NAVIGATORS OF TRANSMIGRANTS". This definition condenses in itself the spirit and vocation of the Italian people from their birth, a birth which was marked by creative ardour, inventive ability, a love of culture and an enthusiasm for transmitting it.

Our peninsula, located right in the middle of the Mediterranean, was for centuries the heart, if not of the world as the ancients believed, at least of the European system; it was the cradle of the highest civilisation which, because of its intellectual and artistic vitality, left a mark on every one of its regions. Invention and creativity have always been for Italy a sign of undoubted value, a distinctive and strongly characterised element recognised throughout the world through products made in Italy. This is the history of our evolution and progress, our capacity to make innovations, and to know how to give fresh lymph and a renewed impulse to our country's economy and to change that very innovation into social wellbeing. Just think of the inventions that in these 150 years of Italian unity have made the life of the Italians simpler, better and more sustainable. In the sphere of inventive capacity, design has an indisputable role; it is an element able to confer an inimitable style on an object – so much so as to make it an icon of its own times – and, at the same time, to make it into a universally accessible product. Italian design, in fact, is a projection of what over the centuries our architecture once was. Design "touches on every aspect of human creativity [...] design has been called 'intelligence made visible' [...] design is to be found where form meets function" (Francis Gurry, *Message on the Occasion of the World Day for Intellectual Property 2011*), and it is certainly what mostly marks us out from the rest of the world, so much so that various design objects have become an integral part of the world's artistic heritage. And if it is true that in principle "a work of art has always been imitable by man [...]" (Walter Benjamin, *The Work of Art in the Age of its Technical Reproducibility. Art and Mass Society*), it is nonetheless fundamental to protect the originality and uniqueness of inventions. Widespread reproduction of an authentic object, following the healthy rules of the market, is quite different from the production of manufactured articles, for which "[...] the authenticity of something is the quintessence of every thing that, right from its origins, can be handed on, from its material duration to its virtue as a historical record (*ibid.*, p. 9)."

A heritage of inventive capacity and of intuition, such as Italy alone can vaunt, would not today have left a trace of itself had we not guaranteed a valid protection for it through the system of industrial property rights which today is a beacon for our economy. Knowing how to invent, innovate and make projects is closely linked to the possibility of seeing one's own ideas protected as a result of that group of norms and laws which today allow us to enjoy a historical development of such extraordinary value, one which already allows us to write the next 150 years of the creative and innovative history of our country.

UMBERTO BROCCOLI

Superintendent, the Cultural Affairs Department of Roma Capitale

There are things that bring us closer together. Objects that eliminate distances. Objects created here in Italy that have united the world.

Just consider the telephone. To speak from one end of the world to another is taken for granted, but years ago whole weeks were needed to have news about someone in another city: there were letters, and this was pleasant, but it was also slow and subject to chance. And then, to hear the voice of someone we love is something else again. Here we find ourselves close together, and we can talk as though we were at home together. What a great gift Antonio Meucci gave us, a gift that is wholly Italian, though this was only recognized much later (in 2002) because, as always, success has many parents (but failure only one).

The Italian didn't have the necessary ten dollars for renewing his temporary patent and so Alexander Bell took over his idea and patented it in his place.

Marconi's radio is another invention we should be proud of: the precursor of all telecommunications and of globalisation. "[...] in recognition of the contribution given to the development of wireless telegraphy." This was part of the motivation given by the Nobel Academy of Science in Sweden.

We can only imagine the emotion when, in the fields near Bologna, the physicist was told for the first time of the reception of a signal received from the firing of a rifle. As Marconi wrote: "I rapidly convinced myself that, if it were possible to transmit and receive in a secure manner these waves or ones similar to them, a new communications system could be realised."

Then there are inventions for which Italy's claim is controversial.

The compass is one of these. According to tradition, Flavio Gioia from Amalfi invented it. But there are those who dissent and say that Gioia was only the chronicler who took note of the invention made by people from Amalfi: this led to a mistaken tradition.

Much the same goes for the pizza and pasta: were the Chinese behind them? It might well be. But the Chinese knew nothing about wheat and they made their noodles with millet. Well, it's not the same thing.

And then pasta is a product made in Italy which is by now known throughout the world: we are famous for our spaghetti as well as for mandolins.

And plastic? In an old TV advert Gino Bramieri, when his wife was busy with her architectural business, had to act the part of a housewife. And here was the answer: "oh mo, mo, mo... Moplen!". Plastic was revolutionary and is used for all kitchen utensils. Today we cannot even think of doing without it. The chemist, Giulio Natta, was its ingenious inventor. He too won the Nobel prize in 1963, and he too was a genuine Italian. "Listen Signora: it has to made from Moplen!"

And so the Italian brand has always been recognised throughout the world, and it has had disciples and imitators. Often it has brought together distant fellow countrymen and even made those on the other side of the ocean feel back at home. Today, now that our Republic is celebrating its 150th birthday, we can feel ourselves a single body under many guises, including the one that has always marked us out: creativity.

EMMANUELE FRANCESCO MARIA EMANUELE
President of the Azienda Speciale Palaexpo

The Palazzo delle Esposizioni is pleased to flank its art exhibitions with this beautiful and intelligent show devoted to the excellence of Italian design.

This will be an opportunity for showing our public the other side of creativity.

I have always believed it to be necessary to think of the creations of visual arts and of design by taking into consideration that they have different functions while, however, keeping in mind that both originate from flair, talent, invention and imagination.

I hope that this show of the winning products of the prestigious premio Compasso d'Oro, started up in 1954 by La Rinascente and, since 1958, organised by the Associazione per il Disegno Industriale, the Italian industrial design association, might lead to thoughts about the complexity and importance of design as well as showing the high quality and the international renown of Italian production. Thanks to the way in which the show has been thought out and structured by the Fondazione Valore Italia – which I thank for the work it has undertaken – it will be possible to reflect on the relationships between design and the visual arts through various significant interconnections; and above all it will be possible to verify the links between creative design and planning that emerge in a work environment where invention, technology and artisan know-how still magically live together and where Italy has an undisputed first place.

And, finally, I hope that the show can offer above all an overview of the history of design of the past fifty years – and not just in Italy, because many of the products exhibited have spread throughout the world. Nothing more than design is part of everyday life. And when we speak about design, apart from referring to exclusive and elite production, we must also and with greater immediacy – the award of the prize demonstrates this – relate it to a shared taste and behaviour that it has helped form. In our society design is democratic: it has allowed us access to greater freedom; it guarantees health, increases the civil values of living together and it is an indication of decorum as well, of course, as luxury. And we can understand the spirit of the times through it. Furthermore, I would like to underline that the show holds a pleasant surprise: it will demonstrate that, despite the dizzy speeding up due to increased technology and consumerism, the contemporary world is still able to create forms – in the case of design, objects – that have the capacity to remain valid over time and to renew the category of what is *classic*.

LUCA MASSIMO BARBERO

Director, MACRO

The show *Italian Uniqueness*, held in the La Pelanda exhibition rooms of the MACRO Testaccio Museum, offers a panorama of one of the aspects of contemporary creativity for which Italy is best known throughout the world: that of industrial design. The show has an added value now when we are celebrating the 150th anniversary of the unification of Italy: it maps out experiments undertaken over the past fifty years and presents the highlights of a positive development and of common growth. Inside an exhibition space already strongly characterised by its industrial architectural forms, recently readapted to hosting an art and culture centre, the design objects from recent years find their ideal setting and can dialogue with the structures and size of a building that maintains its vocation as a producer of contemporary ideas, visions and content. After theatre, performance arts, cinema and the visual arts, design too has now entered a museum always receptive to contaminations, dialogue and meetings in an exhibition that also aims at being a forum for examining and debating the themes of contemporary creativity.

The show, promoted by the Fondazione Valore Italia and by the Associazione per il Disegno Industriale, presents some four hundred Italian objects of the highest quality, selected between 2008 and 2010 by the Osservatorio Permanente per il Design, designs which are in the running for the 22nd premio Compasso d'Oro award. This is a broad and carefully selected collection of contemporary high-quality products which relate not just to the world of production, but also to that of research, experimentation and contamination, themes which are currently topical even in the fields of visual communications and marketing. This is a journey through design that allows us to follow the evolution of its languages and to recognise the contamination between the various arts as well as pinpointing the development of taste and behaviour. These are objects that have become part of our daily life and show themselves to be the signs of Italian society's collective memory which, thanks to them, has become a "new aesthetic society".

What is also important is the collaboration between MACRO and another prestigious Roman institution: the Palazzo delle Esposizioni. This, concurrently with the show in La Pelanda, will be hosting in its own rooms the Compasso d'Oro historical collection of objects and symbols of our national identity. In this way we will be underlining the importance of a dialogue and cooperation between the city's various cultural situations which are all involved and concerned with the common objective of making Rome, once more and even more, a capital of contemporaneity. The collaboration with the Fondazione Valore Italia, concerned with the promotion of products made in Italy and with Italian design, is also completely compatible with MACRO's mission to increase the appreciation of all forms of art.

In this way MACRO confirms its interest in being receptive to all the different forms of art and its commitment to promoting various ways for encouraging the public to participate by stimulating its interest and inviting it to have an increasingly hands-on approach to the vast world of art forms.

GUIDO MARIA RAZZANO
Fondazione Valore Italia

THE ROOTS OF THE *ITALIAN UNIQUENESS* EXHIBITION

The political resurgence of a nation must never be separated from its economic resurgence. The conditions of the two progresses are exactly the same. Civic virtues, the prudent laws that equally protect every right and good political organisation indispensible for bettering the moral conditions of a nation are also the main causes of its economic progress.

Where there is no public life, where national sentiment is weak, then there will never be a powerful industry. [...] The economic conditions of a people are favourable as far as is possible, as long as progressive energy acts in an orderly manner. However, in order to operate and prosper, industry needs freedom; we have no hesitation in stating that its progress is more universal and rapid in a State that, even if undergoing disturbances, has a solid base of freedom, than in one that is tranquil but exists under the weight of a repressive and regressive system [...] We fully believe in the future of Italian industry, not because of the beneficial reforms based on our principles, [...] but mainly because we are confident that out fellow citizens can be awakened and called to a new political life, to that skill, that laboriousness, and that energy that characterised the greatest masters, the powerful and the rich in the Middle Ages when the Florentine and Lombard workshops, and the Genoese and Venetian shipyards were unrivalled in Europe. Yes: we believe in the skill, energy and workmanship of the Italians.

These are the words that Camillo Benso, Count of Cavour, wrote in the first issue of the "Il Risorgimento" newspaper which was issued on December, 15, 1847, and edited by him and Cesare Balbo.

I like the idea of using these thoughts, by the man who was the main strategist of Italian unity, as a starting point for explaining the function that Italian know-how and products made in Italy have developed and continue to develop in reinforcing our sense of identity.

In 1847, at the beginning of his political career, Cavour had already understood that national feelings and industry are bound by an invisible thread that must not be broken, and that, by being based on our predecessors' (the "greatest masters") knowledge of making, Italian manufacturing culture could contribute to "making the Italians": I am paraphrasing one of his most famous sayings, even though its attribution is uncertain (was it by D'Azeglio?), one which he pronounced after the proclamation of the Kingdom of Italy in 1861. We might perhaps say that he had already understood that Italy was to become an important nation as a result of products made in Italy, even though we know that these words were inspired in him by his deep admiration for the British economic and productive system which, at that period, had reached deep industrial maturity.

The scope of the present catalogue and the event which inspired it, is that of making a small contribution to products made in Italy in the 21st century. Its aim is to show how Italian *Uniqueness* is a factor of its *Unity*, and how this *Unity* is necessary for continuing to produce *Uniqueness*.

The idea for the show originated after a note from the presidency of the council of ministers in 2008, which in view of the celebrations for the 150th anniversary of Italian unity – recently declared to be "a great national event" – hoped for the creation of events tending to "recuperate the prerogatives of national unity useful for increasing social cohesion, the processes for building knowledge and the vitality of ideals, as well as to inspire courageous choices for arousing new impulses and trust in the future."

The Fondazione Valore Italia, a department of the ministry for economic development, is by its nature aimed at the study and analysis of the national productive system, with a particular interest in all those sectors showing excellence at an international level and which are at the heart of the success of the made in Italy phenomenon. So from the very start we have considered it necessary to contribute to what the presidency of the council asked for by advancing the uniqueness of our economic and productive system on the world panorama. The occasion of the 150th anniversary was also useful for analysing the situations in which the two previous anniversary celebrations had taken place; in both we discovered a strong sense of feelings of identity and of a great spur towards, and trust in, the future.

The 1911 anniversary, even though it occurred in a period of great social disruption in Italy, was the culmination of a half century devoted to completing the Risorgimento processes: the annexation to the Kingdom of Italy of the Veneto territories (1866) and Rome (1870); the unification of the administrative, monetary, postal and scholastic system of the various pre-unification states; the beginning of the processes for industrialising the country energised by the north-eastern "industrial triangle"; the wish to place Italy among the international powers (1911 saw the end of the war with Turkey for the conquest of Libya); great cultural agitation about national feelings: just think of the work and political involvement (sometimes at first hand in the institutions of the newly formed kingdom) of Manzoni, Carducci, Pascoli, Verdi, D'Annunzio and Salvemini, to mention only a few; and the birth of what we might call the last real avant-garde movement in Italy: Futurism. Throughout the first fifty years of unity all the sectors of Italian public life were pervaded by a strong feeling of national identity. In politics, economy, culture and the great social debates of the time the leitmotif was always the need to "make Italy and the Italians".

If possible, the feeling behind the celebrations of the centenary of unity in 1961 were even stronger. The fifty years from 1911 to 1961 were marked by events that are so well known that it is not necessary to investigate them deeply in order to understand how much they have been influenced, and how much they in turn have influenced, our feelings of national identity. Two world wars, twenty years of Fascism between them, the war for liberation and the building of a new Italy, the change of the form of the state in 1946, the miracle of reconstruction and the economic boom... these were fifty years in which history seems to have speeded up, so different was Italy before and Italy after. The centenary was celebrated with the Lira which had just been awarded the "Oscar for monetary stability", proof of how a country destroyed by war had been able, in just fifteen years, to reconstruct itself from its own ruins, probably managing to "nurture courageous choices for giving a new impulse and faith in the future" as has been requested of us for 2011. And the year preceding the centenary, 1960, had witnessed the success of the Rome Olympics, which gave the world a new idea of Italy and its potential.

Can we say, with respect to the previous two fifty-year periods, that the fifty years terminating with the current celebrations for the 150th anniversary, have seen similar impulses to national cohesion and identification? Undoubtedly no.

The historical, social and political development of Italy since 1961 has meant that national feeing has slowly been on the wane, to the point of making almost anachronistic any kind of event containing any national kind of symbolism, whether flying the national flag, the singing of the national anthem, or the use of the words "homeland" or "nation". A kindly form of consent is only to be seen for great sporting victories, starting with the famous 4-3 victory of Italy over Germany in Mexico in 1970.

Only in recent years has there been any official intention to put a brake on the sense of "decline" that has almost unknowingly entered all sectors of Italian life and that has caused the progressive deterioration of our *idem sentire* and our sense of belonging to the same community.

With this in mind, President Carlo Azeglio Ciampi was the first to want to give Italians a good shaking to wake us up from the apathy into which we were slowly falling. It was he, during his seven years as president (1999-2006), who opened the presidential residence to families, who travelled around the country from top to bottom, province by province, town by town, and who made a firm stand against the inevitable impoverishment of the civic sense and role that Italy can still have in the fields of international culture and economy. And it was President Ciampi who wanted to create a basis so that the 150 years of unity might mark a new point of departure in Italian history and give life to a new drive towards national cohesion and identity.

His successor, Giorgio Napolitano, has followed the path marked out by Ciampi, and the message he sent to us recently is wholly concentrated on the concept that "if we are united we can overcome any difficulty", just as the fathers of the Risorgimento had done.

So where should we start from? From our strong points. And one of these is, without a doubt, our know-how, the capacity our productive system has expressed by uniting creativity to serial production, by mixing quantity and quality, taste and a search for beauty, and by gaining world leadership in many productive sectors.

On the other hand, all of us must at some time or other have come to a halt, proud of being Italian, in front of a high-quality product of mechanics or fashion or food farming or design... and with an even greater sense of pride when that happened abroad and under the eyes of foreign observers, stunned by the *uniqueness* inherent in our products. Above all over the past fifty years, it has been this uniqueness that has underpinned our unity, and it is only by remaining united that such uniqueness can continue to be make itself felt.

This is why the two words unity and uniqueness characterise the celebratory proposal by the Fondazione Valore Italia: we want to emphasise the role they have had in reinforcing our feeling of national identity and in the definition of our being Italian with respect to the rest of the world.

This explains why the subtitle of *Italian Uniqueness* is *The Making of a National Identity*. It illustrates the objective we are aiming for.

In order to do this we have decided to adopt as our fellow companion a part of our national heritage that is still undervalued but which comments faithfully on the evolution of our know-how and on the high points of our productive system: the historical collection of the Compasso d'Oro. The history of the prize and the value of the collection, managed respectively by ADI and the Fondazione ADI, are illustrated in other parts of this catalogue which the reader should peruse. It is the diachronic aspect expressed by the historical collection that allows us to see how, from the post-war period until today, the phenomenon of the made in Italy label has matured, the reasons why it has been able to enjoy global success, and how Italy has changed together with it.

These aspects are the main aim of the part of the show installed in the Palazzo delle Esposizioni in Rome which gives an overview of the third fifty-year period of our national unity.

Our aim has never been limited to a retrospective history but also to opening a debate about what role Italy will play over the next fifty years.

This wish has been reinforced by the observation that, on the basis of data supplied by Istat, the population resident in Italy in 2011 is made up of not much more than 60% of people under the age of fifty. So for almost two thirds of the population the year 2011 is the first occasion in their life for them to celebrate the jubilee of our unification and take time to think about the role of Italy on the map of history. And it is necessary to underline that a large part of this resident population consists of "new Italians" who have come from other countries but who wish to be fully integrated into their new homeland: together with them we are asked to construct the Italy that, in 2061, will celebrate two hundred years of unity.

The present and future are the main players in the show in La Pelanda and in the MACRO Museum in Testaccio, and they are introduced by an exhibition (and this too is an absolute first) of all the objects and projects which, over the 2008-2010 three-year period, have been selected by ADI to take part in the 22nd edition of the Compasso d'Oro prize which is being awarded this year.

The best of contemporary Italian production, then, as a primary basis for a discussion about innovation and the sectors in which we must involve ourselves over the coming years, in order to discover just where Italy might still distinguish itself for its own *uniqueness*, one that can be recognised and be perceptible at an international level.

Our hope is that the *Italian Uniqueness* show, together with the contents of this catalogue, which is an integral part of it, can lead to an open-ended debate about the role that the Italian system will be obliged to play in the near future, and if it can still be the standard-bearer of beauty in a globalised economy. Will we still be the standard-bearers of quality in the tens of manufacturing sectors that are still admired by the rest of the world? Can we manage to find an "Italian path" to development? And central or local governments: what policies must they follow to encourage such a development? And are we consumers still able to recognise quality and place the right value on it without giving in to the temptation of resorting to imitations? Do we have sufficient awareness to allow us to recognise and protect creativity and, therefore, the *originality* of a product?

Our hope is that both the Roman shows will inspire such questions in the visitors and that the 150th anniversary might be remembered as the starting point for a new path for our country.

We do not have any certain answers to the questions just asked but, like Cavour, we can say: "Yes: we believe in the skill, energy, and workmanship of the Italians."

Italian Uniqueness
1961/2011

From Villages to Districts

Antonio Marzano

In Italy we have almost six million businesses: one for every 10 inhabitants. This represents a fascination with business without equal in Europe or the rest of the world. Almost all of these firms are either small or medium sized and they represent 98.5% of the productive network.

In order to understand the characteristics of our productive system, one based on small or medium-sized firms, it is useful to go back to the beginning of the 1950s. In the first years of the decade there was an intense debate in Italy about the size of businesses needed to start off a new model for development after the Second World War.

Many believed that such a model ought to be based on large-scale industries, imagining that the role of small and medium-sized concerns would be marginal. After a lengthy debate in parliament, Law 949 was passed in 1952 which set up the Mediocredito Centrale (the central medium-term credit bank) for financing and giving medium-term help to small and medium-sized firms, and the Artigiancassa for financing and giving credit facilities to artisan businesses.

The Mediocredito Centrale was associated with special credit institutes for financing investments, in particular, with the Mediocrediti Regionali (the regional medium-term credit banks), which had been set up following the passing of Law 949. In this way an interesting form of *ante litteram* federalism was created with regard to medium-term credit because the Mediocredito Centrale, whose endowment fund belonged wholly to the Exchequer, integrated the financial resources of the smallest Mediocrediti Regionali by giving them loans through debenture bonds emitted on the market with sovereign risk.

Since then many things have changed in the credit sector, above all due to the effects of a new banking law which came into effect at the beginning of 1994. But the country's industrial policy has in various ways continued to sustain the system of small and medium-sized firms which are so typical of the whole productive system. With regard to this, mention should be made of the recent strengthening of the guarantee fund, which is also available to artisan firms; the setting up of the national committee for micro-credit; policies for administrative simplification in favour, above all, of small firms. And finally, mention should also be made of the proposal for a "business statute" which is being approved by the Italian parliament and, at a European level, the Small Business Act. With the latter we could say that this (prevalently) Italian experience has been given an important sign of appreciation and recognition by the EU.

The spread and increase of small and medium-sized businesses has many explanations, mainly, though not exclusively, positive. We know that factors exist that impede the increase in size of small firms, and a part of industrial policy is in fact to remove, lessen or compensate for such factors.

But there are many explanations which are positive, according to most evidence. The more diffused the *entrepreneurial spirit* is, which is the ordinary citizen's wish to undertake something, the more difficult the proportionate growth of large businesses is, especially in a relatively small national economy. Then there is the advantage of small and medium-sized businesses' *flexibility*; a greater *control* of the productive process's efficiency; and the greater habit of exploiting the *location advantages* of a specific territory.

And there are limits. Less economics of scale, less cover for banking risks, a reduced interest in becoming international and, of course, in research. But these and other limits have found an answer in Italy that we are forced to describe as brilliant: districts, free aggregations of firms organised territorially and functionally that are able to conserve and strengthen the advantages of being small with some of the advantages of larger firms. And so we have passed from "villages" to "districts".

The subdivision of the Italian social fabric into *municipalities* is known to all, and is the result of the historical processes following the breakup of the Roman Empire. Each small local situation learned to be autonomous and, as far as possible, self-sufficient; each community had its own corporations of arts and trades, and in this context artists and artisans began to operate side by side, transmitting to each other *their search for beauty and their search for what was well-made*. It is sufficient to walk round any Italian museum to see that many utensils, from a certain point onwards, enforce their useful function with an aesthetic function. The explosion of marvellous art and architecture that lasted for centuries in Italy could not but influence those who, on opening the doors of their humble artisan workshops, could measure themselves against the innumerable masterpieces of the Renaissance or the Baroque. This was why in Italy there arose a particular capacity for transmitting experiences and abilities at a local level, involving all the small economic operators in the territory (artisans, merchants, bankers etc.); this capacity was also able to be handed down even with the arrival of the industrial processes of the modern era with the aforementioned change "from village to district".

And all this happened without ignoring that continuous search for beauty, even when making a simple object for daily use: perhaps this is the secret that underpins products made in Italy and is so appreciated by the rest of the world.

But let's return to the question of dimensions. This has to be looked at, not by considering business as a world in itself, but by the relationships it manages to create, manage and control with all the other enterprises and workers in the widest sense, i.e. the market. From this point of view, intermediate and market relationships have a strategic value that is increasing with regard to traditional hierarchies within firms. If we look closer at the nature and intermediate effects of business markets, then we become aware that the problem of dimensions has a different value for our system. A medium size is then not as small as it seems when measured in a traditional way.

And here we must remember the three kinds of relationships between important businesses that give a less fragmented image of our productive system based on small and medium-sized firms.

This is a question of *business groups*, *consortiums* and *industrial districts*. Of course, these three forms of organisation are not divorced from each other and they can happily live together in a more or less interactive way, as experience has shown us. Often the concept of a district contains in itself the idea of a group or consortium. The phenomenon of business groups is widespread in our industrial system. The data we have available indicate that *almost 20% of industrial enterprises with over 10 employees is part of a group*. This phenomenon differentiates according the size of the firms, the sectors they belong to, and their geographical area. According to their size, their diffusion increases from a little under 10% for eleven to twenty employees to over 97% for more employees (over 500). The sectors in which the organisational form of the group is most widespread are those of *high technology* (32%) and economics of scale sectors (22%), sectors which are usually presented as confined to minor businesses. Geographically, this phenomenon is most present in business groups based in the oldest industrialised areas and far less so in other areas, above all in the south of Italy and the islands.

The second form of organisation that allows us to have a different idea of the medium-size of our manufacturing enterprises is represented by consortiums. According to the available data, some 10% of manufacturers with over ten employees *belongs to consortiums*. The greatest difference can be noticed at a geographical level, with a greater concentration in southern Italy and the islands, and a far smaller one in areas of older industrialisation. Consortiums appear far more widespread in the traditional sectors than in the others. The most common typologies are non-specialised kinds of consortiums, followed by credit consortiums, and then by those for exportation. The presence of consortiums for scientific and technological research is, instead, more limited.

The third form of organisation having an effect on the size of firms and, therefore, on their competitive advantages, is districts in the narrowest sense of the word. And now I would like to investigate these more closely. We are dealing with groups of small and medium businesses concentrated in one territory and which are linked by relationships of cooperation and competition and which are part of the same sector. A district can be more efficient than a large business for operating external localisation economies regarding, amongst other things, information and exchange costs, professional training, the spread of technologies, forms of internationalisation and credit guarantees themselves. Such external localisation economies should be improved by the efficient application of information and communications technologies in their various forms: from the simplest to the most complex strategic kind. In this case we are dealing with digital districts.

The elements of cooperation and competition within an industrial district ought to allow a notable reduction of the costs of coordination which generally increase together with the increase of the size of the business.

Empirical evidence indicates among the various strong points of Italian industrial districts, a significantly greater tendency to exportation than for non-district firms; a reduction of informative asymmetries in the relationship between banks and firms; and a greater diffusion of forms of cooperation between such enterprises as consortiums for collective credit guarantees.

The efficient application of information and communications technologies to districts is an important way of overcoming the weak points indicated for smaller businesses. Such an application must concern above all the integration of the various functions of the firm (product development, the supply chain, production, marketing, finance and coordination) with the internal and international market. It is important to note that in our country various "technological poles" have been gathering strength: genuine districts with high technology and research abilities. Currently there are eighteen of them in action, above all in the fields of pharmaceuticals, biomedicine, aeronautics and IT, and they operate in quite different territorial "villages": they extend from the north (Milan, Turin, Varese) to the centre (Bologna, Modena, Rome) and to the south (Naples, Bari, Catania). But in general, there were 156 industrial districts in 2001, as was established by an ISTAT census; today there are some 200 kinds of districts which are recognised and protected by Italian legislation; other sources indicate that there are actually double that number or more. And by now they range from high-tech to food production.

At the beginning of the 1990s, numerous foreign experts, economists and policy makers "discovered" districts. Many countries saw the Italian model of districts as an important successful critical factor for launching and/or re-launching policies for local development. Since then, studies, research and inquiries into the theme of districts have been numerous.

The evolution of the analyses of recent years has introduced certain sensible modifications of the conceptual apparatus typical of districts:

- the hierarchical category with the birth and consolidation of leading or pivotal businesses;
- the "long network" category, the so-called de-territorialisation of districts, i.e. an agglomerative network outside the territory;
- the definition and pinpointing of "meta-districts" of which the distinctive factor is not just manufacturing production but, above all, the production of knowledge. Undoubtedly today the challenge to districts is a tough one. Chinese competition which, to use the terminology of software, we could call "asymmetrical", has a direct impact on Italian specialties which are strongly based, in fact, on districts. The reduction of international market quotas for our traditional sectors, which began at the start of the 1990s, has meant an accumulated loss of great relevance for the percentage of the gross domestic product, and this has led to a loss of work places in the manufacturing industries, a phenomenon aggravated by the de-localisation of costs undertaken by many businesses, even district ones.

Various authors believe that possible answers available for district economies can be indicated by four guidelines:

- greater innovation, not just for processes but also for products (e.g. design) and for organisation, extended to all district businesses;
- greater internationalisation, in the sense not just of export flow, but of collaboration agreements with foreign businesses on a technical, productive and commercial plane; the exchange of patents and licences, programmes of commercial penetration abroad; and direct investment abroad (possibly additive and not substituting existing ones);
- increased training extended to all professionals, entrepreneurs included;
- increased access to credit, in particular to new forms of medium-range financing. These actions are aimed at competitively repositioning and reinforcing districts.

In fact, district firms export an average of over 50% of their output (this figure also includes the indirect exports of micro-businesses). So districts already seem an internationalised industrial structure (in the sense that they sell most of their finished products abroad). But this structure is not yet sufficiently global, if by this term we mean a production chain distributed across many countries, each of which is chosen for the advantages that make it useful for the productive phase it hosts.

In order to pass from internationalisation to a global organisation of the productive chain it is necessary to undertake processes to de-localise the "poor" phases of the chain, with networking or investment strategies aimed at foreign countries in order to have high-quality locations in which new technological and business forms can be created. All these integrated forms of internationalising processes give businesses a better yield-risk combination than firms that are under-internationalised or are only internationalised in the simplest of forms, such as that of exports, for example. But how is it possible to involve in this process the universe of artisan micro-enterprises that has had such importance for the successes of the leading district businesses, and to avoid de-localisations only of "comparative costs" which are an impoverishment of the territory and do not take fully into account the concept of social responsibility for the district system? This is perhaps the next challenge for industrial policy. "Network contracts" favour the collaboration and interaction between businesses and the Small Business Act goes in the right direction.

Italian economic history, from the 1950s onwards, is the result of hundreds of thousands of small businesses, which then became millions. And since the 1960s and 1970s it has been widely interpreted by districts, now numbering many hundreds, including high-tech ones.

It is a history that marks the laborious yet also intense passage from an agricultural economy to an industrial and post-industrial fabric; from a society of emigrants – also from provinces that are now rich – to another with a high rate of immigration; from a country divided into villages to an integrated and interdependent one of territorial districts which are today increasingly networked.

This is a heritage with distinctive characteristics and dynamic potentialities which it would be difficult to repeat in countries different to ours. The success of production can be measured by its volumetric growth in time, by the increase in investments and occupation, and by the profits of the businesses. But it is also measured in some way by the spread of imitations and counterfeiting. However, these might concern certain products but not the creativity which lies at their heart and which will continue unimpeded to produce results from its innovative ideas. They are limits that might also come up against initiatives by external buyers.

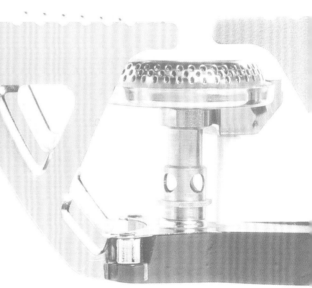

In fact we can say that "villages" have often been thought of as the country's periphery. But the shift from "villages to districts" perhaps shows the opposite. History, culture and tradition have become *products*, they have become competitive factors: and so "villages" have gone from being local to being international.

In the current celebrations of Italian unity, it is pleasant to observe how, in the sense of a greater unity, the phenomena described here have been developing: the proliferation of businesses following a trend that is greater than the European average; the socio-political connotation of a fabric in which business initiative is often undertaken by persons belonging to the working class; the typology of work-relations in small businesses (which are so predominant), and the evolution of the "whole" towards a district-like organisation consisting of coordination, collaboration, interdependence, interaction and networking applications.

At the very least we can perhaps say that divisions and conflicts, even though they exist, might be better for accommodating an economy organised in this way: with a productive, technological and human heritage such as that in Italy.

Italian Modernity

Paolo Mieli

The years from 1961 until today have been distinguished by a profound transformation of our country, with a rhythm of change that in the past could only have happened over centuries. For us, this fifty-year period is still experienced as *news* and it is difficult to attribute to it the chilly notion of *history*. We were there, we experienced all those years, we changed together with Italy, they seem as interminable as our own life... this is why they were fifty long years even though they were part of the context of what has been called "the short century".

Many visions come to mind, and purposely I have decided that, as happens in the news, it might be better to allow them to pile up on top of each other, perhaps in an irrational way, to form a mosaic of images and sounds able to describe the fifty years that have just passed.

The first image that comes to mind is that of an Italy full of youngsters. The youngsters who in the 1950s had something strange about them: short hair, jackets, ties, pleated skirts... they looked like their parents, though a bit younger, and they had with their parents a relationship that was, all things considered, good-natured, remissive, and with the same trust that animated those who, having put the war and hunger behind them, saw the country grow thanks to their own efforts.

How different from the young in the 1960s! These were the years of a genuine youthful revolution, one which culminated in the 1968 movement. For certain aspects the young generation of the 1960s reminds us of the preceding ones which prepared the rebellions of 1848 or that drew Europe and the rest of the world into the First World War in 1914: generations that were sharply contrasted to that of their parents, who wanted to differentiate themselves from them and change social conventions, institutional organisation and territorial equilibriums. And it was this desire for change that erupted in the revolutions of 1968 and 1969. I do not completely agree with those who present the 1968 movement as a reaction to the revolution brought about by the spread of wellbeing and the expansion of the consumer society. In fact, it seems to me that 1968 was, rather, the completion of this process; for the first time the young throughout Italy (as perhaps could previously only have happened – in a completely different context – in the trenches during the First World War) were able to get to know each other, mix together and compare their different experiences as kids from the north or south, rich or poor, from industrial of agricultural families, and have possibilities in life that until just a few years earlier they could not even have imagined. The political character of 1968, which actually was to be very important in the period that immediately followed, was not at first a revolution started by the young.

Many writers have pinpointed in 1968 the roots of the generation of the next decade, the "years of lead"; but I think, rather, that at the heart of the movement was an imaginative, colourful and non-violent anarchic note; only in Italy did it continue to generate leaders, organisers, newspapers and periodicals in the coming years, when by now in the rest of the world the drive of the student movements had been exhausted. And perhaps this characteristic of permanence provoked a degeneration in a political and violent sense, one that caused many young Italians in the 1970s to have a kind of "loss of innocence", and that certainly caused the crisis of rejection in the following generations who, from the 1980s until now, seem distinguished above all by an increasingly cosmopolitan and technological detachment.

But when thinking about the new generation that was about to come to the forefront in 1960, I cannot help remembering another characteristic that indelibly marked the Italy of the first half of the 1960s: the internal migration of people from southern Italy to the north, and from the fields to the towns.

This is something that Italian historians are still debating: were the benefits produced by migration greater than the cost that it inevitably produced in terms of cultural and human uprooting? This was the open-ended conclusion of Luchino Visconti's 1960 film *Rocco and his Brothers*.

There is no doubt that, at the end of the day, the positive aspects were more important than the negative ones in the economic, social and cultural fields. However, it is important to try to highlight the dramatic situation that involved so many Italians in the very years in which the phenomenon of Italian-made production which we are now here to celebrate was being created. This was not a migration similar to that at the end of the nineteenth- or the beginning of the twentieth century, which had as its aim Latin America or the USA. In that case the Italians (many from the north) knew what they were about to come up against: a long journey, another language and different laws, an unknown land. And they had time to prepare themselves emotively for the tremendous difficulties that lay ahead: from the moment they left, throughout the boat journey, until their arrival in a foreign land. The internal migration after the Second World War had, instead, a perception of a less traumatic farewell because the country was the same one, the language was (more or less) the same, the radio and TV programmes were the same, and even the heroes of sport were the same! But instead many of them had to experience the trauma of being rejected, of feeling themselves to be second-class citizens, at times they were even treated as primitive beings. These were tough years for many of them, and yet, thanks to them, Italy experienced a period of growth and wellbeing such as had never happened before in the modern era.

It is useless today to hide how much a new, but equally dramatic, form of migration (that of immigration) counts for our country and just how much the result is always the same: will the costs or benefits be greater?

For this catalogue, perhaps, the theme of the economic boom is central. This is because it touches directly on the birth and affirmation of Italian productive and manufacturing excellence that has made us famous throughout the world. History books place the moment of most tumultuous and miraculous growth in the period between 1957 and 1963, actually comparing it to the "flight of the bumblebee" which, as is well-known, because of its shape, ought not to be able to fly and yet it does fly. To be honest, the boom's roots are to be found in the years immediately following the Second World War as a result of the impulse to reconstruct and of American aid, and its mainspring has to be looked for during the 1950s. In this period, despite all the contradictions, a positive energy accumulated throughout the country which then exploded into a myriad channels: supermarkets, motorways, internal migrations, consumption, television, cars, trains, airplanes, music, advertising, design... In that period millions of Italians started to move, began to consume, and had the impression of a life that would never end, one full of awareness, moments of happiness, possibilities for enjoying themselves and a productive and modern life.

The beginning of our fifty-year period was marked by the image of automobile wheels speeding along the motorways and of infrastructures for which we were the world leaders. In just a few days you could go from one end of Italy to another; the journey in itself was considered as a new way of living (also a tragic one, as in the film *The Easy Life*). The other revolution in life was television, which brought the world into Italian homes and forced Italians in turn to be receptive to the rest of the planet – a receptiveness that was to have its effect above all on industry which then began to produce merchandise even destined to conquer foreign markets; and so there evolved a generation of businessmen and salesmen who began to tour the continents and show our manufacturing skills. It was as a result of this drive that it was understood how serial production, repetitive and propelled by cost-saving, could make our products competitive; it was also possible to introduce elements of beauty and a productive quality that would make our products competitive, thanks to the fascination they exerted and which few consumers in the world were able to resist.

Personally, I clearly realised that times were changing one evening in June, 1965, after a performance by the Beatles at the Teatro Adriano in Rome. That music, the faces I glimpsed, the way of dressing and speaking... I understood that we were really undergoing an epochal change, that the post-war period had finished, that there was a new age to be constructed and that I could make my own contribution, together with others of my age-group, to create a new country.

I remember very well the month that indelibly marked the beginning of the 150th anniversary, mixing fears for the future and the sensation that everything would change. The month was October 1962 during which there happened at the same time the second Vatican council and the Cuban missile crisis: thirteen days during which the world was certain that world war three was about to start. The crisis between the USA and the Soviet Union luckily was resolved, but it convinced the whole world, and perhaps even the bishops at the Vatican council, that we were dancing on the edge of a precipice. It was necessary to move back from the chasm.

Perhaps the Cuban crisis influenced the early stages of the Vatican council; what is certain is that the council changed the history of the Roman Catholic Church. With John XXIII as pope, the Church underwent a process of modernisation, also with regard to its doctrines, which were in sharp contrast to two centuries in which its reaction to the French Revolution and its after-effects had been solidified. Someone has said that in October 1962 a single Church entered the council and that, at the end of 1965, there exited a plural Church, receptive to innovation, in step with the times, and able to perceive the epochal changes that humanity was about to come up against. Perhaps excessively so, according to some... However, I cannot fail to think that such a figure as John Paul II, who so influenced the history of the world, also had his roots in the discussions that took place in that council. And to continue talking about popes, if John Paul II undoubtedly influenced world history, Paul VI had a particular influence on the history of Italy both before and after his period as pope. And the most profound image linked to our history was the one that united Paul VI (Giovanni Battista Montini) and Aldo Moro. Between the two there was a certain difference in age; however their lives were intertwined in a far more intense manner than can be imagined. In the beginning there was FUCI, the Catholic university organisation in which the young Moro was given a deep spiritual and cultural training by monsignor Montini himself, a training that then was to mark the "Moroteo" vision of Catholic politics and political involvement. But what is most impressive and what represents a living picture of Italy in the 1970s, the cruel years of our Republic, was the Greek tragedy that ended the relationship between these two great personalities. From the prison where he was held by the Red Brigades, President Moro pleaded with the pope to intercede in his favour. And Paul VI wrote a memorable open letter to the Red Brigades on April, 21, 1978, published in all the newspapers (unusual for a pope), in which he implored the terrorists "on his knees" to free the Honourable Aldo Moro "simply, without conditions". Those who lived through the period can understand the significance that the letter had – in a country divided between those who pleaded for negotiations and those who were intransigent – with its phrase "without conditions". The pain of the Moro family was such that in the end they wanted a private funeral for their loved one; despite this, Paul VI insisted on a solemn funeral mass for the dead statesman – albeit without the body – with all the most important exponents of Italian politics present. During the mass he preached a sermon which, according to many historians, represented the real end of the first Italian republic.

The first republic was to be characterised by an innovation that in 1960 entered the homes of Italians and changed the relationship between citizens and politics. It was first called *Tribuna elettorale* and then *Tribuna politica*. When this transmission began, only a few people and some political leaders were ever seen on television. For the first time, politics entered into people's homes and it was no longer necessary to listen to public meetings in the midst of supporters without any way of contradicting what was said. Over time, even the politicians had to get used to managing this new means of propaganda, learn to follow the rhythms of television and get used to the rules of quick repartee. What had already been happening for years in the USA (and it was in 1960 that Kennedy tore Nixon – until then the favourite – to pieces in a TV face-to-face programme and so opened the way to becoming the president of the United States) began to happen in Italy too; over time this led political debate to be undertaken outside parliament: from the extra-parliamentary crisis of the 1970s to the "third chamber" of today's television studios. It is impossible to claim that the influence of television does not also extend into political life, but perhaps the shift of politics into television which, from 1961 until today, has involved all Italian politicians, has not been such a good thing for the production of content and proposals, and has led us to the current situation in which, paradoxically, we seem to have gone back more to the post-war period and the elections of 1948 (with the, at times, exaggerated opposition of irreconcilable political forces) than to the electoral tribunes of the 1970s and 1980s. There springs to mind the question if Italian political communications over the next fifty years will be characterised by new networking technologies (the Internet, social networks etc.) and by the progressive loss of the importance of television.

Finally, I would like to mention the emancipation of women which began between the end of the 19th century

and the early years of the 20th, but which in this post-war period has led to results that, until just a few decades ago, would have been unthinkable. The merit for these gains must be awarded above all to the feminist battles of the 1970s and to the activity of such groups as the Radicals who fought for questions of civil rights. If women today (allowed to vote only in the second half of the 1940s, after the Second World War) have important positions and great responsibilities, this is also due to those forms of involvement. However, this does not stop us from thinking that the long march towards equality between men and women has still not ended.

And finally it must be said that that over these past fifty years Italy has undergone an imposing transformation and has travelled a road that would have taken a century to undertake before 1961. Perhaps many centuries. Italians today are in every respect similar to their fellows in the rest of Europe. And if this path continues to be followed with the same rhythm as we were able to summon up over the past fifty years, it is possible that when we celebrate the 200th anniversary of Italian unity we will not only be in step with the rest of Europe, but constitute the avant-garde of our continent.

The Social Impulse in Italian Industrial Production: Enterprise, Creativity and Desires

Giuseppe Roma

Many characteristics that mark out the high quality of a significant part of Italian industrial production derive from the superimposition of social development and economic growth. In all probability we would never have had products with the made in Italy label if, in the fifty and more years it was incubated, grew and matured, there had not been a widespread entrepreneurial spirit together with social behaviour inspired by such values as taste, culture, quality, a good life-style and artisanship. And if a *desire* for rebirth had not motivated the actions of millions of Italians.

The extraordinary capacity to create industrial products with a soul has made Italy one of the leading manufacturing countries in the world and, at the same time, it has made an increasingly evolved and mature social body. This long life-cycle now needs to reinvent its original spirit and provoke a new collective impulse.

THE REALM OF OBJECTS AND THE CONSUMER'S LONG EVOLUTIONARY CYCLE

Our actions and moods are conditioned by the increasingly complex space in which we are immersed. We are permanently surrounded by objects, we continually cross places, we are the object and recipients of images, sounds and messages. If there hadn't developed a planning and design culture together with an enlargement of industrial production, our lives would have taken another direction, one with less emotions, less inclined to enthusiasms, more confused and disordered and, perhaps, more solemn.

In particular, this characteristic has distinguished the manufacturing evolution of our country, which has a particular vocation for linking technology and creativity. In Italy artificers, artisans, architects and artists have historically had high standing, and these are all professions with the prefix "ar" which means "skill and invention in constructing or making".

The third fifty-year period of Italian unity (1961-2011) can rightly be considered the period when, in the social context, there was an incredible evolutionary leap forward for industry, towns, housing and objects. A long cycle that has partly been exhausted, so much so that today we must ask ourselves if we are not faced with a new beginning and if it might not be opportune to stimulate individual and collective needs, the desires of the great mass of individuals, as the basis for a new booming economic and productive period.

Fifty years ago objects were far more limited both in urban and domestic spaces. In 1961 there existed in Italy some two and a half million cars; only eighteen families in a hundred owned one. Today there are thirty-six million circulating for twenty-three million families, a third of which have two or three cars. The increasing pres-

ence of elderly families without a car due to their age makes this proportion even ore striking.

Even scooters, the primary emblem of individual mobility, have tripled in fifty years, but the social reasons for their use have also completely changed. Then, as is currently happening in many countries on the threshold of becoming wealthy, they were the symbols of private emancipation in transport. Today they are the most obvious symptoms of the undesirable effects of an overwhelming individualistic mobility in towns which have grown in a disorderly manner. Again, in 1961 we should note that about twenty families out of a hundred owned a television, and eleven out of a hundred had a washing machine: domestic appliances that, together with many others, are abundantly present in the homes of all Italians.

TEACHING TASTE

Italian society has been capable of generating such a characteristic phenomenon of production as industrial design. At the same time, the application of design to many tools for daily use has helped educate the taste of the public.

The particularity of every culture derives from various historical and anthropological circumstances in which social development manifests itself. For the most part this does not happen in isolation but in relation to other cultures which are the nearest, either for affinity or for contiguity, or else in opposition to the dominant ones. Italy, in the shift from a mainly rural economy to an industrial mechanised society, has used creativity as an indispensible quality for distinguishing, recognising and affirming itself with respect to those cultures which were then the closest: the American and European ones. Without a strong expression of diversity, no human culture really counts: in our case aesthetics has played a fundamental role.

Basing our industrial production on taste and beauty has led to an identifying characteristic, the most efficient tool for reserving a space for ourselves in international competitiveness. Such a paradigm has its roots in the history of our country which has made art the inherent paradigm for expressing the best national qualities and a manifestation of quality that is recognised throughout the world.

The past fifty years of national unity has been a formidable period for accumulating values which, if we look closely, actually go beyond the successful components of that production. The basis certainly consists of two extraordinary components – unique in the world – which have helped each other in turn: the businesses, which at first were small and based on craftsmanship and then became medium-size and multinational, and the planners, technicians, and even the skilled-hands and workers

who have never been "separate" from the process of making, who have never been on the outside. There are well-known cases of the importance of skilled people who, at the beginning of national reconstruction in the early 1950s, invented items for Fiat, Piaggio or Olivetti which then became cult objects. But we certainly owe it to the many designers – Gio Ponti, Gardella, Albini, Bellini, Vico Magistretti and Carlo Scarpa are just a few – who have succeeded one another to the present day, as well as to the emergent talents, if Italy has imposed a style of living; to fashion designers if it is pre-eminent in the luxury and fashion sectors; to car-designers; to technologists and engineers for the machinery and the medium technologies for which we are world leaders. Furthermore, there are the many protagonists for the protection and advancement of the Italian culinary tradition who have created an imposing, all-inclusive chain of high-quality agriculture, traditional products, rural territories and the landscape, refreshment services, tourism for the discovery of wines and ecology, the care for historical town-centres and the advancement of our artistic heritage.

BEAUTY IS USEFUL

In James Hillman's words, beauty is useful, practical and functional; it addresses the mind to permanent values and eternal truths; and it ends up being something simple, pleasing, easy. It is mistakenly believed to be extraneous to economic aims; on the contrary, it is a substantial humanisation of the productive process and of consumer logic because "the artist shows what is extraordinary in the ordinary" and aesthetics shows intentionality without intention.

In the shift from a poor and austere society to one with widespread wellbeing and consumption, a worthy element has then been gained consisting of the intrinsic quality of the goods which Italian families have slowly come to own. And with them there has been a gradual refinement of tastes and fashions; planning and design culture has gained acceptance and recognition, so much so as to become the most appropriate way for satisfying intangible needs and for suggesting new social links.

In what way has design helped Italian society to mature? It might seem excessive to refer to the De Stijl of Rietveld, Oud, Mondrian or Mies van der Rohe and their approach based on the immateriality of space and the proposition of an "anti-materialistic" life-style. But something rather like it has accompanied Italians in their approach to mass consumerism.

LIFE-STYLES AND SOCIAL BEHAVIOUR

To influence life-styles is certainly one of the aims of consumerist society. In Italy, however, changes in behaviour have been deeply tied to the need for safety and protection, and to investment and possessions represented by having a house as one's main possession; here personal identity is shaped and it is here that is placed the greater part of the industrial products for the consumer. The home is the most highly desired and idealised possession in Italy (there come to mind the advertising hoardings in the outskirts in the 1960s and 1970s in praise of the "house of your dreams"). For us a house is a place of comfort and privacy; it is a refuge for affections and family traditions.

Towns have progressively become areas for diversity because public places have been subject to mechanisms which damp down their relational functions, something well symbolised by the piazza. Its latest evolution is further increasing the fragmentation and breaking up of an indispensible collective dimension. Most Italians currently live in large territorial containers, in other words large or medium-sized towns, small-sized residential areas, logistic poles, and centres for large-scale commerce and distribution.

What determine metropolitan areas are the continual movements of individuals rather than the fixity of areas subdivided according to their function. People in movement define the confines of an urban space which by now has become the container or differentiated centres held together by networks of infrastructures.

As with consumption, so we also find a fairly evident cyclic change in towns: after the medium-sized towns, the sprawling manufacturing areas, local systems made in Italy, a substantial integration of district systems and large metropolitan containers is coming about.

INVENTION DESIGN

It can equally be noted how the urban context too shows cycles related to the ways and styles of all the products that interweave without daily life. Standardisation, functionality and saving – even with the risk of giving up creativity – lie at the heart of industrialisation in most Western countries; but in Italy they have been substantially modified since the boom in the 1960s by a particular stylistic care.

With us industrial design has taken the form of creative projects, *invention design*, adding a content closer to the public's needs for the offer of industrial products. Marketing, advertising and sales networks usually take the place of the "producer" of industrial goods. They are the tools, even hidden ones at times, for "selling" and,

in practice, they push the product into second place. Italian-made products are humanised and their symbolic value is increased, obviously without penalising their practical function. Our industrial output allows the emergence of a life-style, it inspires certain models of behaviour, it gives an outlet to repressed desires. So it adds something to technology and the market by widening the range of its properties by underlining their sensorial and chromatic ones.

In fact, some time after the start of the expansion of this kind of industrial production, halfway through the 1980s a thoughtful and eclectic critic of behaviour and design noted a genuine *explosion of colour*: from the colour of clothing to that of street furniture which completely transformed the greyness of the cityscape.

The aesthetic importance of colour in our daily life had been *humiliated* for many years by the greyness or the absolute black and white of interior design, industrial goods and architecture; this was completely swept away by products made in Italy which, already in the first period of mass industrialisation had interrupted the monotony of forms and colours: the Ford T was black, but Alfa Romeos were bright red; black Singer sewing machines were replaced by Necchi's coloured ones, and so on.

More recently the influence of minimalism has returned us to neutral colours, so much so that the prevalent image of the crowds in our cities is black or brown, while white dominates in our homes. A return to colour and rethinking objects through colour too is certainly one of today's challenges, one of the necessary conditions for restarting a cycle.

STIMULATING DESIRES

As has been stated so far, the characteristics of production made in Italy both derive from, and have a strong influence on, social factors, to the point of nourishing each other in turn. We ought to ask ourselves whether today, in the face of a general stagnation, it might not be indispensible to rediscover a motivation for resuming development again, and if this motivation ought not to refer mainly to emotive reasons rather than to rational mechanisms linked to particular interests. And here it is useful to return to Censis's call: *to return to desiring*. *Desire is the attraction of the spirit to whom or what gives pleasure*, a mechanism that inspires us to obtain what we feel a lack of. It is the feeling we undergo *desideris*: when we cease observing the marvel of the stars in the heavens.

A return to aspirations would have the undoubted merit of sparking off dynamics in a static Italian society that is content with the great changes arriving from abroad.

It is only by fostering new desires that vital subjectivity stops shrinking, the spirit of sacrifice becomes a stubborn mark of individual and collective responsibility and society tends to expand. As a great philosopher has said, *desire pushes beyond*; once the impulse to centre an objective has been satisfied it no longer seems enough and we want something more. The creation of business and models and a search for quality in industrial products has given Italy the undoubted advantage of not succumbing to stronger productive systems, and even today we owe the defence of market quotas and our important international role to this capacity. But now it is necessary to be dissatisfied by simply defending the spaces we have carved out: we must go in search of other new ones.

Furthermore, our consumerism has matured and sparked off an Italian way of life that certainly, at least here at home, has taken the place of the more materialistic American model. We are thrifty, tied to the family and domestic spaces that are the repositories of our investments, we Italians are respectful of small towns and historical memory. They are in debt, appropriators, dynamic, mobile, conditioned by advertising and communications, and are obese. They are speedy, we love good food, the wellbeing of thermal baths, and have even become careful of our health and abolished smoking, too much alcohol and a sedentary life.

If the organisation of life in Italian big cities continues to present a problem and everything that is complex risks becoming impossible for our country, still no one can beat us for the level of our quality of life, the size of small or medium towns, the variety of our landscape and our cultural and free-time venues. Inventiveness, beauty, as well as technological intelligence and the capacity to give personalised answers to the global demand for goods, make up the value of Italian production. It is at the heart of our international competitiveness, which, though slowed down by the crisis, is returning to take up its lost position, a mark of the undoubted vitality of our entrepreneurial system. Social behaviour inside the nation does not seem so reactive: the fall in consumption certainly has such objective causes linked to the low dynamics of incomes. But the general sense of tiredness in decidedly facing up to the challenges of the moment call for an indispensible return to desire as a meritorious mechanism for making us see what we are lacking and impelling us to obtain it.

We will discover that, apart from a style of life based on personal wellbeing, today what is indispensible is to rediscover an impulse based on responsibility and duty. And furthermore, just as we have cared for historical memory and the quality of our food, today it is necessary to pay more attention to primary factors and use our en-

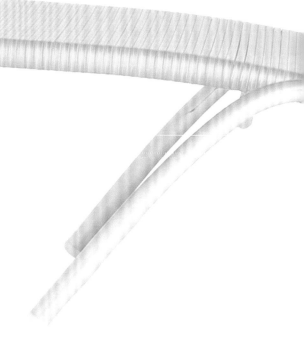

ergy and water more carefully, have greater care for the environment, the quality of the air and for recycling waste, and reconsider the ephemeral freedom of individual travelling. And then, we must lavish more energy on the individual knowledge and training that leads to a wider international receptiveness and a by-now lost relationship between knowledge and action, school and work. And finally, collective involvement would lead to a society open to generational change, to communications and to new information technologies. But this will only come about not because it is a duty but because it is wished for and desired.

Italian manufacture is in good health, perhaps the one aspect of the nation that, during the celebrations for the 150th anniversary of Italian unity, is most healthy. Its competitive strength lies in its international expansion, but its parallel evolution with the dynamics of its society is a guarantee for maintaining its original character intact. And this is why we must arouse our dreams and act so that they become reality.

The Compasso d'Oro Collection and Show

Six Pretexts for a Developing Collection

Enrico Morteo

Usually a collection means something that has been planned from the start and therefore has a method that justifies its content and meaning. But this is not the case with the Compasso d'Oro collection. Its beginnings and ends have other ideas and reasons underpinning its motives and aims.

Unlike a collector (who is usually inspired by an enthusiasm for certain kinds of objects or documents, or by an interest in a particular historical period or simply just inspired by the "beauty" or the "strangeness" of certain materials) or a museum (whose aim is to demonstrate, through the ordering of a selected body of work, the works of some artistic, technical or social phenomenon held to be particularly important) the Compasso d'Oro collection neither starts with a look back nor with the aim of categorising things historically or critically.

In this case the collection began with a straightforward grouping together of objects and projects that have been awarded the Compasso d'Oro prize from its first edition in 1954 up to today. In the by-now twenty-one editions of the prize there are 276 projects which have been awarded the Compasso d'Oro. To these must be added 41 Compasso d'Oro prizes for the careers of the same number of designers, while there have been 36 firms or institutions whose activity has also merited being awarded the prize.

Originated by the La Rinascente chain of stores and, from 1958, managed and organised by ADI, the Italian Association for Industrial Design, the Compasso d'Oro prize aimed to promote the cultural value of consumer goods and renew the range of Italian products in a period of rapid social and economic expansion in Italy. Over time, there no longer being a need to modernise production, this aim has slowly been redefined and the Compasso d'Oro has become a mark of recognition of excellence in Italian design in a wider sense by rewarding technological and typological innovation, research and experimentation, and progress in the use of materials or of production and sales processes.

It is obvious that such a long-lasting phenomenon, one determined by the 12 different juries that have periodically been put together over the past 54 years, cannot boast either of homogeneity or of a constant standard of judgement. Nor has it been able to exploit any consolidated opinion since the juries were coming to grips with the present and rewarded objects that were new and not yet subjected to the judgment of the market or by critics.

I believe that it is for these reasons, rather than for the systematic completeness of a collection, that the image most representative of the totality of projects awarded the Compasso d'Oro is that of an orderly accumulation or, if you prefer, of a significant stratified view of Italian industrial and design culture.

It is to this peculiarity of the collection that we can attribute its limits and merits.

The most obvious limit – one that is often underlined – is that of its incompleteness. In fact, those who think that they can find all the icons of Italian design in the collection will be disappointed. More than once someone has suggested gathering together all the objects that the Compasso d'Oro has overlooked: it has to be admitted that this would be a beautiful exhibition. Apart from the fact that the Compasso d'Oro has always followed a policy of awarding few prizes in order to reward excellence and has made many recommendations for encouraging exploration, it is true that the selection committees have not always recognised the genuine innovation of certain proposals. Furthermore, being organised by an association of professional designers and businessmen, it is not difficult to imagine how much jealousy, envy or strategic balancing acts have influenced the choices.

But these very reasons lie at the heart of the richness of a collection that has never been limited to collecting "beauty" but has been formed from a search for what is best: chosen from a wide range of objects and selected by protagonists and experts and not by journalists or gurus of taste. Such an ample collection does not exist elsewhere in the world; this is a collection that puts side by side objects for domestic use and complex industrial machinery, measuring instruments and toys, cars and decorative textiles, construction systems and the publishing industry, theoretical research and graphic design – to mention just a few of the areas that have been taken into consideration by the prize committee.

What the total collection transmits is a complex and articulated vision of design in which there cohabit materials otherwise relegated to the history of industry or of scientific research, to semiological analyses, the history of costume, fashion, or to the sphere of theoretical experimentation. This kind of design is intimately connected to social and cultural changes: it is not simply an investigation into the beauty of things and objects.

In this sense, the Compasso d'Oro collection is significant both for recording and acting as a commentator; its value overrides the importance of individual choices or of the juries' short-sightedness.

In the face of such a composite and variegated "document", one which is not so much a summary of the recent history of good Italian design but, rather, of the evolution of industrial and material culture in our country, it is possible to imagine multiple analyses and just as many exhibitions.

The most obvious choice, but also the least generous for those who are seeing the collection for the first time, would be to exhibit the collection in a rigorously chronological order. Year after year, edition after edition, the objects would not only be

required to explain themselves but also evoke the climate of a particular moment. But however philologically impeccable, such a choice would oblige the visitors to construct connections between one object and another and to create with their own imagination the landscape of an epoch.

Let's take as an example the objects awarded the Compasso d'Oro in 1964, the eighth edition of the prize and ten years after its start. Prizes were awarded to an item for the office (the CMC7-7004 magnetic character marker designed by Mario Bellini), a beer tap (the Spinamatic designed by the Castiglioni brothers for the Milanese firm Poretti), a Borletti alarm clock (the Sfericlock designed by Rodolfo Bonetto), the interior design and signs for the Milan underground stations (designed by the Albini studio and by Bob Noorda), and a plastic, stackable service of plates (the Compact service designed by Massimo Vignelli for APE). What on earth could all this heterogeneous collection of objects suggest to evoke such different and distant areas of design, ranging in size as they do from something hand-held to architecture? Of course, in the eyes of an expert it would be obvious, for example, that half of the objects are made from plastic. But how many of us still remember that in 1963 Giulio Natta was awarded the Nobel Prize in Chemistry as a result of his research into plastic materials, research that for some time ensured Italian chemical industries a dominant position among the great enterprises of the world and, for small businesses, a relatively cheap material that needed little investment for technology and equipment? Perhaps other visitors, by carefully reading the labels, might realise that five out of six objects were produced by industries in Milan and only one, Olivetti, in Ivrea? But these visitors would have to be very erudite, not to say experts. And then, what could a twenty-year-old say, someone who grew up with computers in a world full of plastic and digital watches?

Incidentally, the tenth anniversary edition – with only six prizes – was one of the most homogenous and compact of all. In other cases, the increase in prize-winning objects symmetrically corresponded to an effect of alienation and apparent contradiction, the logic of which is difficult to understand.

But even more extreme would be a choice where an exhibition focused on individual objects, x-rayed with reference to their executive designs, broken down into their various components, their constructive techniques analysed, and their functional performance and aesthetic-formal value subjected to detailed discussion.

This is an approach always encouraged by those who design for a living and who, therefore, consider projects as a self-sufficient cultural act whose value can be, at most, underlined by some knowledgeable reference to their social and economic context. Given that I consider this kind of exhibition not very communicative, I do not believe that a similar immersion in design details would be capable of explaining the role of design as an accomplice of the evolution of Italian society, often antic-ipating its orientation and offering high-quality models around which there slowly coagulated that totality of initiatives and products that are usually summed up by the not always apt definition of being made in Italy.

In order to allow us to see the strategic centrality of design in the Italian cultural context, I am convinced that it is necessary to reverse our point of view: not to use history in order to speak about the object, but to use the objects to recount history. On the other hand, it is this very unusual structure of the collection that reveals its best qualities. If analysed transversally, the collection, in fact, highlights a fabric consisting of denser groupings, frequent recurrences, apparent divagations and a sudden receptivity that the usual chronological order would not take into account. For instance, you will become aware that domestic furnishing, that group of projects so often evoked as exemplifying the best of Italian design, is strangely under-rep-resented in the collection. On the other hand there are abundant machines and work tools. If lamps are predictably well-represented, it is amazing just how often objects for sport and holidays are to be found. Even those who are convinced that the word design necessarily corresponds to a particular formal universe have to think again when faced with a variety of languages which not only occur over time but which cohabit and dialogue between each other.

It seems to me that in these discontinuities there are traces of various important socio-cultural changes, but also confirmations and correspondences between design research and various moments of great acceleration where innovation and intuition have suddenly nourished and given an aim to the industrial development of our country.

And so, rather than try to compress the tensions and changes of a society in rapid evolution into the tiny dimensions of objects, we have preferred to entrust them with the task of indicating those processes that have modified the human, social, technical and formal Italian landscape over the past fifty years.

With these premises, we have summed up six thematic areas that seem to be par-ticularly representative and around which we have, in fact, reorganised the whole collection, even though we are aware that there will be a certain arbitrariness and that the quality of many objects are not confined to a single thematic area. The themes are: 1. More from less; 2. New Italians, new things; 3. The evolution of design language; 4. The work plan; 5. From research to daily life; 6. Leisure time.

So first, a sense of measure as the distinctive mark of Italian elegance because, in the capacity to obtain the most with the least waste, it is possible to see the positive differential of creativity in a land which has a chronic lack of raw materials.

The new scenarios for consumption because objects do not only contain functions but also habits, expectations and illusions in which we find the mutable horizons of collective behaviour.

The evolution of languages because it is in their changes that it is possible to recognise the speed with which Italian culture has assimilated and surmounted modern myths and anticipated the ways and rules of a post-industrial society.

Work: because it has not only been an alienating tool for production but also a fundamental occasion for social and individual emancipation as well as an engine for transformations.

Applied technology, because, together with technique, it has been an important terrain for Italian design and because we confer on technology a central role in innovation and progress.

Free time, because this is an extremely sensitive indicator of the shift towards a mass society, one structured on its collective myths, fashions, shows and recreations.

Apart from this thematic subdivision, the show presents two different aspects for analysis: one of a narrative kind and the other a way for deeper investigation.

Basically, though without reaching the complexity of a scientific phenomenon, design is indebted to technical factors which can be approached more easily through the mediation of a narration.

In order to create concise historical references we asked twelve protagonists to recount, from their own point of view, the events that marked some of the transformations of Italian society. The words and memories of Maurizio Ferraris, Giampiero Mughini, Elio Fiorucci, Philippe Daverio, Franco La Cecla, Stefano Pistolini, Aldo Grasso, Franco Cardini, Antonia Jannone, Vittorio Marchis, Franco Raggi and Italo Lupi thus become the plot of the same number of stories that will accompany the visitor around the show. Extracts from documentaries and news items, TV advertisements, and fragments of films will evoke moments and events from the economic boom up to the present century.

At the same time we have imagined twelve "micro-stories", two for each thematic area, constructed around various objects awarded the Compasso d'Oro prize. Each micro-story is told in six successive instalments where the objects alternate with architecture, art, research, technology and customs. For example, in the *From research to daily life* section we might start with the Compasso d'Oro awarded in 1959 to the

Olivetti Elea computer, the first wholly transistorised commercial computer in the world, and arrive at the Hyper Search logarithm originated by the mathematician Massimo Marchiori in 1996 and on which the structure of Google, the most famous search engine in the world, has been built. In the middle there could be the innovative knitwear dyeing system introduced by the Benetton brothers in 1962; the Coronado divan designed by Afra and Tobia Scarpa in 1966, based on a special way of processing polyurethane and which allowed the industrial production of padding; the futurist Gran Sasso laboratory requested by Professor Zichichi in the 1970s for intercepting elusive neutrons; the advanced aerodynamic research undertaken by Pininfarina and awarded the Compasso d'Oro in 1979.

This is not a question of an organic narration but, rather, of an attempt to allow a glimpse of that tight network of phenomena which have helped determine possibilities for change. Twelve "micro-stories", each in six instalments: a total of 72 episodes which certainly do not aim at exhausting the range of Italian design in the past fifty years and even less do they account for all the notable events which in some way or other have helped define the aim of high-quality. More simply, it is a scheme corresponding to a wish to show how the world of design has participated in wider transformational scenarios, but also how these have been reflected by the vicissitudes of design.

To round off the scheme proposed by the show there are two symmetrical and mirroring views, one of our recent past, and another of the near future. With the collaboration of the Ugo Mulas Archive, the exhibition proposes a significant range of images by this great photographer devoted to the sphere of work and production. A survey through the eyes of one of the greatest Italian photographers of the second half of the 20th century: a tribute to Italian know-how, to the persons and skills that have, over the past decades, constructed the best of the country we live in today. With the collaboration of the Centro Sperimentale di Cinematografia, the exhibition also offers a group of three brief views by young film directors who have been chosen as representatives of all young Italians. We have asked them – they being the only part of tomorrow that we have access to – to ask themselves questions about our present and our immanent future so as to inspire aspirations and fears, expectations and hopes in a different, affluent, and fragile society.

We have worked on this project clearly keeping in mind that it ought not be a show of design but, rather, a show about design. A subtle distinction but, I believe, one not without significance. It means choosing to consider design as a receptive discipline, and projects as a moment for the meeting and synthesis of diverse situations. It means placing arguments within a framework in which everyone can find their own key to understanding. It means recognising that in the design of objects there are reproduced the same dynamics as are to be found in a wider cultural debate.

But it also means accepting that over the past fifty years design itself has changed a lot and that today it finds itself facing a need to bring into play knowledge, contexts and abilities. Today the value of Italian design has been consolidated into a heritage that by now belongs to history, and history can help explain it. But it can and must also be a resource, a reserve of attitudes, methods and procedures which we can trust in so as to reinvent our future.

It is for these reasons that we wanted to collect together in this catalogue a series of outside views, a kind of circumnavigation of design, carried out through a group of essays that also note its faults and implications. Rather than ask critics to tell us what is or was design, we have given involved writers, anthropologists, art critics, sociologists, scholars of imagery, experts in law, work historians, restorers of modern objects and research managers in order to understand how and where design touches on their particular interests, what aspects for them are the most interesting, and in what way design can once again undertake the function of creative innovation and how we can conserve its masterpieces or defend their value.

But then how can we forget that, if the first edition of the prize was originated and organised by a large store in Milan which promoted the cultural value of useful objects and recognised design's ability to encourage the modern renewal of Italian products, this 22nd edition of the Compasso d'Oro is being held in Rome thanks to the collaboration of ADI and the Ministry of Economic Development with the aim of backing the Italian industrial system, but also with the aim of celebrating the 150 years of Italian unity?

More from Less

Italy, unlike other countries, has never had an abundance of raw materials or sources of energy. Therefore its development has been centred on manufacturing rather than heavy industry. In the absence of raw materials, the fortunes of Italian firms are based on commercial abilities and workmanship

The key factors of their success are imagination, awareness of market trends and a talent for applying technical improvements. This success has been based on the ability of making the best of things by working on quality rather than quantity.

Italian industry was stretched to its limit by the autarchy imposed by the Fascist regime in 1936, but it still managed to respond and develop successfully in cutting-edge areas like organic chemistry, aeronautics and lightweight alloy processing. In the post-war period these capacities became the strong points of reconstruction.

Quality of design and simplicity of the project remain a hallmark of Italian design, able to transform assembly into a compositional technique, to give a simple sign meaning, to give value to lightness or obtain complex performances from something simple.

1.

2.

3.

Gino Sarfatti
1. **MOD. 559**
desk lamp
Società in Accomandita
Arteluce
photo cscdo Archive
I. COMPASSO D'ORO 1954

Franco Albini
2. **LUISA**
chair
Carlo Poggi
II. COMPASSO D'ORO 1955

Salvatore Alberio
3. **A-A**
round table with metal support
Arform
II. COMPASSO D'ORO 1955

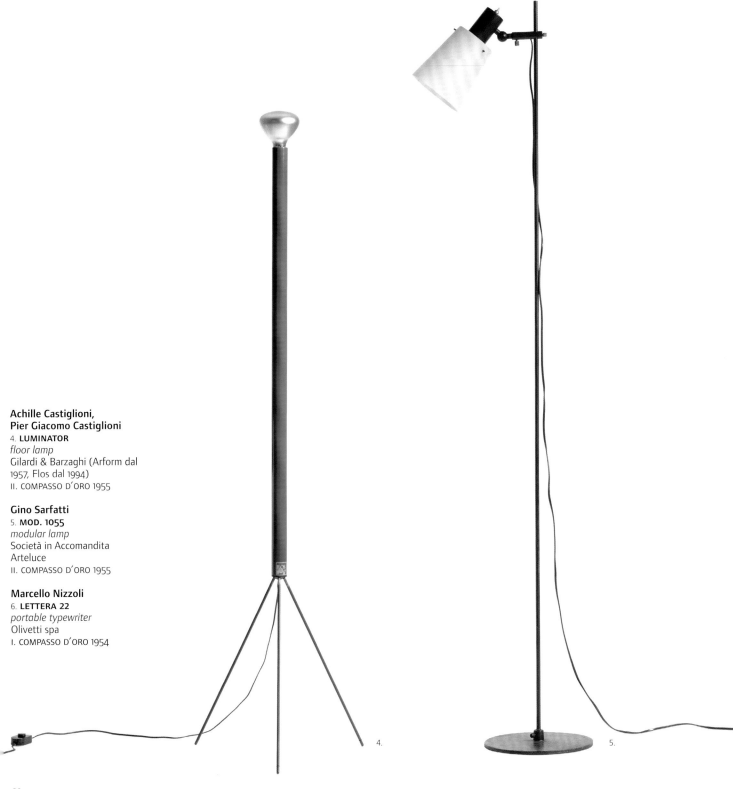

**Achille Castiglioni,
Pier Giacomo Castiglioni**
4. **LUMINATOR**
floor lamp
Gilardi & Barzaghi (Arform dal
1957, Flos dal 1994)
II. COMPASSO D'ORO 1955

Gino Sarfatti
5. **MOD. 1055**
modular lamp
Società in Accomandita
Arteluce
II. COMPASSO D'ORO 1955

Marcello Nizzoli
6. **LETTERA 22**
portable typewriter
Olivetti spa
I. COMPASSO D'ORO 1954

4.

5.

6.

7.

Gino Valle, Nani Valle
7. **CIFRA 5**
electromechanical clock
R. e C. Solari
III. COMPASSO D'ORO 1956

Dante Giacosa
8. **FIAT 500**
car
FIAT spa
V. COMPASSO D'ORO 1959

Gino Colombini
9. **K.S. 1171/2**
dismountable dish rack
Kartell srl
VI. COMPASSO D'ORO 1960

Richard Sapper
10. **STATIC**
clock
Lorenz spa
photo cscdo Archive
VI. COMPASSO D'ORO 1960

8.

9.

10.

11.

12.

13.

14.

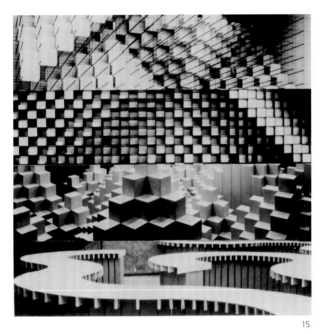

15.

16.

Mario Bellini
11. **TABLE**
table
Sandro Pedretti & F.llo
VII. COMPASSO D'ORO 1962

Massimo Vignelli
12. **COMPACT**
melamine set
Articoli Plastici Elettrici
photo cscdo Archive
VIII. COMPASSO D'ORO 1964

**Franco Albini, Bob Noorda,
Franca Helg, Antonio Piva**
13. **MILAN UNDERGROUND
SIGNAGE AND SET UP**
*Milan Underground signage
and set up*
Metropolitana Milanese spa
photo cscdo Archive
VIII. COMPASSO D'ORO 1964

Roberto Mango
14. **1964-1967 DESIGN
RESEARCH**
research
Facoltà di Architettura
di Napoli
IX. COMPASSO D'ORO 1967

Enzo Mari
15. **INDIVIDUAL DESIGN
RESEARCH**
individual research
photo cscdo Archive
IX. COMPASSO D'ORO 1967

Vico Magistretti
16. **ECLISSE**
desk lamp
Artemide spa
IX. COMPASSO D'ORO 1967

17.

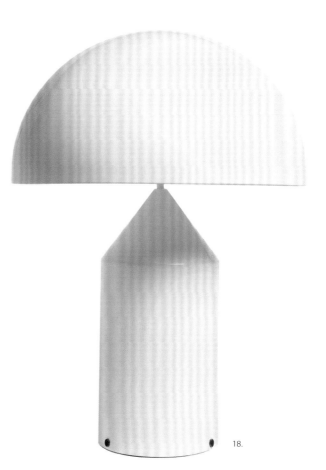

18.

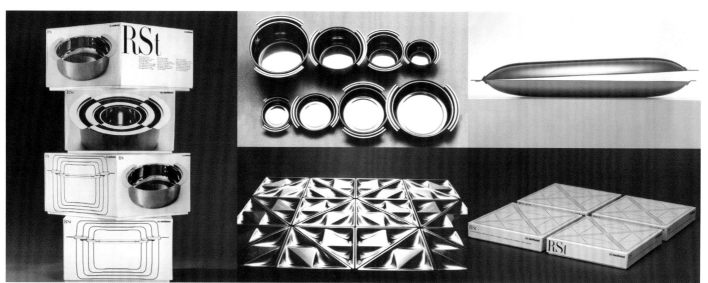

19.

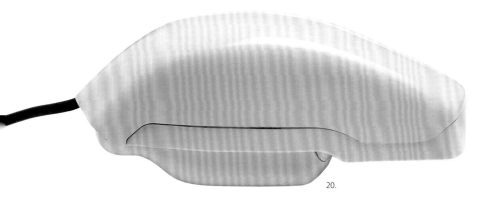

20.

21.

22.

Bob Noorda, Roberto Sambonet, Pino Tovaglia
17. **LOMBARDIA REGION CORPORATE IDENTITY**
visual design
Regione Lombardia
XI. COMPASSO D'ORO 1979

Vico Magistretti
18. **ATOLLO 233/D**
desk lamp
OLuce srl
XI. COMPASSO D'ORO 1979

Roberto Sambonet
19. **8 PIECES STAINLESS STEEL TRAY, FISH KETTLE, 32 PIECES APPETIZER, CORPORATE IDENTITY FOR PACKAGING**
(stainless steel) fish kettle and trays
Sambonet
photo CSCDO Archive
X. COMPASSO D'ORO 1970

Marco Zanuso with Richard Sapper
20. **GRILLO**
telephone
Siemens
IX. COMPASSO D'ORO 1967

Mario Bellini
21. **LE BAMBOLE**
armchairs
B&B Italia
XI. COMPASSO D'ORO 1979

Achille Castiglioni, Pio Manzù
22. **PARENTESI**
suspension lamp
Flos spa
XI. COMPASSO D'ORO 1979

23.

24.

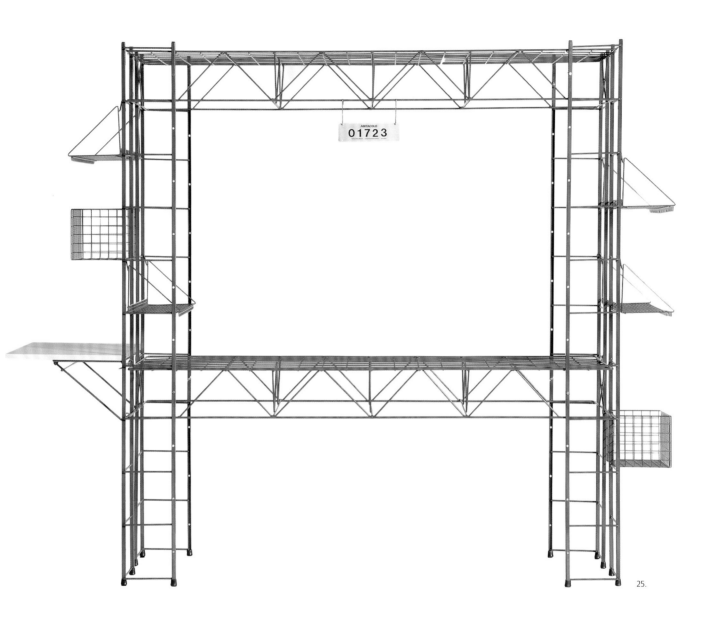

ABITACOLO
01723

25.

Enzo Mari
23. **DELFINA**
chair
Soc. Driade spa
XI. COMPASSO D'ORO 1979

Jonathan De Pas, Donato D'Urbino, Paolo Lomazzi
24. **SCIANGAI**
clothes stand
Zanotta spa
XI. COMPASSO D'ORO 1979

Bruno Munari
25. **ABITACOLO**
modular furniture
Robots spa
XI. COMPASSO D'ORO 1979

26.

27.

28.

29.

30.

31.

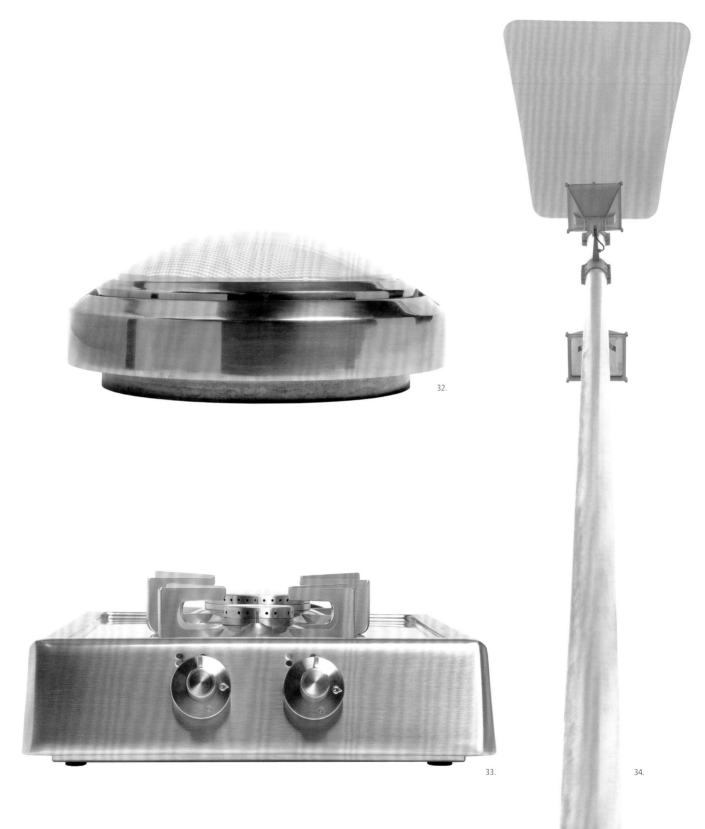

32.

33.

34.

35.

**Paolo Rizzato,
Alberto Meda,
Riccardo Sarfatti**
32. **METROPOLI**
*series of wall and ceiling
lamps*
Luceplan spa
XVII. COMPASSO D'ORO 1994

Domenico Moretto
33. **FOLDING COOKING HOB**
cooking hob
Alpes Inox spa
XVIII. COMPASSO D'ORO 1998

**Renzo Piano Design
Workshop**
34. **NUVOLA**
outdoor lighting fixture
iGuzzini Illuminazione srl
XVIII. COMPASSO D'ORO 1998

Riccardo Blumer
35. **LALEGGERA**
chair
Alias srl
XVIII. COMPASSO D'ORO 1998

36.

37.

38

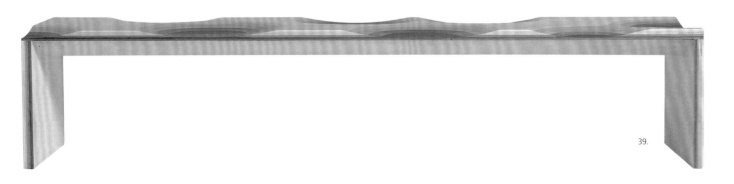

39.

**Giulio Iacchetti,
Matteo Ragni**
36. **MOSCARDINO**
disposable cutlery
Pandora Design
XIX. COMPASSO D'ORO 2001

Studio Cerri & Associati
37. **TITANO**
dining table
Poltrona Frau spa
XIX. COMPASSO D'ORO 2001

Konstantin Grcic
38. **MAY DAY**
utility light fixture
Flos spa
XIX. COMPASSO D'ORO 2001

Toyo Ito
39. **RIPPLES**
bench
Horm srl
XX. COMPASSO D'ORO 2004

Enzo Mari
40. **LEGATO**
table
Driade spa
XIX. COMPASSO D'ORO 2001

40.

MICHELANGELO PISTOLETTO, VENERE DEGLI STRACCI (THE RAG VENUS)

**STUDIO ALBINI - BOB NOORDA,
MILAN UNDERGROUND SIGNAGE AND SET-UP**
COMPASSO D'ORO 1964

BRUNO MUNARI, FALKLAND LAMP, DANESE

In 1950, Milan had 1,300,000 inhabitants and was fourteenth on the UN list of the biggest cities in the world, behind Beijing, but in front of Berlin. Milan was an expanding and lively city in the middle of an area with a high economic development rate.
To keep up with the liveliness of a rapidly growing city the city council launched impressive transformation projects that redesigned the relationships between residential, industrial and service areas, as well as public transport, which was expanded with an underground rail system and different levels of the road network which were expanded with a new set of ring roads. 1961 marked the launch of the first underground line, the red line. Franco Albini's studio was awarded the design of the new underground stations. Albini immediately involved Bob Noorda to whom he handed over the study of the graphics for signs and routes. Noorda chose maximum legibility fonts, decided on the positioning of signs and their hierarchy and selected colours and finishes that would avoid reflective glare from the lighting. He then concentrated it all in a coloured strip that he included in the design in agreement with Albini.
His strong and simple sign system, apparently just made up of colours and letters, was so efficient that Noorda would later be asked to reproduce the scheme for the Sao Paolo and New York subways. E.M.

In 1957, Bruno Danese decided to increase his production, switching from the very small-scale artisan ceramics he had started making with artist Franco Meneguzzo to objects designed to be serially produced.
For this new enterprise, Bruno Danese and his wife Jacqueline Vodoz chose Bruno Munari and Enzo Mari, two designers known to pay particular attention to production methodology during design.
Both trained artists, Mari and Munari looked critically at conventional industrial production methods and aimed at increasing the intelligence of the average product by respecting working methods and an imaginative use of materials. This translates into simplified compositions, almost completely devoid of finish and shapes influenced by assembly sequences.
However, if Mari made the design project into a theorem, Munari considered it as an experiment causing irony and matter-of-factness to live side by side.
By applying these rules systematically Munari designed objects that hovered between the extremes of useful and amusing features, artistic and industrial aspects, and reality or fantasy.
Surprising and evocative objects fit here, like the Falkland lamp, an invention just made from nothing except tubular elastic fabric which takes on a three-dimensional form thanks to a series of metal rings in different diameters that give it shape and keep it taut. E.M.

"When my urge to understand became clear, I instinctively identified all the opposites which were part of the system that creates polarities. Looking at art, I felt I was torn between an abstract mental part and a concrete physical part."
Right from the start, and even berore any official recognition, (Oggetti in meno/ Fewer Things) Pistoletto proved to be one of the moving lights of Arte Povera.
Venere degli Stracci [The Rag Venus], made out of polishing rags which he had used for his earlier mirror paintings, is the most representative work of the artist, besides the whole movement.
This most famous work by Pistoletto features an assembly of multicolour rags, toward which the neoclassical Venus is facing, revealing a shapely and sensual back. The installation is based on the contrast between the perfection of the still and immortal female nude, symbol of absolute beauty, and the physical deterioration of the pile of old clothes which provides the evidence of a vulnerable existence. The perfect face of Venus, living outside real life and time, is spectacularly immersed in this heap of opaque old rags full of the ephemeral evidence of those who have used them in the past. Pistoletto created an effect of ironic vitality, showing how our cultural identity emerges from the past. A.M.S.

Michelangelo Pistoletto
Venere degli stracci, 1967, cement, mica, rags, 150 × 280 × 100 cm
Collection Museo d'Arte Contemporanea, Rivoli -
Photo P. Pellion

VICO MAGISTRETTI, LAMPADA ATOLLO, OLUCE
COMPASSO D'ORO 1979

On his way back from a round of clients and shops, one of Vico Magistretti's young assistants reported on the feedback that he had received about their most recent designs as well as suggestions regarding objects that should be redesigned or rethought from scratch.
Among other things, he reported a request for a living room lamp, to be put in the corner between two sofas placed at right angles, usually occupied by a low square table. At the time, there were very few lamps available on the market and they were quite dated.
To explain the request better, he took a piece of paper and drew a hasty sketch of a cylinder with a hemispherical shade. Magistretti looked at the sketch and swiftly added two lines, giving the cylinder a more elegant conical top; just two lines to draw an easy yet strikingly apt shape that in its satisfying simplicity became an icon of Italian design. E.M.

GIORGIO ARMANI, WOMEN'S COLLECTION

Giorgio Armani's career started at the end of the 1950s, amid the exuberant mood that characterised Milan's great department store, La Rinascente. As a young window-dresser, Armani collaborated with graphic designers and architects such as Munari, Sambonet, Steiner, and Huber, who was hired to ensure that the store windows passed on a precise message and an image that did far more than simply show off the merchandise.
Armani's career as a clothes designer, however, began in 1965 when he was taken on by Nino Cerruti.
In 1975, now experienced and determined to develop his own personal style, he started his own business.
Intent on creating a modern woman who is sporty and natural, he began by changing the very structure of the clothes and progressively defining a carefully matching colour palette. First, he destructured the traditional tailoring of the jacket, doing away with padding and the inner lining, redesigning the geometry of the cut and the buttons. He then bathed the result in a range of colours varying from black to beige, through grey, and his signature blue.
It was in 1980 that his quest came to total fruition, though. For the professional career woman Armani imagined an androgynous wardrobe made up of jackets and trousers. While femininity was ensured by soft and floaty shirts, it was the cut of the jacket that supported the whole composition: lightly padded shoulders were enough to convey the image of a strong and decisive woman. Two tiny bits of padding, almost nothing, and yet sufficient to embody the spirit and impression of the contemporary woman. E.M.

LUISA BOCCHIETTO, VAS-ONE VASE, SERRALUNGA

Rotational plastic moulding is a technique that exploits rotation in pre-heated moulds to distribute heated liquid plastic evenly.
This method isn't new and it has often been used for producing low cost and low quality goods, for example tanks, cisterns, road bollards and some of the moving parts of looms used in the textile industry in the area around Biella. The crisis in the textile industry pushed Serralunga, a company that specialised in this kind of goods, to try and export this production technique to other areas nearer the design world.
Since the rotational technique only makes hollow objects, Serralunga decided to start with a vase collection, a type of product similar to furnishings, but not in direct competition, thus permitting the use of the same distribution channels. Famous designers were engaged to design this collection and when launched in 2008 it was an immediate success.
Behind lay a huge research effort, essential to improve the quality of the finished products: complex moulds, a wider range of plastics, particularly uniform surfaces with different textures, undercut details and sharply defined corners and edges.
Designed by Luisa Bocchietto, who was in charge of the Serralunga collection for a long time, Vas-One brings together all the best features of the project. Within its very traditional shape it hides a lamp for outdoor environments, with a special effect only achieved by the translucent quality of polyethylene, which plays with expectations and appearances. At the same time reassuring and spectacular, Vas-One is a perfect example of contemporary design, reinventing our everyday landscape thanks to technology and imagination. E.M.

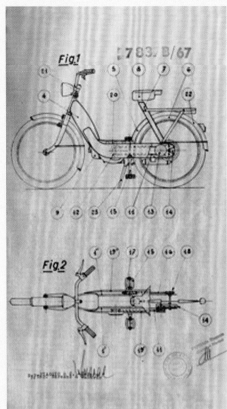

VICO MAGISTRETTI, SELENE CHAIR, ARTEMIDE

FRANCO ALBINI, LUISA CHAIR, POGGI
COMPASSO D'ORO 1955

Franco Albini was a cultivated, modern architect with a love for aeronautics. And yet when designing perhaps his most famous chair, he chose what seems like a rather conventional solution.

Albini worked on the design for the Luisa chair for about twenty years, searching for a way to make front legs, arms and back out of a single continuous piece. He then designed sloping back legs to support the arm rests.

In later versions Albini no longer used a single piece of curved wood or metal, separating, instead, the various components of the seat and reverting to more traditional carpentry methods.

Rather than opting for the modern solution of the single piece which would allow for mass production and costly equipment, Albini shifted his attention to the linking features. It is the joints that control components and govern the wooden sections, searching for adequate surfaces among the recesses.

And it is the rhythm of the joints that restore to the design that level of refined technology that post-war Italy would otherwise have been unable to accommodate. E.M.

CIAO MOPED, PIAGGIO

In the early 1960s, the spread of small cheap cars changed the role of motorcycles and mopeds and the way they had been hitherto used. They ceased to be looked on as a practical way of going from A to B, and became the first specifically teenager's means of transport, preliminary to the coveted driving licence. This evolution is reflected in the design and the spirit of many of these lightweight vehicles which shed the complexity typical of mechanical objects and instead become very easy to operate and maintain.

The Ciao by Piaggio is an emblematic case. This moped, despite its quite evident design ancestry in the humble bicycle, is equipped with a generous 49cc engine and, more importantly, a new automatic, constantly variable transmission, able to instantly adjust the transmission ratio according to load, speed and slope. Perfect for town, for both boys and girls, the Ciao was even simpler than the Vespa and the Lambretta, the perfect symbol of that younger generation who made freedom and independence their way of life. E.M.

Ciclomotore Ciao, Piaggio & C. spa, 1967
Technical drawing attached to patent, MICA, UIBM, fasc. 123038

Vico Magistretti designed the Selene chair for Artemide in 1969. Masterfully designed to produce a small, elegant, yet strong structure from a thin sheet of plastic, the first version was practically crafted, using hand shaped fibreglass, dyed and then varnished. Its minute proportions and elegant design gave it a classical understated look that probably made it an unexpected success.

The company quickly set up a production line using a complicated mould giving a finished chair ready for sale in a single process. Selene was the first plastic chair moulded in a single piece to be produced in Italy.

Futuristic, shiny, and in assorted colours, Selene was comfortable, without bowing either to tradition or to science fiction.

The natural ability to dialogue between tradition and innovation is the hallmark of Vico Magistretti's work. As well as being the symbol of an enlightened bourgeoisie, he also experimented with the unconventional and surprisingly formal. "I believe that embracing technology wholesale is quite foolish. Technology is just a tool like a hammer. The extraordinary quality of good design is that it enables us to see antique or modern things, shapes and techniques in a new light." E.M.

RICHARD SAPPER, TIZIO LAMP, ARTEMIDE

Richard Sapper designed the ultramodern and simple Tizio in 1972. It was a very unconventional looking table lamp, a bare skeleton of weights and counterweights, all function and technology. The whole design was aimed at making the most of the qualities of the new low voltage halogens. It consisted of a small incorporated shade which housed the light bulb; a heavy base that housed the transformer; no connecting wires as the current travelled directly down the light metal strips of the structure; functional counterweights in aluminum that balanced it; perfect dynamically jointed movement. The forerunner of new techniques, Tizio did not at first meet with success, since it took ten years for its futuristic shape to be accepted and to be appreciated by accompanying taste.

A real status symbol of contemporary design, Tizio has become a fixture on many movie and television sets, often representing the stile of the prosperous 1980s, symbolising new economic power and the new consumer culture. E.M.

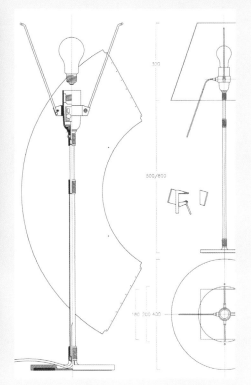

PAOLO RIZZATTO, COSTANZA LIGHT, LUCEPLAN

When the Costanza light designed by Paolo Rizzatto for Luceplan first appeared, many critics and observers were fooled: the return of the lampshade – widespread in traditional lighting but little used in the stylish world of design – seemed like a revisiting of the past, with little innovation or design about it.

In reality, instead, the Costanza denotes the ability to reinvent and update the absolute archetype of the light: the 'abat-jour'.

Indeed, it was with the lampshade that polycarbonate made its debut in the world of lighting and design. This sophisticated, and then still costly, material was used at the time for car dashboards and airplane instrument panels. It was thanks to close association with the technicians from Bayer (and the fact that the company agreed to buy ten years' worth of material in advance) that the Germans were persuaded to develop a 7/10 millimetre sample which would be inflexible enough and create the right opalescence for the lampshade. No less innovative was the introduction of a dimmer touch sensor, which uses the conductors in the body to turn the lamp on and off and regulate light intensity. A simple shape with complex technology, the Costanza did not win the Compasso d'Oro, but in the wake of endless copies it has become a classic of contemporary design. E.M.

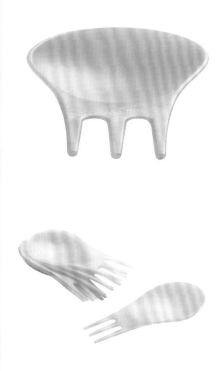

GIULIO IACCHETTI - MATTEO RAGNI, MOSCARDINO CUTLERY, PANDORA DESIGN
COMPASSO D'ORO 2001

Hovering between natural instinct and consumerism, food is an excellent gauge of changes in collective behaviour. A necessary and cultural act, eating represents the values of a society, and captures its public and private rites.

When they designed a *double-face* piece of cutlery, Giulio Iacchetti and Matteo Ragni exactly captured the change in contemporary eating habits, caught between the need for speed and newly discovered environmental concerns. Moscardino was made to be handled, either as a tiny fork or a spoon, halfway between good table manners and eating with one's fingers. Perfect for buffets, cocktails, and aperitifs, Moscardino represents a new kind of socialisation, brief meetings and quick exchanges rather than conversations. At the same time it is made of a completely biodegradable material, which is disposable and zero impact, thus also satisfying the requirement for environmental awareness. E.M.

79

New Italians, New Things

Although still inferior to most other European countries, the percentage of women in employment in Italy has risen from the 28% of 1960 to the present 46%. In 1960 only 55% of Italians owned a refrigerator, while today no house is without one. From an automobile fleet of 2,000,000 circulating cars in 1960, today Italy is the European country that has the most cars with 35,000,000 million registered vehicles. These figures alone are enough to show a society in rapid evolution.

Over a few decades, family and work structures have changed, likewise domestic habits and the perception of the landscape. These profound changes have coincided with the decline of agriculture, women's emancipation, the improvement in education levels and the decrease in family size. This evolution has influenced the shape of houses, objects and consumer goods which have reflected or occasionally raced ahead of the evolution of the country. Italy has seamlessly passed from traditional rural models to widespread industrialisation and then to the dynamics of an elusive supermodernity incorporating advanced service industries and involving a high level of workforce mobility.

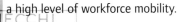

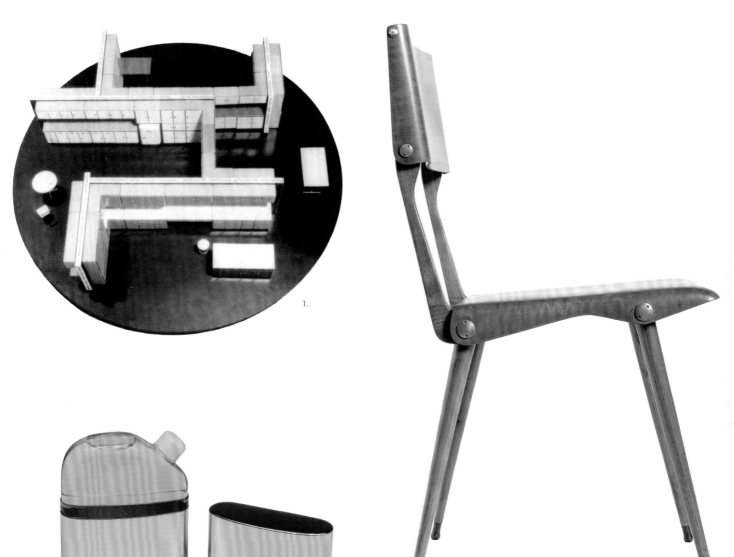

1.

2.

3.

Augusto Magnaghi
1. **FITTED KITCHEN**
fitted kitchen
SAFFA spa
photo cscdo Archive
I. COMPASSO D'ORO 1954

Franco De Martini
2. **TRAVEL PERFUME FLASK**
travel perfume flask
Atkinsons J. & E. spa
photo cscdo Archive
I. COMPASSO D'ORO 1954

Carlo De Carli
3. **MOD. 683**
chair
Ditta Figli A. Cassina
I. COMPASSO D'ORO 1954

4.

5.

6.

Max Bill
4. **METHACRYLATE**
TOILETTRIES PROVISION
toilettries provision
Verbania srl Di Cannero
Riviera - distribuzione Kristall
photo cscdo Archive
III. COMPASSO D'ORO 1956

Ubaldo Dreina
5. **DOLOMITI**
nylon waterproof
Impermeabili San Giorgio spa
photo cscdo Archive
II. COMPASSO D'ORO 1955

Gino Colombini
6. **KS 1146**
polyethylene bucket with lid
Kartell-Samco srl
photo cscdo Archive
II. COMPASSO D'ORO 1955

Bruno Munari
7. **MOD. 510**
table ice bucket
Tre A Attualità Artistiche
Artigiane
II. COMPASSO D'ORO 1955

7.

8.

9.

10.

11.

12.

Gino Colombini
8. **PLASTIC TUB**
plastic tub
Kartell-Samco srl
photo cscdo Archive
IV. COMPASSO D'ORO 1957

Massimo Lagostina,
Adriano Lagostina
9. **STAINLESS STEEL**
KITCHENWARE IN GIFT PACK
stainless steel kitchenware
in gift pack
Ing. Emilio Lagostina spa
photo cscdo Archive
III. COMPASSO D'ORO 1956

Roberto Menghi
10. **GRADUATED POLYETHYLENE**
BUCKET WITH SPOUT
bucket
Smalterie Meridionali spa
III. COMPASSO D'ORO 1956

Marco Zanuso
11. **MOD. 1102**
automatic sewing machine
F.lli Borletti spa
III. COMPASSO D'ORO 1956

Marcello Nizzoli
12. **MIRELLA**
sewing machine
Vittorio Necchi spa
IV. COMPASSO D'ORO 1957

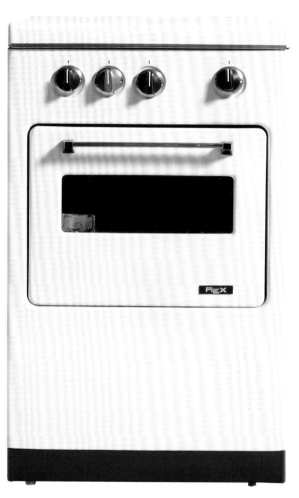

13.

14.

15.

Uffici Progettazione del Dipartimento elettrotermodinamici della divisione beni di consumo
13. **CASTALIA**
washing machine
CGE Compagnia Generale di Elettricità
photo CSCDO Archive
VI. COMPASSO D'ORO 1960

Ufficio Progetti Rex
14. **MOD. 700**
gas cooker
Industrie Antonio Zanussi
VII. COMPASSO D'ORO 1962

Achille Castiglioni, Pier Giacomo Castiglioni
15. **PITAGORA**
coffee machine
La Cimbali Giuseppe spa
VII. COMPASSO D'ORO 1962

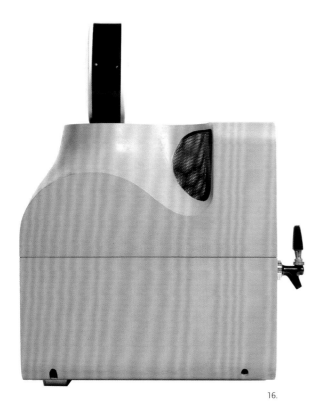

16.

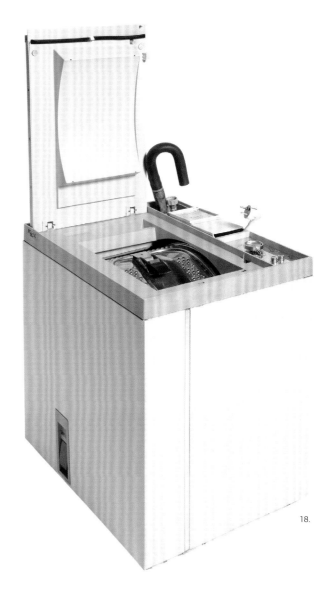

18.

17.

**Achille Castiglioni,
Pier Giacomo Castiglioni**
16. **SPINAMATIC**
beer spigot
Splügen Bräu della Poretti spa
VIII. COMPASSO D'ORO 1964

**Marco Zanuso,
Richard Sapper**
17. **DONEY**
television
Brion Vega Radio Televisore sas
VII. COMPASSO D'ORO 1962

**Ufficio Disegno Industriale
Zanussi**
18. **MOD. P5**
automatic washing machine
Zanussi
IX. COMPASSO D'ORO 1967

19.

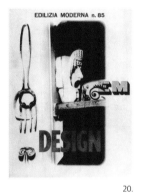

20.

21.

Joe Colombo
19. **AIR CONDITIONER**
air conditioner
Candy
X. COMPASSO D'ORO 1970

Vittorio Gregotti
20. **DESIGN MONOGRAPHIC**
DOSSIER
research
Edilizia Moderna
photo CSCDO Archive
IX. COMPASSO D'ORO 1967

Lodovico Acerbis,
Giotto Stoppino
21. **PROGRAMMA SHERATON**
storage units
Acerbis International
XI. COMPASSO D'ORO 1979

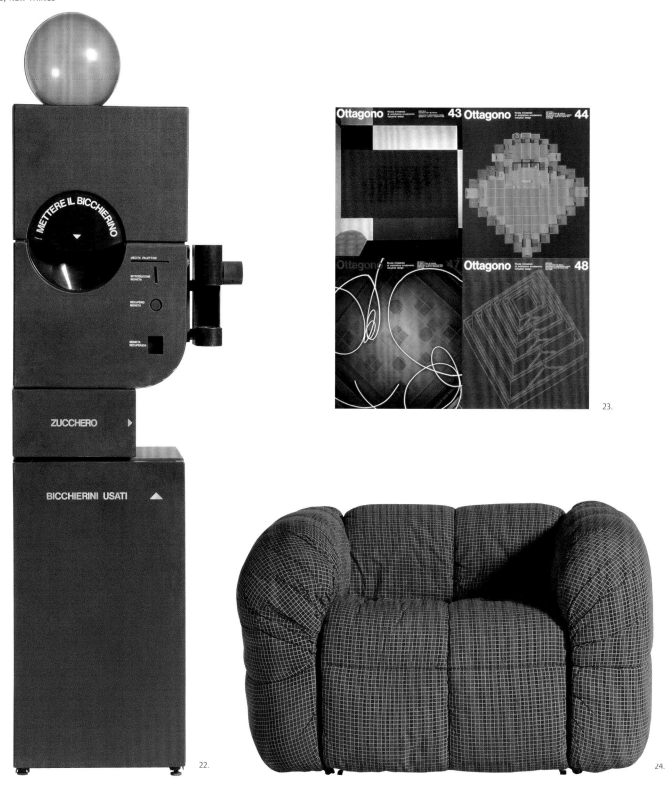

22.

23.

24.

25.

Mario Bellini, Dario Bellini
22. **BRAS 200**
coffee vending machine
Bras spa
XI. COMPASSO D'ORO 1979

**Giuliana Gramigna,
Salvatore Gregoretti,
Sergio Mazza**
23. **OTTAGONO**
magazine
CO.P.in.A. Editrice srl
photo cscdo Archive
XI. COMPASSO D'ORO 1979

Cini Boeri, Grizziotti Laura
24. **LA FAMIGLIA DEGLI STRIPS**
armchair
Arflex spa
XI. COMPASSO D'ORO 1979

Afra Scarpa, Tobia Scarpa
25. **SORIANA**
armchair
Cassina spa
X. COMPASSO D'ORO 1970

CENTROKAPPA

26.

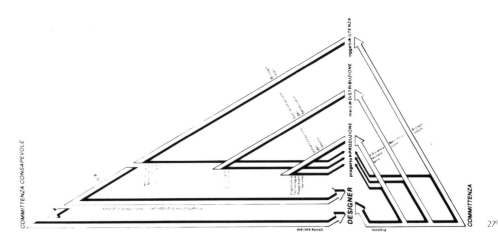

27.

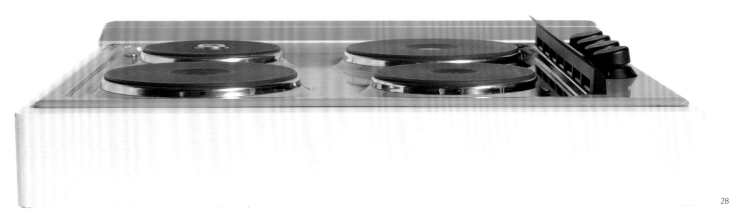

28

29.

30.

31.

Centrokappa
26. **CENTROKAPPA**
research
Centro di ricerca,
progettazione, promozione e
sviluppo dell'immagine
photo CSCDO Archive
VII. COMPASSO D'ORO 1979

ISIA – Roma
27. **TEACHING DIAGRAM**
research
ISIA, Roma
photo CSCDO Archive
XI. COMPASSO D'ORO 1979

Makio Hasuike
28. **OSA**
home appliances
Merloni spa
XI. COMPASSO D'ORO 1979

**Rodolfo Bonetto,
Giancarlo Illiprandi**
29. **INTERIOR TRIM FOR FIAT 131
SUPERMIRAFIORI**
interior trim for car
Fiat
photo CSCDO Archive
XI. COMPASSO D'ORO 1979

Ugo La Pietra
30. **L'OCCULTAMENTO 1972**
bedroom with table
Arosio Giacobbe e Figli, F.lli
Viscardi
photo CSCDO Archive
XI. COMPASSO D'ORO 1979

Vico Magistretti
31. **MARALUNGA 675**
armchair
Cassina spa
XI. COMPASSO D'ORO 1979

Angelo Cortesi
32. **308**
bedroom furniture system
Tosi mobili spa
XII. COMPASSO D'ORO 1981

Piero Polato
33. **SCHOOLBOOK**
text
Edizioni scolastiche Bruno
Mondadori
photo cscdo Archive
XII. COMPASSO D'ORO

Claudio Salocchi
34. **METROSISTEMA**
*equipment for houses and
communities*
Alberti Arredamenti Cucine
photo cscdo Archive
XI. COMPASSO D'ORO 1979

**Giorgetto Giugiaro-SIRP spa,
Italdesign**
35. **PANDA**
car
Fiat Auto spa
XIX. COMPASSO D'ORO 1981

Marco Zanuso
36. **ARIANTE**
fan
Vortice Elettrosociali spa
XI. COMPASSO D'ORO 1979

Alessandro Mendini
37. **MODO**
magazine
RDE Ricerche Design Editrice
srl
XI. COMPASSO D'ORO 1979

32.

33.

34.

35.

36.

37.

39.

40.

41.

38.

**Gianni Arduini,
Lorenzo Bonfanti,
Gianfranco Salvemini**
38. **FB 33**
floor polisher
Vorwerk Folletto
XIII. COMPASSO D'ORO 1984

Studio Kairos
39. **SISAMO**
closet
B&B Italia
photo CSCDO Archive
XIII. COMPASSO D'ORO 1984

Ettore Vitale
40. **TV THEME MUSIC**
tv theme music
RAI
photo CSCDO Archive
XIII. COMPASSO D'ORO 1984

Francesco Soro
41. **SIGLO 20**
sofa
ICF spa
XII. COMPASSO D'ORO 1981 1981

**Francesco Trabucco,
Marcello Vecchi**
42. **BIDONE LAVATUTTO**
floor polisher
Alfatec spa
XV. COMPASSO D'ORO 1989

Luciano Valboni
43. **DOMINO**
*hotel tourist area beverage
vending machine*
Zanussi Grandi Impianti spa
XV. COMPASSO D'ORO 1989

Anna Ferrieri Castelli
44. **K 4870**
stackable chair
Kartell spa
XIV. COMPASSO D'ORO 1987

Enzo Mari
45. **TONIETTA**
chair
Zanotta spa
XIV. COMPASSO D'ORO 1987

42.

43.

44.

45.

47.

48.

49.

46.

51.

52.

50.

Michele De Lucchi, Giancarlo Fassina
46. **TOLOMEO**
series of lamps
Artemide spa
XV. COMPASSO D'ORO 1989

Giovanni Baule, Wando Pagliardini
47. **LINEA GRAFICA**
graphic design and visual communication magazine
Azzurra editrice srl
XIV. COMPASSO D'ORO 1987

Ettore Vitale
48. **ENVIRONMENTAL CONDITION REPORT**
book
photo CSCDO Archive
Ministero dell'ambiente
XVI. COMPASSO D'ORO 1991

Italo Lupi
49. **IF**
cultural magazine
Fondazione IBM Italia
XVIII. COMPASSO D'ORO 1998

Mario Bellini
50. **THE BELLINI CHAIR**
stackable chair
Heller Incorporated
XIX. COMPASSO D'ORO 2001

Antonio Citterio, Oliver Low
51. **MOBIL**
chest of drawers system
Kartell spa
XVII. COMPASSO D'ORO 1994

Giorgietto Giugiaro
52. **PUNTO**
subcompact car
Fiat Auto spa
photo CSCDO Archive
XVII. COMPASSO D'ORO 1994

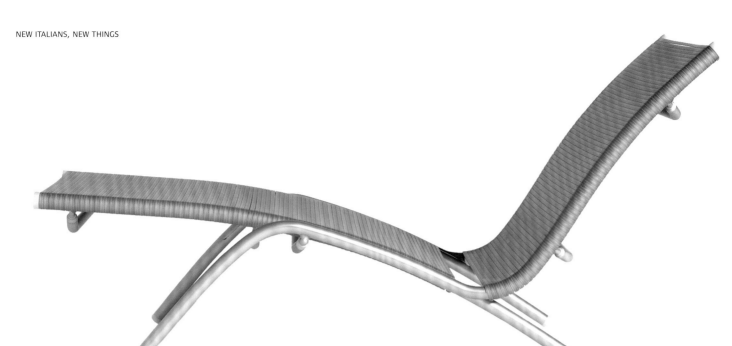

53.

54.

55.

56.

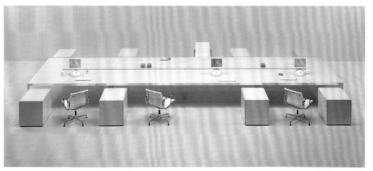

58. 57.

Franco Bizzozzero
53. **BIKINI**
chaise longue
Bonacina Pierantonio snc
XIX. COMPASSO D'ORO 2001

Centro Stile Fiat,
Stile Bertone,
I.DE.A. Institute
54. **NUOVA PANDA**
car
Fiat Auto
photo cscdo Archive
XX. COMPASSO D'ORO 2004

59.

Monica Fumagalli,
Giancarlo Iliprandi
(Iliprandi Associati)
55. **L'ARCA**
monthly magazine
l'Arca edizioni
XX. COMPASSO D'ORO 2004

Stefano Casciani,
Anna Del Gatto
and Maurizio Malabruzzi,
conductor Ugo Gregoretti
56. **LEZIONI DI DESIGN**
television programme
RAI Educational
XIX. COMPASSO D'ORO 2001

Marc Sadler
57. **BIG**
bookcase
Caimi Brevetti
XXI. COMPASSO D'ORO 2008

Pierluigi Cerri,
Alessandro Colombo,
Studio Cerri & Associati
58. **NAÒS SYSTEM**
system of multipurpose tables
unifor
photo CSCDO Archive
XX. COMPASSO D'ORO 2004

Lorenzo Gecchelin
59. **LATINA**
squeezer
F.lli Guzzini spa
XX. COMPASSO D'ORO 2004

Bartoli Design e Fauciglietti
Engineering
60. **R606 UNO**
chair
Segis spa
XXI. COMPASSO D'ORO 2008

Giorgetto Giugiaro,
Italdesign Giugiaro
61. **BRERA**
sport car
Alfa Romeo
XX. COMPASSO D'ORO 2004

60.

61.

AUGUSTO MAGNAGHI, MODULAR KITCHEN, SAFFA
COMPASSO D'ORO 1954

The SAFFA kitchen successfully combined the typical modular features of the American-style kitchen with the logic of the German one. Unlike the former, though, it was not made of expensive, heavy metal units and, unlike the latter, it foreshadowed the idea of electrical appliances fitted between the cupboards. Suitable for light industry and compatible with the chronic lack of raw materials, the SAFFA kitchen was a practical example of how the Italian home could be modernised.

By eliminating the old rural stove and hearth, but without trying to copy the spacious kitchens of the large middle class homes, the Saffa kitchen embodied the features of the Italian-style kitchen of the future. Indeed it was not long before the size of the electrical appliances and that of the modular units would be standardised to become the classic 60x60x85 cm, ensuring perfect integration between containing units and technical elements. The design was completed by the introduction of the continuous work surface made of laminate, or wood, marble or granite in the more costly versions. This practical design was to guarantee the Italian kitchen and home appliances industry long-lasting leadership on the international market. E.M.

**ANGELO BIANCHETTI - MARIO PAVESI,
AUTOGRILL PAVESI, FIORENZUOLA**

The entrepreneurial talent of Mario Pavesi, famous confectionery manufacturer from Novara, is quite obvious, as the mere mention of the famous Pavesini biscuits (a packaged version of a traditional Novara biscuit) should be enough. But Mario Pavesi owed a lot of his business success to commercial acumen, which was always ahead of the times.

In 1947 he decided to open an outlet for his products at the Novara entrance of the Milan-Turin motorway. Italy needed rebuilding, but Mario Pavesi foresaw future developments, and decided to invest in bars and restaurants along the incomplete stretches of motorway inherited from before the war. At the same time, Pavesi understood that travelling isn't only a necessity but also an experience and a break from everyday routine.

With the constant help of the architect Bianchetti, Pavesi imagined surprising, creative and carefree architectural forms for his Autogrills.

Hence, when the Autostrada del Sole route between Milan and Naples was announced, he was one of the first industrialists to win the contract for a series of restaurants to be built next to the service stations along the motorway.

With far reaching insight, Pavesi and Bianchetti imagined a bridge structure that was both spectacular and rational. Not a restaurant at the side of each carriageway but a single panoramic and dramatic lookout floating above the traffic. In 1959 the bulldozers were still at work on the Milan-Bologna tract but the Fiorenzuola d'Arda Autogrill was already under construction, the first bridge restaurant to be built in Europe.

While fitted American-style kitchens became part of Italian homes and the Fiat 600 took to the roads, Pavesi Autogrills suggested new eating styles and new consumption patterns to accompany these changes in the behaviour and lifestyles of Italians.

Between 1958 and 1977, the architect Angelo Bianchetti built eleven bridge Autogrills, seventy restaurants in motorway service areas and four motels for the Pavesi group. E.M.

Autogrill Pavesi, Fiorenzuola d'Arda, 1959, the first of the bridges.
Designer, the architect Angelo Bianchetti
Photo Archive of the architect Jan Jacopo Bianchetti

**UGO LA PIETRA, L'OCCULTAMENTO 1972,
EXPERIMENTAL DOMESTIC INTERIOR**

In 1969, the three main unions called a general strike over the right to decent and affordable housing for everyone, rather than for work or pay issues. That strike marked the highest point of post-war economic expansion, since shortly afterwards, the 1973 petrol crisis and the accompanying slump were to pull in the opposite direction.

A few years later, Ugo La Pietra looked at popular housing with new interest, noticing how far the basic structure of popular housing had dropped behind the changed needs of a society in rapid transformation. Apartments intended to simply house workers at rest could not satisfy the new generations with their more casual and freer lifestyles. Intending to shock, La Pietra designed an adaptable space holding beds, mattresses and storage space below the level of a new raised and moveable floor. Here, he actually conceived a dwelling halfway between the principle of the Japanese *tatami* and a situationist installation. In line with the radical design of the time, La Pietra did not create a house for everyone, but a house for each of us, predating the notion of the American loft. E.M.

FIAT-GIUGIARO ITALDESIGN, PANDA CAR
COMPASSO D'ORO 1980

Launched in 1980, the Fiat Panda was a real novelty on the car scene at the time. The Panda did not fall into any known category for, despite being quite spacious, it had a small engine, it was too large and spartan to be considered a city-car in the wake of the famous Mini Minor and not spunky enough to become close to its sister car the Fiat 127, the Volkswagen Golf, or the popular Renault 5, too minimal for a family car and too small to be a forerunner of the later trend for people carriers.

While Giorgetto Giugiaro designed it, the Fiat management inspired the main idea of this car. In those years of great social tension within and outside factories, the company wanted a car suitable for the new young and casual market, to tempt with a car that oozed confidence and was easy to run. At the same time the car had to be easy to assemble and, above all, have extremely low production costs. It was murmured that Giovanni Agnelli himself had set its production cost at a million lire at the most. Giugiaro interpreted these requests in a very acute way, focusing on extremely versatile and spacious interiors. With light and easily foldable seats, the Panda's interiors were incredibly adaptable, from being a living room to becoming a bedroom, from a nursery to a load carrier. A very simple outer body enclosed this living space, all taut lines and flat surfaces, including the windows, windscreen and rear window without any curvature.

Leaving behind the myths of speed and rampant aerodynamics, the Panda reinvented cars from the inside, with a design centred wholly around the quality of its interiors, in exchange for the spartan simplicity of its bodywork. Tough, versatile and cheap, the Panda was an immediate success and had already sold its millionth model by July 1984. E.M.

BARILLA - GAVINO SANNA,
MULINO BIANCO BARILLA ADVERT

Food consumption grew steadily from the early 1950s, in response to previous malnutrition and shortages. According to official Censis statistics, this increase started coming down only at the beginning of the 1980s. Actually it wasn't a decrease in absolute terms, since Italians still happen to be the Europeans with the highest calory consumption a day.

What changed were tastes and habits; a decline in the use of traditional fresh food and ingredients of the Mediterranean diet together with the emergence of supermarkets and the appearance of the first American fast food chains. These are all symptoms of changing lifestyles and family dynamics in which nobody seems to have the time or desire to spend time cooking. So while the dreary trio of salmon, rocket and shrimps took over restaurants, the 1980s marked the triumph of fast food, soft drinks, frozen food, packaged snacks, crackers, cakes and biscuits.

Two opposite phenomena, both bearing strong connotations, partially compensated for this trend. On the one hand there were the proposals of the famous Nouvelle Cuisine chefs, dishes that mostly populated the pages of glossy magazines and seemed to be made especially to inspire the imagination, while on the other hand new advertising campaigns came to the fore, created by advertising designers who had strong opinions about both the stomach and the heart requiring nourishment.

The prototype for this form of communication is the advertising campaign designed by Gavino Sanna for a new line of baked foods from Barilla through which the Mulino Bianco brand became a place of healthy sentiments, family peace, rural tranquillity and simple everyday joys. It was a mellow and reassuring representation that combined simple and traditional Italian values with the affluent present; nostalgia and optimism at the service of the new consumerism. E.M.

ALESSANDRO MENDINI, ANNA G CORKSCREW, ALESSI

While the 1980s put paid to the idea of design purely based on the rational concept of needs and functions, the 1990s marked the consolidation of highly narrative and emotional design.

Convinced that design can help to build affectionate relationships between objects and people, Alberto Alessi took a gamble when he launched new product lines with high empathy value. Almost like comic strip characters, the Alessi items were figures that populated the kitchen and the home like playfellows.

Emblematic was the corkscrew designed by Alessandro Mendini, the mind behind the new semantics introduced by Alessi. Without doubt the most famous corkscrew in the history of design, Anna G is a fond portrait and a homage. Its success was such that it led, between 1994 and 2001, to a small family of objects.

Despite occasionally yielding to the language of the status-symbol and the odd concession to neo-kitsch taste, Mendini and Alessi won the bet. A whole experimental workshop was established that successfully combined financial rewards and the freedom of a privileged observatory through which to transform contemporary design. E.M.

MARCO ZANUSO, RICHARD SAPPER,
DONEY TELEVISION SET, BRIONVEGA
COMPASSO D'ORO 1962

GAETANO PESCE, UP ARMCHAIR, C&B

Just eight years after the start of regular television programming by the RAI, Marco Zanuso designed the Doney, the first transistorised Italian television, for Brionvega.

Thanks to the miniaturisation of its electronic components, the Doney was quite small, easy to carry and reasonably light.

It was produced just two years after the first Japanese-made portable transistor television, thus demonstrating the technical prowess of Italian Industry in an advanced sector like televisions.

While the layout imitates the American and Japanese style technically, with the circuiting well distributed around the cathode-ray tube, in the design of the body Zanuso and Sapper were ahead of all international competitors. Entirely made of plastic, the external shell was simply made from two plastic caps of which the front one was transparent and protected the screen. This made the shape of the television coincide with the screen profile, emphasizing that, alongside the technical part, images are the main purpose of a television. E.M.

ACHILLE AND PIER GIACOMO CASTIGLIONI,
ARCO LAMP, FLOS

Designed in 1962, the iconic design of the Arco lamp was not simply an example of advanced technology. It created new relationships between objects, forms and space.

Arco is a floor light with all the advantages of ceiling suspension. This new freedom allowed the Italian home to break away from the traditional living room, making it possible to focus light on new areas. Suitable for a dining table, Arco also provides discreet atmospheric illumination, ideal for conversation zones. Versatile and multifunctional, the Arco lamp by the Castiglioni brothers has all the adaptability required for contemporary living.

Made of a stainless steel shade, it features an adjustable lamp arc and Carrara marble base with a hole to allow two people to lift and carry it without risk. E.M.

In 1969, Gaetano Pesce designed a really astounding armchair for C&B. Like the Italian furniture industry which had been exploring the limits and possibilities of expanding resins of German origin, Pesce had been working with polyurethanes for a while. These materials seemed easy to work and perfect for both serial production and individual creations.

In the UP series, Pesce blended technology with artistic performance. The armchair is sold looking like a large flat pill in a vacum packed bag. To the buyer's amazement, on the pack being opened, the air entering finalizes the chemical reaction of polymerisation of the polyurethane, thus flexing the elastic fabric and blowing it into shape. This game or magical trick demonstrates the perfect interdependence between technology and form. But also a technological virtuosity that shows the ability of Italian industry to masterfully use better than anyone else the possibilities offered by new plastic materials. This game or magical trick demonstrates the perfect interdependence between technology and form. Here a technological exercise also showed how expertly Italian industry profited from the possibilities offered by the then new plastic materials. E.M.

RISCHIATUTTO TELEVISION PROGRAM, RAI

A new quiz show was aired for the first time at 9.15 pm on February 5, 1970, on the second channel of the RAI, the state Italian radio and television company, that would change Italy's relationship with television. *Rischiatutto* was presented by witty Mike Bongiorno. It was certainly not the first Italian television quiz, but the set, the narrative style and the presence of other personalities besides the presenter gave the programme a new and less formal approach.

Stills and films accompanied the questions; one of the authors would intervene with notarial functions; the youthful beauty of a very young Sabina Ciuffini in the novel role of assistant all constituted dynamic elements that brought television right into everyday Italian life.

Unlike the previous RAI quiz programme, *Lascia o raddoppia* (Double Your Money), *Rischiatutto* was not aimed at a rural Italy and its villages. It revealed a contemporary Italy instead, with its new consumer society myths and a sense of the first generational conflict embodied by the polite banter between the forty-five-year-old presenter and his assistant who politely represented the 'ye-ye' generation of those years, as the go-go was known in Spain and Italy.

While the seriality of television always favours some sort of familiarity between the public and television personalities, the programme's smoothness apparently cancelled the distance between reality and representation. Above all, there was Mike Bongiorno – who, as Umberto Eco noted, was always ready to seem simple, vague and the author of embarrassing mistakes which were not necessarily spontaneous.

Despite its traditional quiz show framework, *Rischiatutto* opened the door to instant television, no longer proposing educational models, but following the average pulse of its public and therefore able to capture the attention and curiosity of its spectators. The last episode was shown on the May 2, 1974. E.M.

Rai Teche

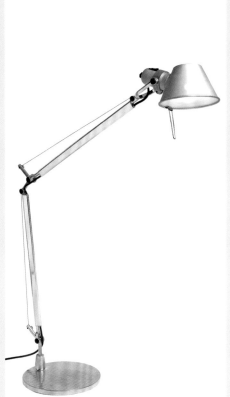

MICHELE DE LUCCHI - GIANCARLO FASSINA, TOLOMEO LIGHT, ARTEMIDE
COMPASSO D'ORO 1989

Not so much a study of form, the design of the Tolomeo light embodies an image in movement. De Lucchi describes how the idea of a diagram in motion came about by watching a fisherman pulling in his rod: "Everything materialised [...] when I made up my mind not to simply design a light but to create a modern version of the extremely famous, widely sold, and widely used arm-light, Naska Loris, the so-called architect's light". De Lucchi is well aware that this is a redesign, but his approach does not just address the form but the technical and operative means as well.

While the basic principle is that of the spring, De Lucchi does not highlight the visibility of the mechanism, playing instead on the idea of a mysterious trick. Like human muscles, the springs are hidden within the structure of the aluminium arm, and all that remains visible is a slender aerial steel cable that works like a tendon.

Designed in 1987 in association with Giancarlo Fassina, Tolomeo is an assembly regulated by elegant joints. Simple, logical and lightweight, the lamp is an icon of Italian design.

And, above all, it is not just a naive piece of machinery but a sophisticated household item. E.M.

MAURIZIO CATTELAN, LA NONA ORA (THE NINTH HOUR)

"I never thought that my Pope was a mere provocation. Like all my work, *La Nona Ora* is first and foremost about me and my sense of inadequacy... It's a very religious piece: a work that lays bare the Pope revealing his human side. It's a way of showing that even the Pope is subject to a form of authority."

Here, Cattelan explained one of his most controversial works. Made for the Apocalypse exhibition in London, the work shows Pope John Paul II on the ground, hit by a meteorite. The artist has accustomed the public to irreverent situations. He often uses the language of the mass media, bending it to his cruel and unforgiving irony, prompting considerations on some of our acquired and encoded behaviour that often conceals quite different meanings.

Opinions about his work are quite controversial: some consider him one of the most significant artists of the 20th century, while others think he is a parasite, an impostor who aims more at shocking than producing a real work of art.

All the same, this work was sold at Christies in New York for US$ 886,000 on May 17, 2001, and was later sold to Phillips De Pury & Co on November 11, 2004. In turn, they sold it for US$ 3,032,000 and established the current record quotation for the artist's work. A.M.S.

Maurizio Cattelan
La Nona Ora, 1999
Painted wax, fibreglass structure, fabric
Photo Attilio Maranzano
Courtesy Maurizio Cattelan Archive

The Evolution
of Design Language

For the first time at the end of World War Two, Italy was a free and optimistic country. It was, however, very backward in comparison with countries having more advanced economies. Since major industries were suffering from the consequences of the war and the limitations imposed by peace treaties, the development occurred through Italy's small-scale industries.

This framework of smaller industries proved to be extremely flexible and dynamic. It constantly forsaw consumer behaviour and its further evolution, as well as technical innovation, suitably in tune with the rapidly changing society. Italian firms do not produce mere objects but foster collective images of a future overflowing with beauty, freedom and optimism, thus showing that design can go beyond immediate functionality.

It was precisely this attitude that enabled Italian designers to sense the new post-industrial trends in affluent contemporary society before anyone else. Wherever the emphasis has shifted from the production of goods to image creation, Italian design has shown itself capable of offering solutions involving high quality and cultural excellence, following the move from practical needs to real or presumed desires.

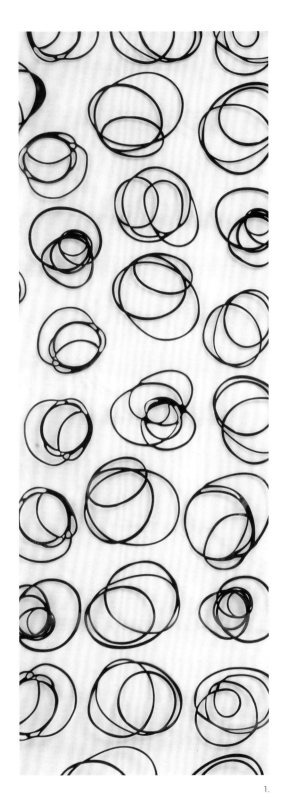

Max Huber
1. **MOULDED PLASTIC**
moulded plastic
Stabilimento Ponte Lambro
spa
I. COMPASSO D'ORO 1954

Flavio Poli
2. **MOD. 9822**
glass vase
Seguso srl
I. COMPASSO D'ORO 1954

Giovanni Gariboldi
3. **TABLE SET UP IN COLUMN**
table set up
Società Ceramiche Richard
Ginori spa
I. COMPASSO D'ORO 1954

2.

1.

3.

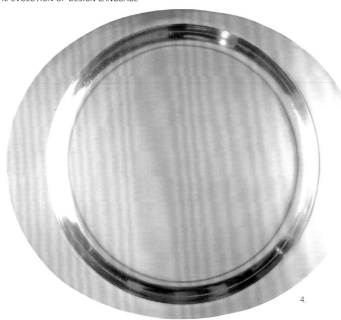

4.

5.

Roberto Sambonet
4. **SERIES OF STAINLESS STEEL TRAYS**
series of trays
Sambonet spa
III. COMPASSO D'ORO 1956

Ruth Christensen
5. **ALTA MAREA**
textile
Manifattura JSA
photo CSCDO Archive
IV. COMPASSO D'ORO 1957

Giuseppe Ajmone
6. **JUNGLA**
carpet
Figli di Guido Pugi
photo CSCDO Archive
III. COMPASSO D'ORO 1956

Gianni Dova
7. **NOVOSHANTUNG PERLISA ARCOBALENO P.496**
textile
Manifattura JSA
photo CSCDO Archive
II. COMPASSO D'ORO 1955

Umberto Nason
8. **TWO-TONE DRINKING GLASSES AND BOWLS**
drinking glasses and bowls
Cristalleria Nason & Moretti
II. COMPASSO D'ORO 1955

6.

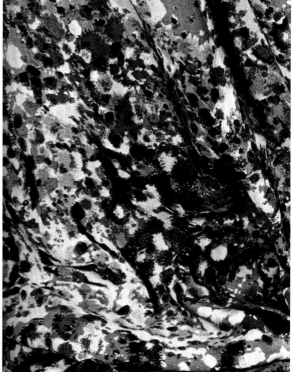

7.

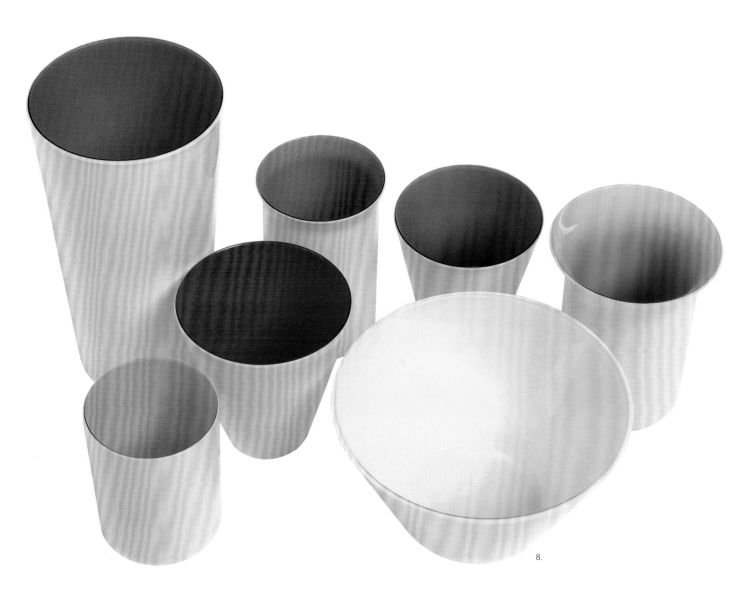

8.

9.

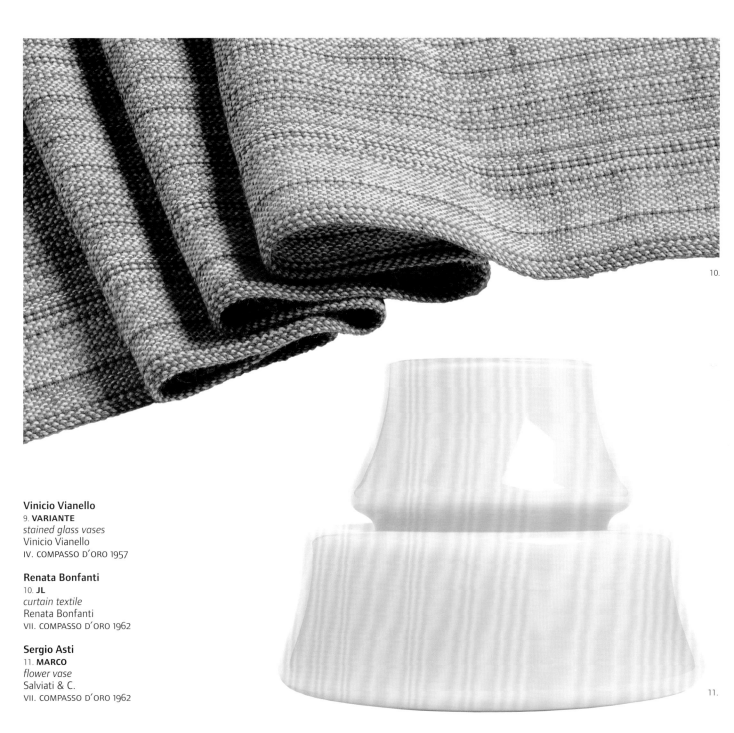

10.

11.

Vinicio Vianello
9. **VARIANTE**
stained glass vases
Vinicio Vianello
IV. COMPASSO D'ORO 1957

Renata Bonfanti
10. **JL**
curtain textile
Renata Bonfanti
VII. COMPASSO D'ORO 1962

Sergio Asti
11. **MARCO**
flower vase
Salviati & C.
VII. COMPASSO D'ORO 1962

12.

13.

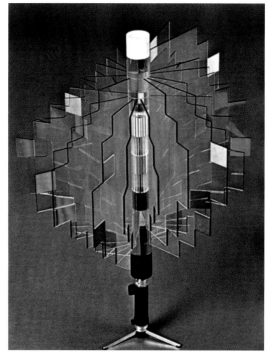

14.

Richard Sapper
12. **9090**
espresso coffee machine
F.lli Alessi spa
XI. COMPASSO D'ORO 1979

Ennio Lucini
13. **TUMMY**
series of pots
F.lli Barazzoni spa
XI. COMPASSO D'ORO 1979

Andrea Branzi,
Clino Trini Castelli,
Massimo Morozzi, CIM
14. **MERAKLON SISTEMA**
FIBERMATCHING 25
manual
Centro Design Montefibre
photo cscdo Archive
XI. COMPASSO D'ORO 1979

Riccardo Dalisi
15. **RESEARCH FOR ITALIAN**
COFFEE MAKER
MANUFACTURING
research for Italian coffee
maker manufacturing
Alessi spa
XII. COMPASSO D'ORO 1981

15.

16.

17.

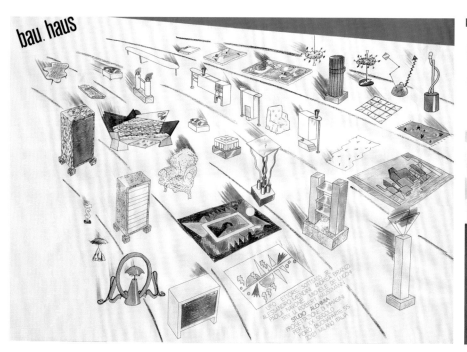

18.

19.

20.

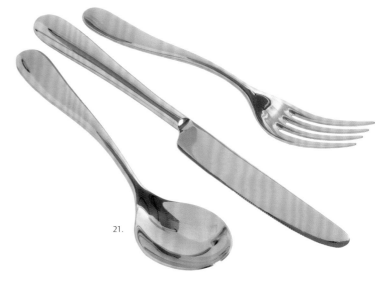

21.

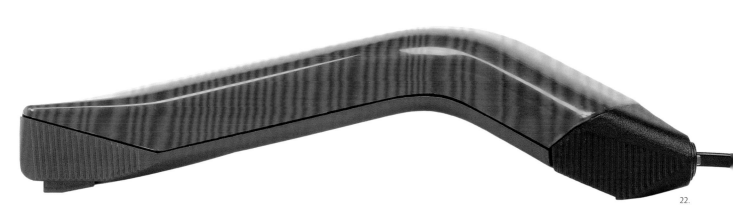

22.

Achille Castiglioni
16. **DRY**
cutlery set
Alessi spa
XIII. COMPASSO D'ORO 1984

Richard Meier
17. **TEA AND COFFEE SET**
tea and coffee set
Alessi spa
XIII. COMPASSO D'ORO 1984

Studio Alchimia
18. **DESIGN RESEARCH**
research
Studio Alchimia
XII. COMPASSO D'ORO 1981

Ettore Vitale
19. **ITALIAN SOCIALIST PARTY CORPORATE IDENTITY**
corporate identity
Partito socialista italiano
photo cscdo Archive
XIII. COMPASSO D'ORO 1984

Foster Associates
20. **NOMOS**
system of tables and office desks
Tecno spa
photo cscdo Archive
XIV. COMPASSO D'ORO 1987

Ettore Sottsass jr.
21. **NUOVO MILANO**
cutlery set
Alessi spa
XV. COMPASSO D'ORO 1989

Pasqui e Pasini Associati
22. **COBRA**
telephone
Italtel Telematica spa
XIV. COMPASSO D'ORO 1987

23.

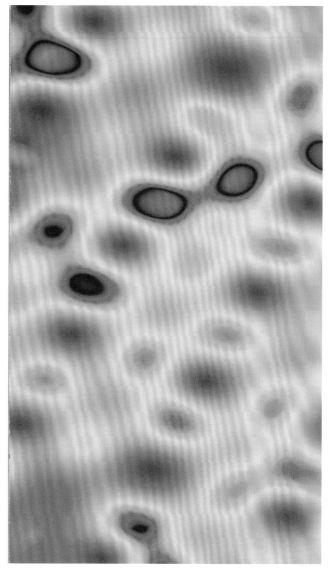

24.

**Sinopico, Dudovich,
Cappiello, Nizzoli, Nespolo**
23. **1860/1990 - 130 ANNI
DI STORIA DELLA GRAFICA
CAMPARI**
graphic design
Campari spa
photo CSCDO Archive
XVI. COMPASSO D'ORO 1991

**Centro Ricerche Abet
Laminati**
24. **DIAFOS**
HPL decorative rolled sections
Abet Laminati spa
XIV. COMPASSO D'ORO 1987

Direzione Tecnica Piaggio
25. **SFERA**
moped
Piaggio V.E. spa
photo CSCDO Archive
XVI. COMPASSO D'ORO 1991

25.

26.

27.

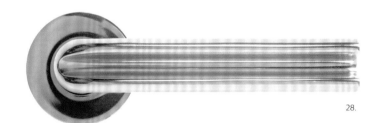

28.

Giuseppe Raimondi
26. **DELFINA**
chair
Bontempi spa
XIV. COMPASSO D'ORO 1987

Richard Sapper
27. **COBÀN**
espresso coffee machine with coffee mill
Alessi spa
XVIII. COMPASSO D'ORO 1998

Giotto Stoppino
28. **ALESSIA**
series of door knobs and coat hooks
Olivari B. spa
XVI. COMPASSO D'ORO 1991

Anna Ferrieri Castelli
29. **HANNAH**
cutlery
Sambonet spa
XVII. COMPASSO D'ORO 1994

Gianluigi Landoni
30. **WING**
soap dispenser
Rapsel spa
XVIII. COMPASSO D'ORO 1998

29.

30.

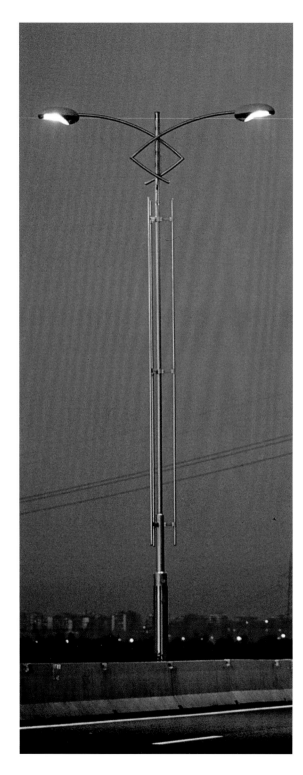

31.

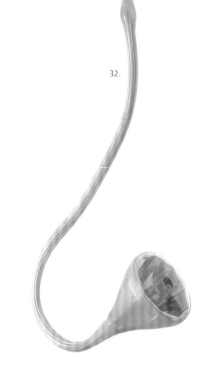

32.

33.

Emilio Ambasz
31. **SATURNO**
streetlamp
Ilva Pali Dalmine Design
Community srl
photo cscdo Archive
XIX. COMPASSO D'ORO 2001

Herzog & De Meuron
32. **PIPE**
suspension lamp
Artemide spa
XX. COMPASSO D'ORO 2004

Philippe Starck
33. **BUBBLE CLUB**
sofa and armchair
Kartell spa
XIX. COMPASSO D'ORO 2001

Harri Koskinen
34. **MUU**
series of seats
Montina srl
XX. COMPASSO D'ORO 2004

34.

35.

36.

Culdesac
35. **NEOS**
watch
Lorenz spa
XXI. COMPASSO D'ORO 2008

Bruno Rainaldi
36. **PTOLOMEO**
bookcase
Moco Divisione Minotti Italia
Trading
XX. COMPASSO D'ORO 2004

Ron Arad Associates
37. **MT3**
rocking chair
Driade
XXI. COMPASSO D'ORO 2008

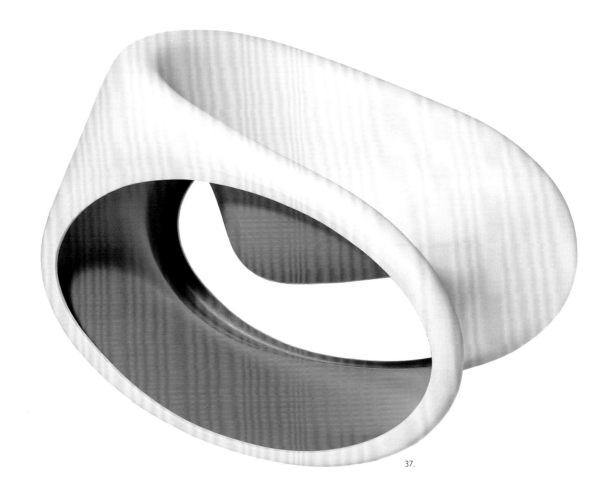

37.

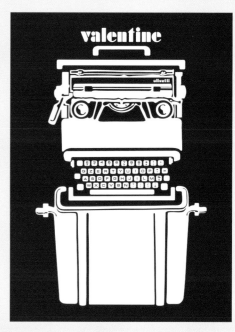

GIOVANNI GARIBOLDI, COLONNA TABLEWARE, GINORI
COMPASSO D'ORO 1954

Efficient and economical solutions in industrial logic have always responded to the requirements of serial production. However, starting from the 1950s, this approach stopped being simply utilitarian and acquired a genuine aesthetic value, to accompany new casual and informal lifestyles.

Tableware is typical of this change. Traditionally it came in sets but it eventually became a strictly modular system. Intended for houses that no longer housed homely kitchen ranges but efficient workshops in which everything had its place, tableware found new shapes and followed new logics.

In 1952, Giovanni Gariboldi designed his stackable tableware set for Richard Ginori, using space saving as a pretext to create a solution that played on the surprise effect by overdoing the stackability of the elements. His design minimised separation between the single units giving the illusion of a single unit when stacked, a smooth and very simple column, a sort of modular whole.

The same playful attitude also surfaces in Massimo Vignelli's impeccable Compact set in 1963. The severe geometrical shapes, all sharp corners and perfect circles, have been softened by plastic and bright colours, with which Vignelli created almost monolithic cylinders. Roberto Sambonet applied the same approach to pots and pans in 1963 when he designed a modular system of eight concentric stainless steel vessels. Each pan was matched with a corresponding shallow one that could also be used as a lid or a tray in a play of recesses which Sambonet designed as a single unit, a concentric pattern of hollows and solids. E.M.

PIETRO DEROSSI, PIPER CLUB, TURIN

The Piper was a forerunner of a look which was made famous ten years later in Stanley Kubrick's *A Clockwork Orange*. The Piper was a flexible and versatile club and it suited many purposes: dancing, theatre, cinema, exhibitions, meetings and happenings.

Avant-garde, a radically alternative image to the established appearance of modern and functional architecture, spatially the Piper corresponds to the idea of an extremely open and socially interactive place.

The design used modular industrial structures and mobile fittings, with shiny, coloured plastic furniture and offered a different way of interpreting social interaction.

Designed to accommodate changing necessities, the Piper was not a neutral container but a highly spectacular stage set. The entrance staircase was created as an actual sound experience thanks to an installation by Sergio Liberovici who had set up forty magnetic tracks on which he had recorded music, sounds, speeches and noises which were randomly mixed as people passed by. The main hall offered projections, audio reproduction and lighting and a light machine suspended from the ceiling, designed by Bruno Munari, that could cross the whole space thanks to an electrified rail while producing dynamic coloured light effects.

Designed in Turin by Piero Derossi, the Piper hosted avant-garde theatre – the Living Theatre performed there for the first time in Italy – and contemporary art exhibitions, and was a disco club shaped on the new languages and behaviour of a rapidly changing younger generation. E.M.

ETTORE SOTTSASS, VALENTINE TYPEWRITER, OLIVETTI

The Olivetti directors asked Ettore Sottsass to design a new portable typewriter, hoping to repeat the successful image of the famous Lettera 22. Sottsass's response was astonishing for its intelligence, sensitivity and capacity of interpreting not so much the actual product, but rather its context. Sottsass was far more interested in its "portable" aspect than in the typewriter itself, "portable" being an adjective that reflects the change in attitude of the late 1960s, from the structured work sphere to individual leisure time.

When the Valentine was introduced to the public it was immediately clear that it was not a typewriter in a case, but a case of words or rather possible stories. "Its name is Valentine and it was invented to be used anywhere except at work, to forget the boredom of the working day by keeping poetry lovers company on restful Sundays in the country or by adding a note of colour to a study at home."

Rather than designing an object, Sottsass interprets casually confident behaviour as if the Valentine were a fashion accessory to be worn with studied nonchalance.

A handle and a red box, two elastic clips to close it, a stripped down case that left the keys bare like legs in a miniskirt, the Valentine is a very serious and cheerful toy with two bright orange spots that look like a robot's eyes. It was an anti-machine not for experts and technicians, but easy and usable, a pop item. As a product it did not satisfy Olivetti's requirements, but the "personal" philosophy behind the design made it a world-wide communication success. E.M.

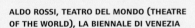

LUCA RONCONI, PRODUCTION OF THE LAST DAYS OF HUMANITY BY KARL KRAUS, THE TURIN THEATRE COMPANY

ALDO ROSSI, TEATRO DEL MONDO (THEATRE OF THE WORLD), LA BIENNALE DI VENEZIA

Despite being a fragile and ephemeral construction, the Teatro del Mondo by Aldo Rossi was also a very solid example of Italian architectural thinking. It was commissioned by Paolo Portoghesi, director of the 1979 Venice Biennale. This was an important Biennale which had the task of tracing the limits between the final fading of modernity and the emergence of more recent and still tentative movements.

This was the context in which Aldo Rossi launched his floating theatre, a combination of Venetian-ness with the alien qualities of rationalism and fantasy, symbolising this postwar Italian architectural debate. Should Venice be a heritage site or should it be continually rethought and renewed? Rossi's Teatro del Mondo showed the need for a new kind of urban planning, and while Rossi tried to heal the breach beween past and future so poetically, the Biennale exhibited its irreverent post-modernity at the Arsenale.

Actually things went differently, and today architecture seems to be part of a global taste for sensationalism. Although strongly symbolic of Italian innovation at the end of the 20th century, the Teatro del Mondo was demolished as soon as the Biennale was over. E.M.

La Biennale di Venezia
Photo Giorgio Zucchiatti

The Last Days of Mankind by Karl Kraus was staged at Turin's Teatro Stabile between November 29 and December 21, 1990. With its 792 pages, this in some ways extraordinary play directed by Luca Ronconi is a tragedy in five acts that sets itself apart right from the start.
A satirical fresco of the decline of the Western world, Kraus's original work relies on the power of speech and, unabridged, it would entail hours and hours of performing.
Ronconi stripped the text bare, however, reinstating through stage direction and visual effects what the cuts removed from the universal nature of the play. Rather than simply an arbitrary revisiting, Ronconi shifted the meaning from word to image.
Performed in the old foundry of Turin's Lingotto, the building itself became the protagonist and the public was transformed into a crowd besieged by a multiplication of scenes, almost as if in the overlapping sounds and images the performance gave voice to the sound of the world.
With the hybrid nature of its language and its stage layout the play provided an example of theatre that united performance and invention, experimentation and classicism. The Last Days of Mankind represented a unique symbol of Italian theatre at the turn of the millennium. E.M.

Gli ultimi giorni dell'umanità di Karl Kraus, produced by Luca Ronconi, Teatro Stabile di Torino, Ex Sala Presse Lingotto, 29 November 1990 Photo Tommaso Le Pera, courtesy Centro Studi Teatro Stabile di Torino

JACQUES HERZOG AND PIERRE DE MEURON, PIPE LAMP, ARTEMIDE
COMPASSO D'ORO 2004

We still need something more from lighting since the problem of lighting was solved by having an infinite variety of lamps available to put on the floor, ceiling, wall or table, or in the bathroom and kitchen, not to mention reading lamps, and by a just as wide variety of light sources like cold neon, cutting edge LED, low and high tension halogens and metal halides lamps.
Through lighting, we want to shape space and create ambience as lighting has become a fundamental aspect of our everyday scape. Besides being a source of light, a lamp should be a bright and hopefully eye-catching object.
Following the tendency of design to be increasingly interested in controlling functions as elements of a general spatial layout, lamps have become the focus of research that blends aesthetics, new technologies, visual attraction and energy saving.
The famous contemporary architects Jacques Herzog and Pierre de Meuron are no exception to the rule. They combined the new LED light sources with a silicone lining and a flexible steel pipe, thus creating an efficient, yet futuristic lamp that can easily be used on the floor, on walls or on the ceiling. E.M.

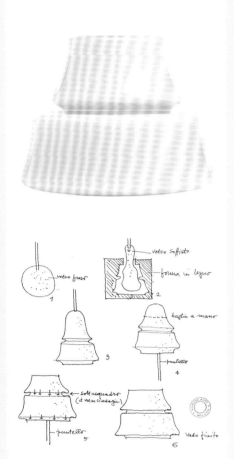

ALTO GRADIMENTO, RADIO PROGRAMME, RAI ITALIAN BROADCASTING CORPORATION

The first broadcast of *Alto Gradimento* began on the notes of the famous song *Rock Around the Clock* on the second RAI radio channel at 12:30 on July 7, 1970.
Nothing like it had ever been broadcast on public radio before, much less in a time slot not aimed at younger audiences
In fact *Alto Gradimento* was very different from other music programmes that Buoncompagni and Arbore had already conducted on the radio for young people.
Alto Gradimento was defined as an open workshop for new kinds of media language and communication.
While the music and carefree attitude of the presenters were typical of exchanges between young people, the programme mixed a variety show structure and curtain raisers with improvised happenings.
Helped by a motley crew of assistants with a biting wit – the architect Mario Marenco, Giorgio Bracardi, an irreverent comedian, and his musician brother, Franco – the two presenters seemed to have picked up slapstick and surreal aspects from the 1960s youth movements, summed up in the famous slogan "laughter will bury you".
Political ideology and social criticism were not included; it was just pure unadulterated fun behind which, however, lay a sharp and corrosive satire.
Hovering between Nanni Loy and *Hellzapoppin'* as well as between Neapolitan song and the Blues, *Alto Gradimento* captured an Italy struggling with modern developments that needed the right language and expressions to carry the collective heritage of popular culture into the pop forms of mass society.
On air five days a week for ten years, *Alto Gradimento* helped bring radio and television up to date, leading to programmes like *L'Altra Domenica* [The Other Sunday] (Renzo Arbore, 1976), *Discoring* (Gianni Boncompagni, 1977), *Pronto Raffaella?* [Hello, Raffaella?] (Gianni Boncompagni, 1983), *Quelli della notte* [People of the night] (Renzo Arbore, 1985), *Indietro tutta* [Full steam Backwards] (Renzo Arbore, 1988), and *Non è la Rai* [This is Not the RAI] (Gianni Boncompagni, 1991). E.M.
Rai Teche

SERGIO ASTI, MARCO VASE, SALVIATI & C.
COMPASSO D'ORO 1962

Decorative glass design has become a fixture of the Italian design universe since the Milanese Paolo Venini landed on the island of Murano in the 1920s with the precise intention of renovating the tradition of blown glass.
It is a difficult area where control over shape is constantly challenged by the chemical alchemy of colours, unexpected reactions of the material and artisan production methods.
Instead of imposing a rigid control over all the possible variables, Sergio Asti has accepted an ingredient of uncertainty, making it the basic element of the design.
This glass vase begins life in a wooden cast, the only aid used in controlling shape. However, once extracted from the cast, the glass paste tends to change shape because of its weight and the fluidity of the material which is still very hot.
This involuntary deformation is the main characteristic of this design, which conjugates and blends the serial approach of the cast with the freedom of the kind of workmanship which is still manual. E.M.

GATTI-PAOLINI-TEODORO, SACCO CHAIR, ZANOTTA

Made famous by Paolo Villaggio's Fracchia television sketches, the Sacco chair was designed by three young and relatively unknown designers from Turin: Piero Gatti, Cesare Paolini and Franco Teodoro. The three designers imagined an elementary device standing for a non-conventional, easy and free lifestyle that broke the traditional domestic model of sitting room and sofa.
The design disregarded all conventional relationships between form and function and consisted of a sack half filled with little polystyrene balls, its shape and use wholly determined by the weight of the person sitting on it. "We wanted to design objects as flexible as possible, that could adapt to different situations, behaviours and physical structures – we started thinking about materials... and fresh snow onto which you collapse and leave your imprint came to mind...".
The first prototype made in their studio with a transparent nylon sack was photographed and published in an American magazine. The article caught the eye of Macy's department store, which then ordered 10,000 units. Caught unprepared, the three designers decided that the only person who could deal with such a project was Aurelio Zanotta.
And so Sacco became part of Zanotta's collection, Zanotta being one of the firms best able to carry out these experiments in unconventional, irreverent and daring design, thus transforming imagination into the real thing. E.M.

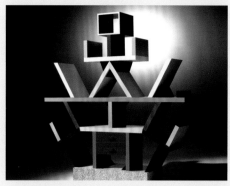

PATRICIA URQUIOLA, BISQUIT TABLE, BUDRI

STUDIO ALCHIMIA, DESIGN RESEARCH
COMPASSO D'ORO 1981

Halfway through the 1970s, the driving force of radicalism and countertendencies in art began to weaken. A pause for critical thinking followed the need to shock. In Milan in 1976, Alessandro and Adriana Guerriero established Alchimia with designers like Alessandro Mendini, Ettore Sottsass, Andrea Branzi, Lapo Binazzi, Michele De Lucchi, and artists of the Transavanguardia movement such as Cucchi, Paladino, and Chia, as well as members of alternative theatre groups such as the Magazzini Criminali [Criminal Warehouse] and Falso Movimento [Fake Movement]. Alchimia scrutinised the question of modern projectuality looked upon as a way of transforming reality, in favour of restraint in design, decoration, aesthetics and emotions. Their most famous slogan was perhaps "towards a project-free existence". Having acknowledged the end of modernity, Alchimia concentrated on dismantling its heritage, toppling its icons and confusing its tenets by superimposing trivia brought in from high or pop art, somewhere between kitsch and technicolor. These superficial adjustments meant ironic or cosmetic changes rather than anything that went deeper.
Designed by Alessandro Mendini, the most characteristic totem of Alchimia, was Proust, a poetic exaggeration of an armchair. "To begin with, I had thought of only designing a Proust material for Cassina, inspired by literature, with the idea of achieving the image of a surface rather than a three-dimensional form. Having read about and researched Proust's visual and material world, I thought of creating a possible armchair for him. I found a fake 18th-century chair, and chose a detail from a painting by Signac that became the texture covering the armchair and a nebulous obscuring of its original shape". It was striking but very intellectual, created from a fake piece and a copied detail. E.M.

ETTORE SOTTSASS, CARLTON BOOKCASE, MEMPHIS

In 1979, Ettore Sottsass and a few of his friends (Andrea Branzi, Marco Zanini, Michele De Lucchi, Matteo Thun, Barbara Radice, Martine Bedin, Nathalie Du Pasquier, Aldo Cibic and George Sowden) amicably broke away from the Alchimia group. Although he shared its principles, Sottsass was searching for a closer contact with the marketplace, convinced as he was of the need to bring the language of production and design up to date. Not a walk among the ghosts of modernism but an embracing of minority, esoteric or primitive cultures – societies that were either budding, forgotten, or mythological.
Although at the outset the defectors had had no specific plan, by the autumn of 1979 their minds were busy. What they wanted was simply to design objects and projects without restraint. There were so many ideas that they decided to hold an exhibition and Ernesto Gismondi, owner of Artemide, revealed himself to be a visionary entrepreneur. The story goes that the name of the group comes from a Bob Dylan song: "Oh, mama, can this really be the end / To be stuck inside of mobile / With the Memphis blues again..."
In actual fact the group's official debut came about in Milan in September 1981. The object/symbol of the collection was Carlton, a brightly-coloured laminate bookcase that occupied the home almost like a domestic monument. Designed by Ettore Sottsass, Carlton overturns the logic of rational design, placing its symbolic value before any technical or functional priorities. It is not a question of style but an ethical comment on the value of each and every object and every one of our decisions. Sottsass captures exactly the tragic dimension of the deadlock reached by the allegory of modernity, but he fills the void with cheerful optimism and the prospect of a new opening.
Not only furniture but watches, glass, and wholly new graphics: not a subversive operation, but, for the first time, a radical proposal with the power to create something new.
The effect is explosive and design is projected into a new and undefined postmodern dimension. Many more joined the original group, including Hans Hollein, Michael Graves, Iosa Ghini, Arata Isozaki, Shiro Kuramata and Javier Mariscal, making design transnational, transcultural, and transgenic. E.M.

It all started with a rock. Rather, with a flint that, skillfully chipped, became first a rudimentary tool and then, gradually, trimmed into many more specialised and sophisticated tools: axes, knives, scrapers and razor-sharp scalpels.
Perhaps wooden objects haven't actually survived but we could argue that people began to shape their environment armed with a sharp and pointed rock.
Then about two million years later, through all the digging, beating and heating, they realised that some types of stones would become pliable when heated and could be given different shapes. Metal, which was tougher and more flexible, was quite easy to shape and a lot more versatile than flint, obsidian or porphyry, and therefore gradually replaced stone.
No longer essential to technical progress, stone took other directions. It did not however disappear from our lives to became the material of history and memory. Stone makes the monuments that defy time, stone builds the most sacred and important places and the busiest streets and squares. But stone is also used for fountains, pestles and mortars, grindstones, and hearths, as if faith in eternity and the reliability of daily life lived on in it.
Italian designers, among others, have renewed its image by offering contemporary designs in marble and stone, reflecting both traditional and modern industrial practices.
Designers such as Enzo Mari, Tobia Scarpa, Sergio Asti, Ettore Sottsass, Aldo Rossi, Achille Castiglioni and Angelo Mangiarotti have transfered many qualities to marble, including a conceptual simplicity, a surprising transparency, echoes of the past, playfulness and the evocative power of symbols.
Currently we are witnessing further acceleration. A new generation of designers, aided by computerised machines, are eliminating the differences between design and decoration, objects and their parts, design and architecture. CNC machines and laser cutting make both lace and tunnels without waste. Here, the work of Patricia Urquiola is typical. She is capable of making her entire design from contemporary decorative elements. Precise work, surgically precise cuts, and the new adhesives enable stone to be layered in a mosaic forming arabesques, outdoing any functional considerations. A surprising lightness and transparent airiness is thus produced from stone scraps and parings. E.M.

The Work Plan

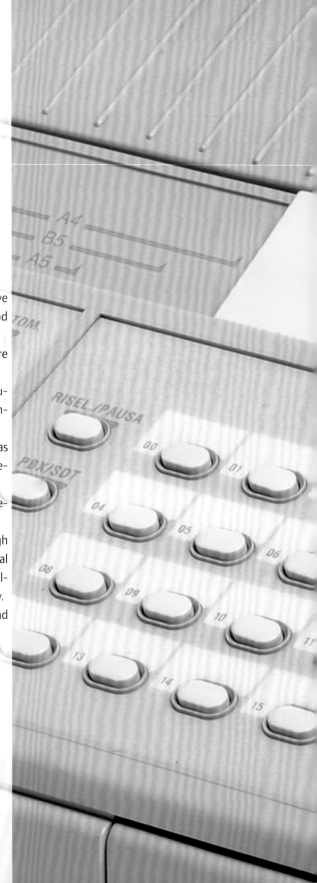

Theoretically, each of us is engaged in work for only eight hours a day for five days a week. However, in the last fifty years work dynamics have had a profound impact on Italy's human and social relations.

To begin with, the economic boom coincided with the rapid decline of agriculture and a marked growth of industry and, later, of the service sector.

This caused an internal migration which radically changed Italy's makeup. Thousands of people left the poorer areas of the country attracted to urban and industrial centres.

At the same time, thanks to the new system of compulsory education (which was increased to the age of 14 in 1962), the general level of education rose while television contributed to forming a new common identity and language.

Women gained new social roles and economic independence while prosperity became widespread.

The changes in work practices set the rhythm for Italy's modernisation, although often traumatically; not just in industry and large firms, but as part of an original widespread entrepreneurship which came into being thanks to skills that developments in the workplace had first triggered and then made available generally.

Today, Italy faces a new global scenario where resourcefulness, know-how and flexibility are indispensable for competing successfully on this scale.

1.

2.

3.

Ambrogio Carini
1. **LG T/2**
microscope
Officine Galileo
photo cscdo Archive
V. COMPASSO D'ORO 1959

Gastone Rinaldi
2. **DU 30**
*chair made of sheet metal,
iron and foam rubber*
Rima di Mario Rinaldo spa
I. COMPASSO D'ORO 1954

Giovanni Fontana
3. **(BUSINESS) OVERNIGHT BAG**
(business) overnight bag
Valextra spa
I. COMPASSO D'ORO 1954

4.

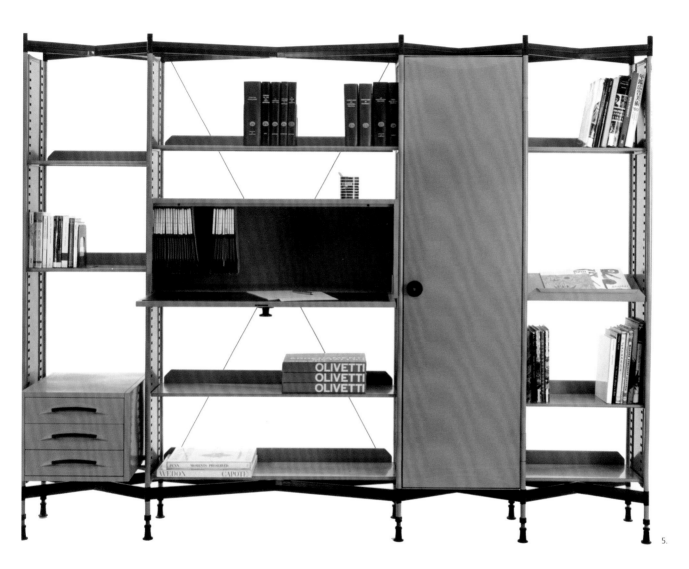

5.

Luigi Caccia Dominioni,
Achille Castiglioni,
Pier Giacomo Castiglioni
4. **T 12 PALINI**
school chair
Palini Industria Legno srl
VI. COMPASSO D'ORO 1960

Lodovico Belgiojoso,
Enrico Peressuti,
Ernesto Nathan Rogers
5. **SPAZIO**
series of metal office furniture
Ing. C. Olivetti & C. spa
photo cscdo Archive
VII. COMPASSO D'ORO 1962

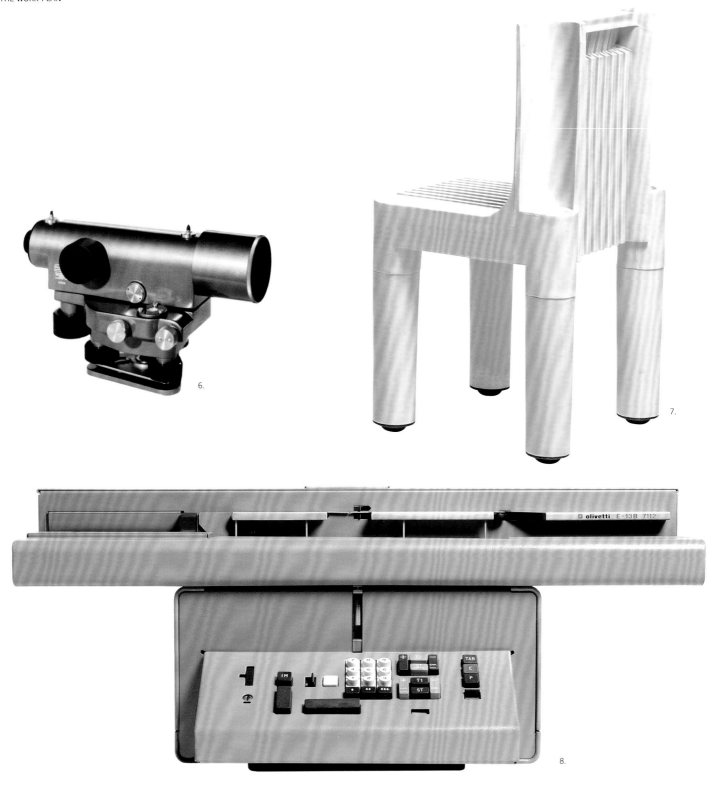

6.

7.

8.

Ufficio Tecnico Salmoiraghi
6. **MOD. 5169**
precision level instrument
Filotecnica Salmoiraghi spa
photo cscdo Archive
VII. COMPASSO D'ORO 1962

Marco Zanuso,
Richard Sapper
7. **K 1340**
chair
Kartell srl
VIII. COMPASSO D'ORO 1964

Mario Bellini
8. **CMC7-7004**
magnetic seal press
Ing. C. Olivetti & C. spa
VIII. COMPASSO D'ORO 1964

Rodolfo Bonetto
9. **AUCTOR MULTIPLEX**
MUT/40A
machine tool
Olivetti
IX. COMPASSO D'ORO 1967

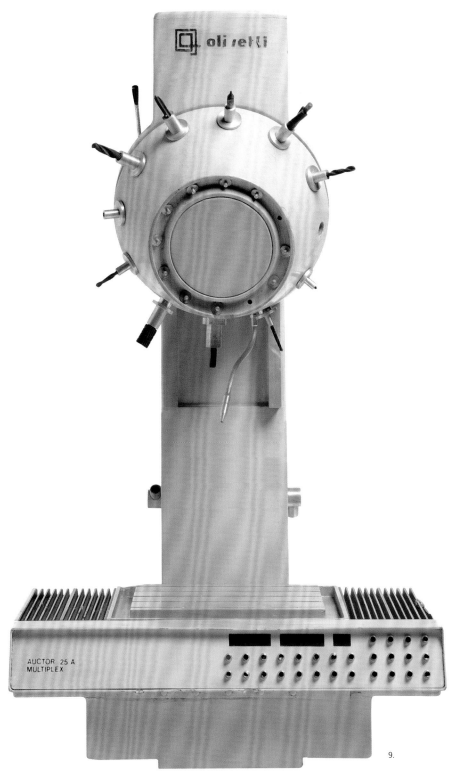

9.

10.

**Achille Castiglioni,
Pier Giacomo Castiglioni**
10. **SIX LINES SIMULTANEOUS
TRANSLATION HEADPHONES**
*six lines simultaneous
translation headphones*
Phoebus Alter
IX. COMPASSO D'ORO 1967

**Gilbert Durst
in collaboration
with Wilmath Pramstraller
and Joseph Hollrigl**
11. **DURST A 600**
photo enlarger and player
Durst spa
IX. COMPASSO D'ORO 1967

Rodolfo Bonetto
12. **AUTOMATIC MICROFILM
APPARATUS**
*automatic microfilm
apparatus*
BCM
photo CSCDO Archive
X. COMPASSO D'ORO 1970

**Francesco Mazzucca
with Ufficio Progetti Elvi**
13. **ELVI 390**
*preset cycle units system
for semiautomatic multiple
analysis*
Elvi
X. COMPASSO D'ORO 1970

11.

12.

13.

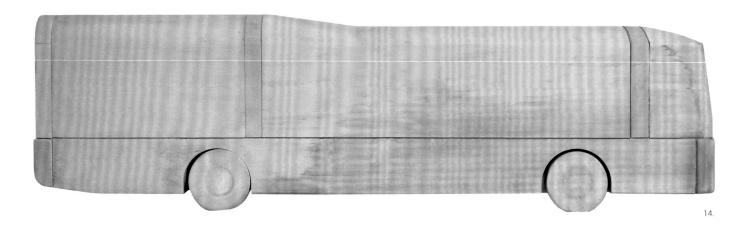

14.

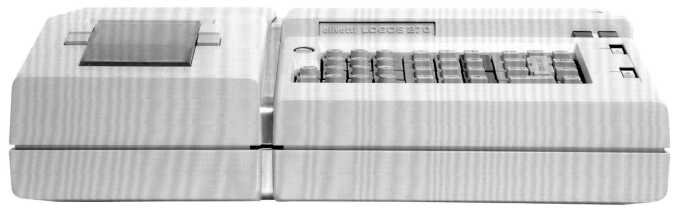

15.

Alberto Rosselli, Isao Hosoe
14. **METEOR**
tour bus
(model by Giovanni Sacchi)
Fiat - Carrozzeria Orlandi
Modena
X. COMPASSO D'ORO 1970

Mario Bellini
in collaboration
with Sandro Pasqui
15. **LOGOS 270**
table writing calculator
Ing. C. Olivetti & C. spa
X. COMPASSO D'ORO 1970

Ettore Sottsass jr.
with David Higgins Lawrence
and Monk John Lawrence
16. **G 120**
electronic computer
Honeywell Information
Systems Italia
photo cscdo Archive
X. COMPASSO D'ORO 1970

Ettore Sottsass jr.,
Hans Von Klier
17. **MC 19**
electric adding machine
Ing. C. Olivetti & C. spa
X. COMPASSO D'ORO 1970

16.

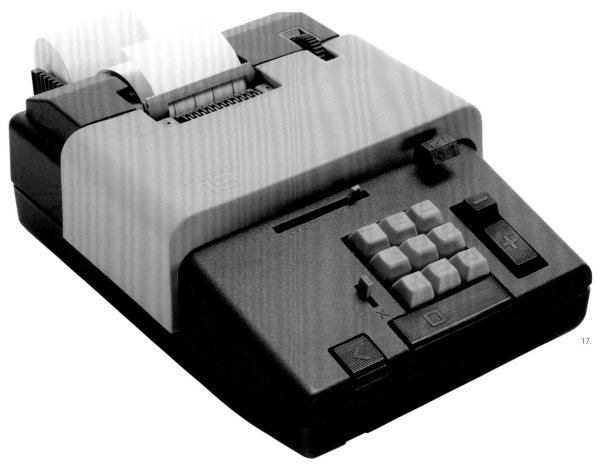

17.

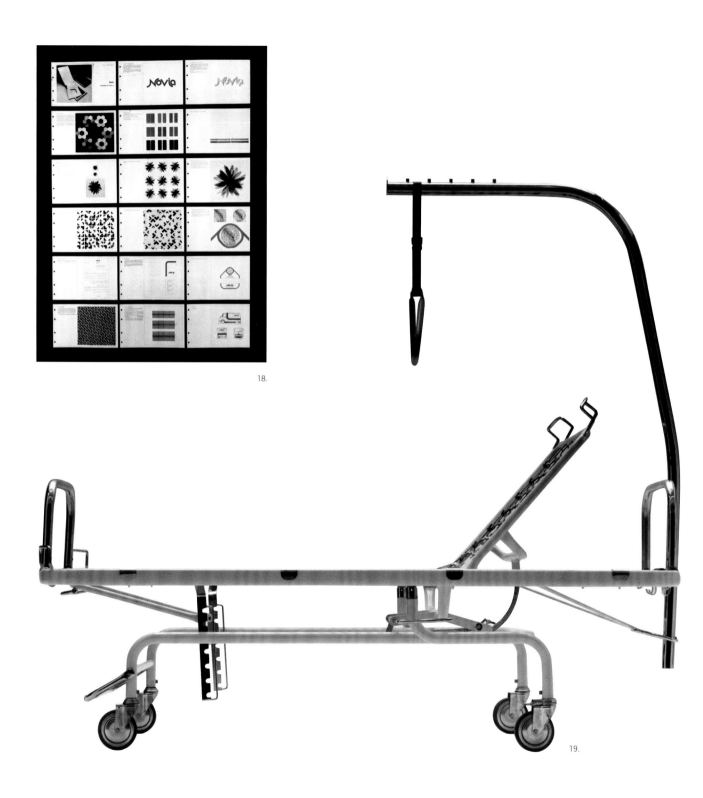

18.

19.

Antonio Barrese
18. **MARCA NOVIA**
manual
Bassetti spa
photo cscdo Archive
XI. COMPASSO D'ORO 1979

**Achille Castiglioni,
Giancarlo Pozzi,
Ernesto Zerbi**
19. **TR 15**
hospital bed
Omsa spa
photo cscdo Archive
XI. COMPASSO D'ORO 1979

**Luciano Agosti,
Giovanni Brunazzi,
Franco Grignani,
Giancarlo Ilibrandi,
Bruno Munari, Ilio Negri,
Gianni Parlacino,
Pino Tovaglia**
20. **MODULO**
print
Società Nebiolo
photo cscdo Archive
XI. COMPASSO D'ORO 1979

Design Group Italia
21. **TRATTO CLIP
AND TRATTO PEN**
pen - felt tip
Fila spa
XI. COMPASSO D'ORO 1979

ABCDEFGHIJKLMNOPQR
STUVWXYZ abcdefghijk
lmnopqrstuvwxyz

ABCDEFGHIJKLMNOPQR
STUVWXYZ abcdefghijk
lmnopqrstuvwxyz
1234567890
$&?;:'![«(*HOx+:-=

ABCDEFGHIJKLMNOPQR
STUVWXYZ abcdefghij
klmnopqrstuvwxyz
1234567890
$&?;:'![»(*HOx:+-=

ABCDEFGHIJKLMNOPQR
STUVWXYZ abcdefghijk
lmnopqrstuvwxyz
1234567890
$&?;:'![«(*HOx:+-=

ABCDEFGHIJKLMNOPQR
STUVWXYZ abcdefghij
klmnopqrstuvwxyz
1234567890
$&?;:'![»(*HOx:+-=

ABCDEFGHIJKLMNOPQR
STUVWXYZ abcdefghij
klmnopqrstuvwxyz
1234567890
$&?;:'![«(*HOx:+-=

20.

21.

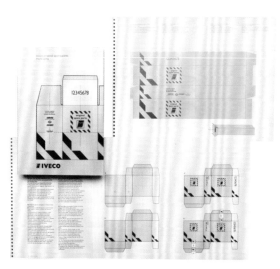

22.

2

Giovanni Brunazzi
22. **IVECO CORPORATE IDENTITY**
corporate identity
Fiat Iveco
photo cscdo Archive
XI. COMPASSO D'ORO 1979

Olivetti - Direzione Relazioni Culturali - Disegno Industriale - Pubblicità
23. **DESIGN PROMOTION**
corporate identity
Olivetti & C. Spa
photo cscdo Archive
XI. COMPASSO D'ORO 1979

Rodolfo Bonetto, Naoki Matsunaga
24. **INSPECTOR MIDI 130 W**
measuring machine
Olivetti & C. spa
photo cscdo Archive
XI. COMPASSO D'ORO 1979

Isao Hosoe, Antonio Barrese, Antonio Locatelli, Pietro Salmoiraghi, Angelo Torricelli
25. **SPAZIO**
coach
(model by Giovanni Sacchi)
Carrozzeria Emiliana Renzo Orlandi
XI. COMPASSO D'ORO 1979

Giorgio Decursu
26. **MEC 2**
machine tool
Officine Meccaniche San Rocco srl
XI. COMPASSO D'ORO 1979

24.

140

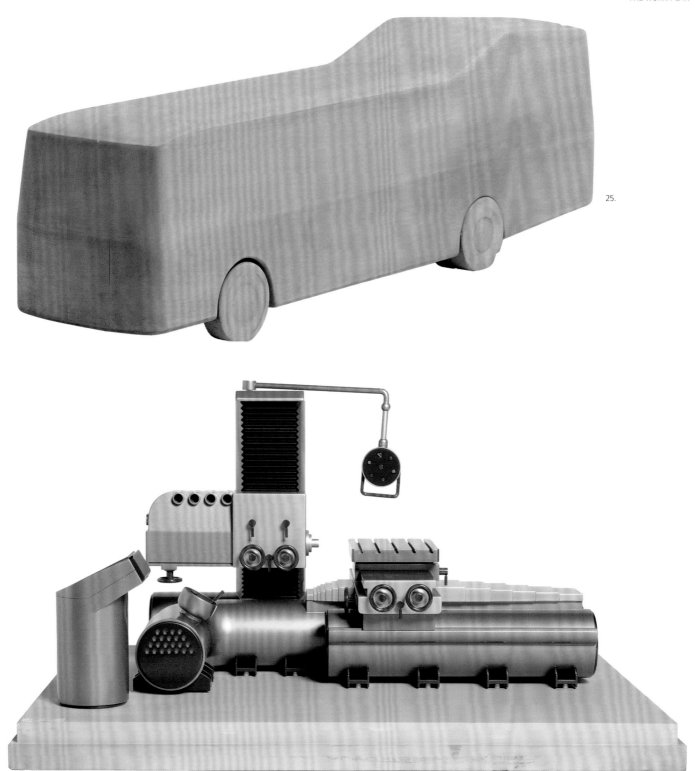

25.

26.

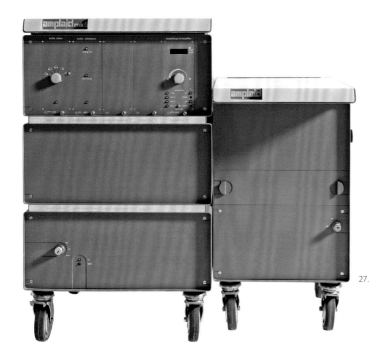

27.

Carla Venosta
27. **MARK 5**
microprocessorised system for
bioelectric data capture
Amplaid spa
XI. COMPASSO D'ORO 1979

Luigi Bandini Buti,
Gabriele Cortili,
Franco De Nigris,
Enrico Moretti
28. **IL DESIGN ERGONOMICO**
research
SEA
photo cscdo Archive
XII. COMPASSO D'ORO 1981

Mario Bellini
29. **PRAXIS 35**
portable electronic typewriter
machine
Ing. C. Olivetti & C. spa
XII. COMPASSO D'ORO 1981

Paolo Parigi
30. **A.90**
drafting machine
Heron Parigi
photo cscdo Archive
XI. COMPASSO D'ORO 1979

Emilio Ambasz,
Giancarlo Piretti
31. **VERTEBRA**
office and institutional chair
Castelli spa
XII. COMPASSO D'ORO 1981

28.

29.

30.

31.

32.

Mario Bellini
32. **MERCATOR 20**
cash register
Olivetti spa
photo cscdo Archive
XIII. COMPASSO D'ORO 1984

**A. Cortesi, G. Facchetti,
U. Orsoni, M. Fantoni,
P. Pataccini**
33. **CORPORATE IDENTITY AND
STAND DESIGN FOR ALITALIA
TRAVEL AGENCY**
corporate identity
Alitalia
photo cscdo Archive
XIII. COMPASSO D'ORO 1984

Rodolfo Bonetto
34. **AUCTOR 400**
*vertical (axis) machining
centre*
Olivetti OCN
photo cscdo Archive
XIII. COMPASSO D'ORO 1984

Richard Sapper
35. **DALLE NOVE ALLE CINQUE**
furniture system for office
Castelli spa
photo cscdo Archive
XIV. COMPASSO D'ORO 1987

Bob Noorda
36. **FUSITAL CORPORATE
IDENTITY**
corporate identity
Fusital
photo cscdo Archive
XIII. COMPASSO D'ORO 1984

**Gianfranco Zaccai
con Design Continuum**
37. **ACL/AUTOMATED
COAGULATION LAB.**
coagulation analyser
Instrumentation Lab.
photo cscdo Archive
XIV. COMPASSO D'ORO 1987

33.

34.

35.

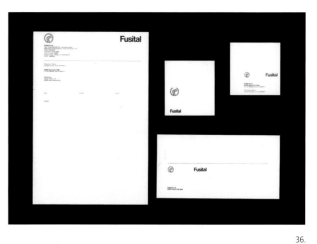

36.

37.

38.

39.

Giorgio Decursu
38. **U CONTROL**
*electronic device for
positioning boring and facing
heads*
D'Andrea spa
XV. COMPASSO D'ORO 1989

Centro Studi Castelli
39. **GUYA**
seating system for office
Castelli spa
XV. COMPASSO D'ORO 1989

Antonio Barrese
40. **CORPORATE IDENTITY
APPLICATION MANUAL**
manual
Università Commerciale Luigi
Bocconi
XV. COMPASSO D'ORO 1989

Giugiaro Design
41. **ISOTRON**
dental equipment
Eurodent Industrie spa
XVI. COMPASSO D'ORO 1991

40.

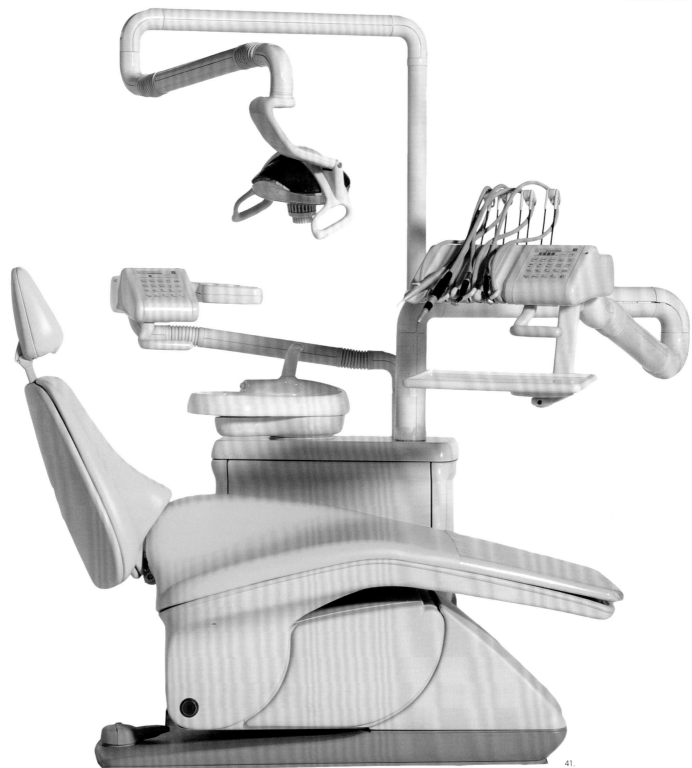

41.

42.

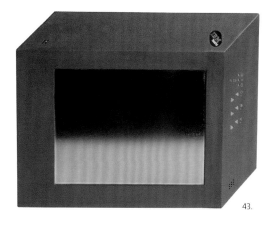

43.

Giorgio Decursu
42. **ECW. 375** e **EWW. 240**
handwheels
Elesa spa
XVII. COMPASSO D'ORO 1994

Richard Sapper
43. **LEAPFROG**
laptop
IBM Corporation
XVII. COMPASSO D'ORO 1994

Giorgio Decursu
44. **T200/I200**
*series of thermoplastic
injection moulding presses*
BM Biraghi spa
XVI. COMPASSO D'ORO 1991

**George Sowden,
Simon Morgan**
45. **OFX 420**
fax (device)
Olivetti Design
XVI. COMPASSO D'ORO 1991

Emilio Ambasz
46. **QUALIS**
series of office armchairs
Tecno spa
XVI. COMPASSO D'ORO 1991

Giancarlo Piretti
47. **PIRETTI COLLECTION**
series of community seating
COMS Coop.
photo CSCDO Archive
XVI. COMPASSO D'ORO 1991

44.

45.

46.

47.

48.

49.

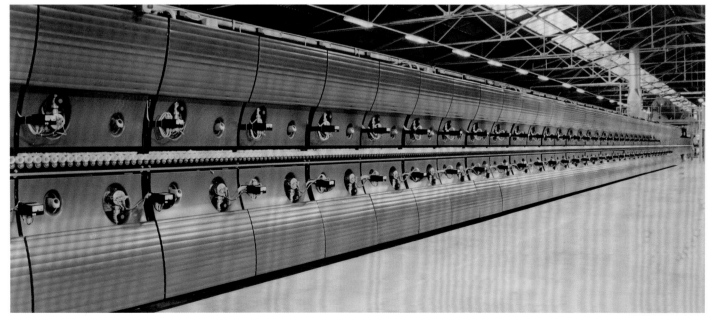

50.

51.

Luciano Marson
48. **HORM: ISTRUZIONI
DI MONTAGGIO**
manual
Horm srl
photo cscdo Archive
XIII. COMPASSO D'ORO 1998

Pininfarina Studi e Ricerche
49. **BLITZ/DRAGO**
forklift truck
Cesab Carrelli Elevatori spa
photo cscdo Archive
XVII. COMPASSO D'ORO 1994

Isao Hosoe Design
50. **FMP 270 PULSAR**
*single layer ceramic tile kiln
and control room with process
supervision software*
Sacmi Forni
photo cscdo Archive
XVIII. COMPASSO D'ORO 1998

**Luciano Pagani,
Angelo Perversi**
51. **MOVE** and **FLIPPER**
office furniture
Unifor spa
XVIII. COMPASSO D'ORO 1998

**Philips Corporate Design,
Stefano Marzano**
52. **INTEGRIS H5000
CARDIAC SYSTEM**
x-ray system
Philips Electronics
XVIII. COMPASSO D'ORO 1998

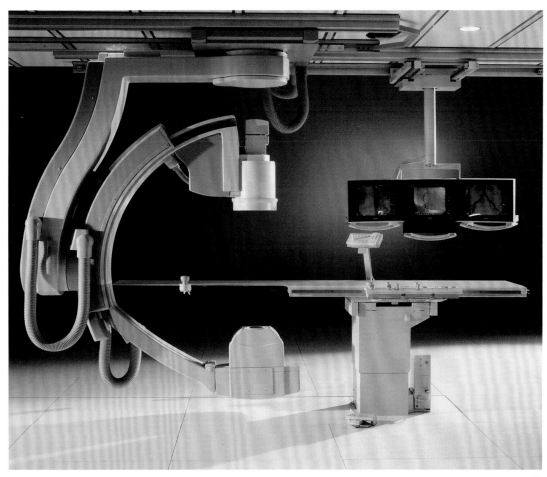

52.

53.

54.

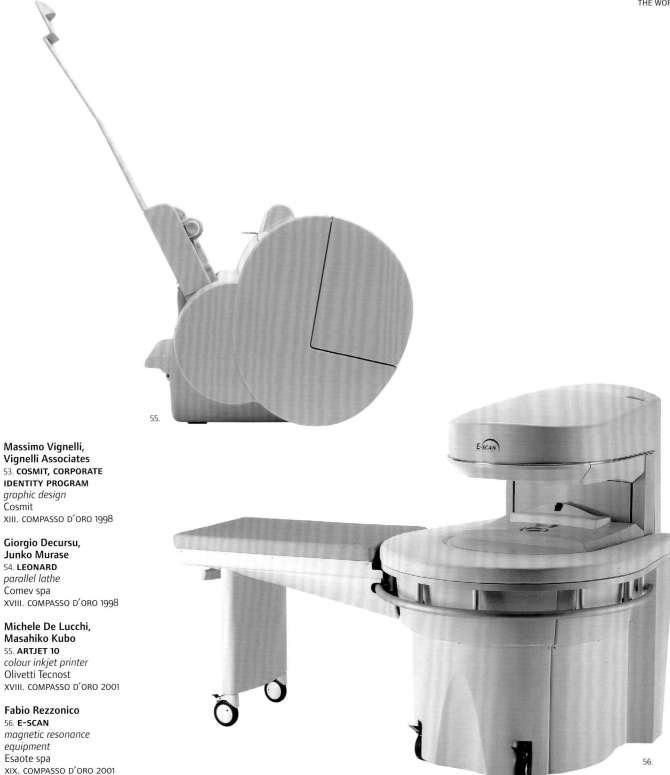

55.

56.

**Massimo Vignelli,
Vignelli Associates**
53. **COSMIT, CORPORATE
IDENTITY PROGRAM**
graphic design
Cosmit
XIII. COMPASSO D'ORO 1998

**Giorgio Decursu,
Junko Murase**
54. **LEONARD**
parallel lathe
Comev spa
XVIII. COMPASSO D'ORO 1998

**Michele De Lucchi,
Masahiko Kubo**
55. **ARTJET 10**
colour inkjet printer
Olivetti Tecnost
XVIII. COMPASSO D'ORO 2001

Fabio Rezzonico
56. **E-SCAN**
*magnetic resonance
equipment*
Esaote spa
XIX. COMPASSO D'ORO 2001

RODOLFO BONETTO, AUCTOR MULTIPLEX TOOL, OLIVETTI
COMPASSO D'ORO 1967

Right from the 1908 establishment of the company, Camillo Olivetti had decided not just to assemble components, but also control the whole production progress, from design to sales, from the actual production of components to the necessary tools. Therefore, along with calculators and typewriters, Olivetti also produced milling cutters, lathes, presses and other complex machinery meant to be used all day and designed to reduce risks and effort as far as possible for the workers operating them.

Working conditions and machinery changed with the introduction of electronics in the 1960s. The machines were now pre-programmed and could handle the work independently to a great extent, manage the production cycle, automatically switch jobs and use the right tools for the various operations. In the same way, the operator was now required to substitute muscle power and precision with organisational and supervisory skills.

In 1963, Rodolfo Bonetto was asked to supervise the rather delicate passage from human to machine labour, winning over the understandable resistances of the workers.

He was no ordinary designer, not having an artistic temperament, was self-taught, soundly analytical and very thorough in establishing hierarchies between form and function within complex operative processes.

He managed to compensate the workers with a working safety plan. His machines, although huge, highlight the relationships between parts, focus attention on the control panels, on the tool paths and on those of the components being worked upon.

An approach to design that is a far cry from the customary creative stereotype, maybe closer to the work of an engineer, a process programmer or a systems analyst but all the same satisfying people's real needs. E.M.

DESIGN GROUP ITALIA, TRATTO PEN, FILA
COMPASSO D'ORO 1979

In the 1970s, Fila, a firm which had always produced pencils, crayons and ball point pens, decided to expand into the then new field of felt tip pens, taking advantage of new Japanese high quality writing tips. Fila chose the Design Group studio, who specialised in mass consumer products, for their Tratto Pen project.

The design they opted for was extremely simple; reducing details and variants to an absolute minimum, it consisted of a straight body, rounded ends with a classically elegant, hemispherical top, and with careful attention paid to the diameter required for a comfortable grip. Entirely made of methacrylate and then later polypropylene of an asphalt-like colour, the body of the pen was monochrome, because the founder of Design Group, Marco Del Corno, wanted a neutral object that was suitable for all possible uses. The only contrasting features were the coloured end indicating ink colour and the ridged cap edge.

The Tratto Pen is extremely versatile and suitable for work, play, drawing or writing.

Later, other versions were added, including versions with a pocket clip and with different tips and coloured versions to appeal to the marketing side. E.M.

CARLO PETRINI STARTS SLOW FOOD

In 1989, Carlo Petrini founded the international Slow Food Association in Paris. Based on his experience gained in the Arcigola association in Bra in 1986, Slow Food originated with the aim of promoting, communicating and studying the tradition of food, to preserve the universal right for enjoyment. Behind this "hedonist" idea, however, the role of the association in actual fact was a great deal more serious. Its duties were to educate the taste-buds, and to teach people nutrition and food science, safeguarding biodiversity and the traditional foodstuff production this entailed, but also respect for ecosystems, the pleasure of eating and quality of life. It supported a new style of nutrition respectful of the environment and cultural identities, able to close the gap between consumer and producer and creating a virtuous network of international relations and a greater sharing of knowledge.

Originally an opinion movement, Slow Food has gradually become an innovative cultural experience of global standing. Slow Food has influenced tastes and consciences but it has also notably improved Italian food production processes, restoring ethics and economics to today's farming. E.M.

MICHELE DE LUCCHI, NEW POST OFFICES POSTE ITALIANE

At the end of the 1980s while privatisation and business reorganisation were in the air, Poste Italiane launched a radical modernisation process, guided by a management team that came from private industry with new ideas on the concept of service and customer relations.

What had been for decades a dusty if reassuring home ground of the relationship between central government and citizens was suddenly shaken up by a desire for renewal.

By redesigning the entire logistic territorial network, priority mail was introduced to face the then chronic delays in correspondence delivery. On the savings and accounts side, an effort was made to shift towards modern banking methods. This involved a series of changes that would obviously also be reflected in a new image of the postal service and its capillary network of post offices all over the country.

The Fragile design studio studied a new, brighter, more modern image for Poste Italiane, while Michele De Lucchi designed the new layout for the new post offices. The main theme of the design appeared to be openness, as the tall barriers that separated the public from the workers were abolished and a marked division was made between financial and postal services. There were ample waiting areas, as well as separate cubicles for private transactions and for savings management. All were enclosed by glass partitions, with light colours and an efficient design for tills and surfaces.

The design of a workspace and the development of a new relationship with the public were not the only ingredients involved; a modern meeting place had also been conceived. E.M.

ISAO HOSOE, TUNNEL KILN, SACMI
COMPASSO D'ORO 1998

In 1935, Filippo Marazzi was a wealthy merchant from Sassuolo in his sixties who had learned to understand and interpret the aspirations of the emerging provincial middle classes. Those were the years in which Natalino Otto sang "If I had a thousand lire a month" and went on to dream about "a young and pretty wife" and "buying a little house on the outskirts of town".

In this atmosphere of measured optimism, Marazzi understood how the home was the ultimate aspiration of a country that dreamt of stability and security. So, he courageously launched himself into manufaturing ceramic tiles.

The plains around Modena are rich in clay and hence brick works, but Marazzi was ambitious and created a factory. The first factory was built incorporating a stand of poplars, the plants having been cut with geometrical precision: the trunks of two lines of trees became the columns on which he set the roof of the workshop. Ceramics are versatile and easy to work and proved the perfect material for enlarging his business from artisan to industrial production. They involve decoration and large quantities, research into aesthetics and technical improvements, and both manual labour and automation.

Filippo Marazzi had excellent foresight and other factories flourished round that early factory, not just dealing with manufacture, but research centres, art schools, technical laboratories and centres making machine tools for tiles.

A concentration of industries became an actual industrial estate after World War Two, making Sassuolo the world's most important ceramic production centre.

Hence, It is no coincidence that Sacmi Forni, which specialises in producing ceramic kilns, is based in Salvaterra Casalgrande (Reggio Emilia), just a few kilometres from Sassuolo.

When Sacmi asked Isao Hosoe to design a new model of industrial kiln with a series of requirements (digitised control processes, maximum heat recovery, no fumes) Hosoe complied. He went beyond his brief, however, and also designed a safe and ergonomic kiln, which although huge, he designed bearing in mind the scale of the people who were to use it. E.M.

HELICOPTER AGUSTAWESTLAND AW-101

In 2005, after a complicated series of tenders, competitions and appeals, the United States president ordered the new fleet of helicopters for the White House from the Italian firm Augusta-Westland.

It was not the first time that Italian companies had won contracts for US police and army supplies. In 1968, Moto Guzzi had managed to convince the Los Angeles Police Department to include the famous Guzzi V7 in its fleet.

Other American cities followed suit, making this Italian motorcycle famous overseas. In 1990, Beretta had managed to wrest an important contract for the standard issue Beretta M9 semiautomatic pistol from the American army which caused endless arguments and protectionist disputes.

The case of the American presidential helicopter, officially named US-101, is much more significant given its complex and highly technological development. This was a particularly important achievement because military development is known to be a research laboratory and testing ground for civil industry, and radar, transistors and recent synthetic fibres such as Kevlar® are just a few examples of new technologies of military origin.

The development of the Marine One was based on the proven AW 101 helicopter, a multi-purpose three-turbine helicopter, developed for both military and civilian uses. Originally developed as a joint-venture agreement signed in 1979 between the British Westland and the Italian Agusta, this helicopter has proved particularly versatile and reliable. Since the acquisition of the English firm by Agusta in 2004, the company is now completely owned by the Finmeccanica group.

The development of US-101 Marine One was made in collaboration with the American Lockheed, the company entrusted with the installation of the interiors, communication suites, and mission equipment.

Although US Defense Secretary Gates recommended the cancellation of this contract due to budget concerns, currently Agusta-Westland has delivered the first 11 aircraft, fulfilling the first part of the contract. E.M.

LUIGI CACCIA DOMINIONI–ACHILLE AND PIER GIACOMO CASTIGLIONI, SCHOOL CHAIR, PALINI
COMPASSO D'ORO 1960

The chair was presented in 1960, in conjunction with the 10th Milan Triennale dedicated to Home and School.

Begun in 1923 in Monza and transferred to Milan in 1933, the original aim of the Triennale was to examine the boundaries between the arts, paying particular attention to architecture and the minor or decorative arts, which were experiencing rapid change during this period of formal and cultural renewal.

After the war, however, the Triennale became an important centre for the theory and practice of a wider range of subjects directly linked to the urgent need for reconstruction.

At the heart of the questions raised by the Triennale in the first two decades following the war were the matters of rebuilding the city, social housing, the modernisation of production processes and the birth of the consumer goods industry.

More than just expositions, these were veritable workshops attended by both public administration and private enterprise, with architects, town planners, economists, sociologists and philosophers all united by a common desire to contribute ideas to the new forms, structures and institutions of the newly-born Italian Republic. It was a burst of activity that was thwarted by the protests of 1968, however. The constructive role of the Triennale was brought to a halt, and subsequently acquired a more conventional function as a simple exhibition site.

In itself, the chair designed by Caccia Dominioni and the two Castiglioni brothers is extremely simple: a painted curved iron tubular structure with plywood seat and back, devised for the mass market. In actual fact, the real interest in its design is that it caters to the earliest attempts in Italy to abandon the strictly traditional school chair – epitomised by the tall school desk in dark wood with incorporated chair – in favour of a freer and more participatory approach. More than just a new chair, it foreshadowed a new concept of schooling. E.M.

UGO MULAS, PHOTO REPORTAGE: THE WORKING WOMAN

In 1962, Olivetti asked Ugo Mulas for a photo report on work in its factories. It was quite an ordinary request from a firm that was determined to build a modern image, which would reflect and illustrate the modernity of its products. Similarly, it had already employed photographers like Henry Cartier-Bresson, Fulvio Roiter and Gianni Berengo Gardin. Mulas decided to focus his lens above all on the female workers and staff. In Italian society, these women were at the forefront of a real anthropological revolution. No longer mothers or wives subject to male authority, the women depicted by Mulas are determined and seductive, besides being strong and frivolous. His camera catches the exact moment of change; it captures an artfully crafted hairdo, the whiteness of a collar that stands out from a black work apron, but also the assuredness of a new social and economic autonomy.

As new stars of a changing society, women would soon be challenging the traditional family structure, demanding new roles and responsibilities in the workplace and public life and causing a deep transformation of Italian society that is by no means over yet. E.M.

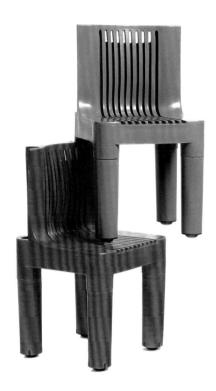

ZANUSO-SAPPER, K 1340 CHAIR, KARTELL
COMPASSO D'ORO 1964

In 1959, Milan City Council asked Marco Zanuso to design a series of furnishings for primary schools. While the desk design was straightforward, Zanuso struggled with the problem of the chair: neither the wood chosen for the desk, nor plywood or metal seemed suitable. He went round in circles without solving the problem, and in 1961 the city council finally lost interest in the project. Instead, Zanuso had developed a keen interest in the design and was working on a very small chair, more suitable for a kindergarten than a primary school. Zanuso contacted Kartell and experimented with plastic as a material, first with polyester and later with polyethylene. The chair finally saw the light of day in 1964. Zanuso had designed a highly interactive spatial element, a play unit, modular, stackable, buildable and coloured. It weighed 2240 grammes and was made of polyethylene, measured 27 × 27 × 49.5 cm, had four removable legs, and the seat and back were a single piece. Midway between a construction game and ordinary furniture, the chair became whatever the children wanted it to, providing the main component of many different scenarios. E.M.

MARISA BELLISARIO APPOINTED PRESIDENT OF ITALTEL

In 1981, Marisa Bellisario was called by the then Minister of State Holdings, Gianni De Michelis, to guide Italtel, a large, publicly owned industrial group formed by thirty electro-mechanical companies with thirty thousand employees, in great difficulty and in need of radical restructuring.

It was the first time that a woman had held such an important position in a large and important company in Italy.

Marisa Belisario became president of Italtel after a career that had begun in the electronics division of Olivetti in 1959. When the electronics branch of the firm passed to General Electric in 1965, Marisa Belisario moved to the United States, and her expertise eventually took her to join the management of Honeywell. In 1979, there was a first rapprochement with Italy and Olivetti, when Carlo De Benedetti offered her the presidency of the Olivetti Corporation of America.

The experiences and skills gained in America in a cutting edge sector like the electronics industry made her the ideal candidate for CEO of Italtel.

In this new post Marisa Bellisario faced a difficult situation. The unions did not support her, as they were sceptical about her reorganisation plans, and neither did the executives, as they feared her managerial outlook. They were not actually wrong in fearing her, as Marisa Belisario changed 180 of the 300 executives, set up new projects and in three years managed to turn the company's budget around, changing it into a company with a 1300 billion lira revenue besides a modern electronic industry.

But then a possible merger between the newly restored Italtel and Telettra, a Fiat company in the same sector, was proposed and Turin vetoed her as CEO and the project collapsed. In Italy, perhaps the role was still considered too important to be entrusted to a woman.

However, Marisa Bellisario had an extraordinary career, all built on merit and skills. Probably, without the opening of the Olivetti and her achievements during the American experience it would not have been possible to reach such a level.

Marisa Bellisario wrote in her autobiography: "I never lived feminism as an activist; in its most important years I was committed to my work abroad and then in Ivrea. I was working and making a career for myself, showing that I could do what men did, and maybe do it better". Certainly, though, when she arrived at Italtel, university graduates constituted only 5% of the workforce, and thanks to her, after a few years, they increased to 27%. Hers was a practical feminism, demonstrating profound change in Italian society. E.M.

Marisa Bellisario, Fondazione Marisa Bellisario

"NEWSWEEK", ARTICLE ABOUT THE NURSERY SCHOOLS IN REGGIO EMILIA

In December 1991, the American weekly magazine, *Newsweek*, dedicated almost an entire issue to a report featuring the best schools in the world.

Starting from the observation that the American model had been unable to address the collapse of the family and the dominant role of television, journalists took a look around the world for the best examples to copy in an attempt to remedy the crisis back home. In the end, only two American universities were spared (one in California and one in Pittsburgh), but they found an excellent reading and writing programme in New Zealand, the best mathematics and foreign language courses in Holland, the best science teaching in Japan, the best lycées and secondary schools in Germany, and the best adult-learning classes in Sweden.

In Reggio Emilia, instead, they found the best pre-school education.

The article began: "All glass, the Diana nursery school in the north of Reggio Emilia looks more like a pleasant greenhouse than a state school. The children's drawings are everywhere, on the walls, painted on the windows, hung from the ceiling and scattered over the tables."

Starting the network of municipal pre-schools, of which there were then thirty-three, had, until 1985, been an enthusiastic Loris Malaguzzi. His approach to learning was embodied in one simple but dazzling observation: "School should be somewhere for all children. It should not be based on the idea that all children are the same, but on the fact that all children are different."

Great freedom and a wide range of stimuli solicited by the teachers are the features of these nursery schools, where not just creativity is cultivated but relationships as well: each class has a communication centre made of cardboard boxes, each with the name of a child or teacher: three-year-olds can use them to give a slice of cake or a piece of coloured paper to a friend; the older children use them to send proper letters. It is splendid training for school and life, concluded the authors of the study. E.M.

RESTORATION PROGRAMME FOR DU 30 CHAIR
COMPASSO D'ORO 1954

Thanks to financial backing by the Miroglio Texile Group, in 2010 the Fondazione ADI - Compasso d'Oro signed an agreement with the Friends of the Venaria Restoration Centre (Associazione Amici Centro Restauro di Venaria) to undertake conservation of the objects awarded the Compasso d'Oro, currently conserved by the Fondazione.

After a detailed report on the condition of the entire collection carried out by the experts at the Venaria Centro Nazionale del Restauro, the agreement comprises a plan to restore or safeguard all the items in the collection.

The project entails careful examination of all the objects as well as a case by case study to ascertain the most appropriate restoration methods.

Awarded the first edition of the Compasso d'Oro prize in 1954, the DU 30 chair by Gastone Rinaldi provides a perfect example of Italian design of the period. Its multi-textile composition including metal, fabric and expanded resin offers a significant example of the technology and skills of the Venaria centre.

Faced with modern technical everyday items, restorers have to decide where to draw the line between conservation and reconstruction; whether to make the piece work again or, rather, to conserve its original appearance. As such, the restoration laboratory is a place for pondered research, advanced technology and tradition. E.M.

From Research to Daily Life

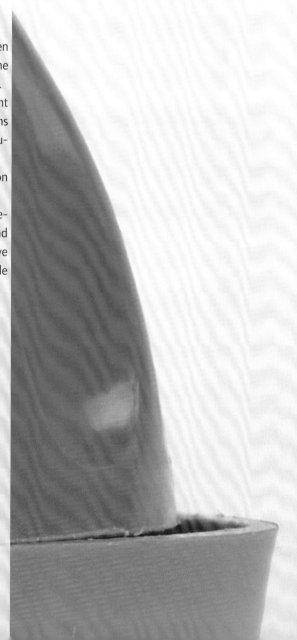

This is easier said than done. This proverb perfectly illustrates the distance between an invention and its practical application. Or, as an alternative, it demonstrates the distance between a brilliant technical solution and a practical object in daily use.

Here the necessary work is not limited to the effort necessary in finding efficient and functional solutions but requires the development of languages and forms which make technical novelties acceptable, comprehensible and preferably beautiful too.

This can only be achieved through finding common ground between innovation and production, research and industry, and culture and design.

Faced with the rapid pace in developments during the post war period, Italian design has taken on the role of a valuable clearing house where the intuitions and successes of Italian research have been transformed into functional and evocative objects, recreating technology in the shape of an everyday environment accessible to us all.

Ezio Pirali
1. **V.E. 505**
fan
Fabbriche Elettriche Riunite
I. COMPASSO D'ORO 1954

Giovanni Varlonga
2. **THERMOVAR FEAL VAR/M3**
heaters
FEAL Società Fonderie
Elettroniche Alluminio Leghe
sas
VI. COMPASSO D'ORO 1960

Marcello Nizzoli
3. **BU**
sewing machine
Vittorio Necchi spa
I. COMPASSO D'ORO 1954

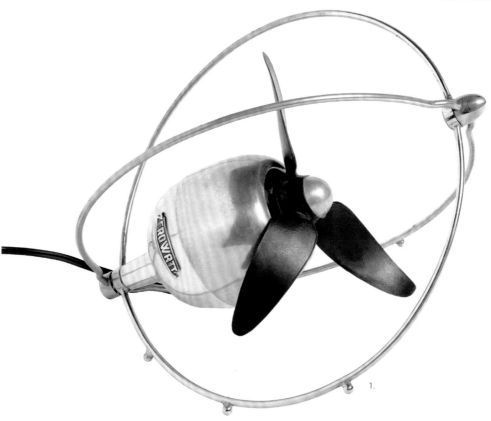

1.

2.

3.

4.

5

Giuseppe De Goetzen
4. **ELCHIM**
vacuum cleaner brush
F.lli Chiminello srl
II. COMPASSO D'ORO 1955

Sandro Bono
5. **WATERPROOF CAN**
waterproof can
Fratelli Bono spa
V. COMPASSO D'ORO 1959

Oscar Torlasco
6. **GENOVA 4053**
street light fixture
Fabbrica Apparecchi
Illuminazione Greco spa
V. COMPASSO D'ORO 1959

6.

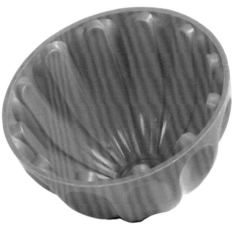

7.

8.

Gino Colombini
7. **KS 1481**
lemon squeezer
Kartell srl
V. COMPASSO D'ORO 1959

Ettore Sottsass jr.
8. **ELEA**
electronic calculator
Olivetti & C. spa
photo CSCDO Archive
V. COMPASSO D'ORO 1959

Joe Colombo
9. **SPIDER**
floor and table lamps
OLuce srl
IX. COMPASSO D'ORO 1967

Rodolfo Bonetto
10. **SFERYCLOCK**
alarm clock
F.lli Borletti spa
VIII. COMPASSO D'ORO 1964

Ufficio Tecnico Marelli Aerotecnica
11. **CUPOLINO**
extractor fan
Marelli Aerotecnica
photo CSCDO Archive
VI. COMPASSO D'ORO 1960

Gino Valle
12. **ALPHANUMERIC INDICATORS FOR TRAIN STATIONS AND AIRPORTS**
alphanumeric indicators for train stations and airports
Solari & C. spa
photo CSCDO Archive
VII. COMPASSO D'ORO 1962

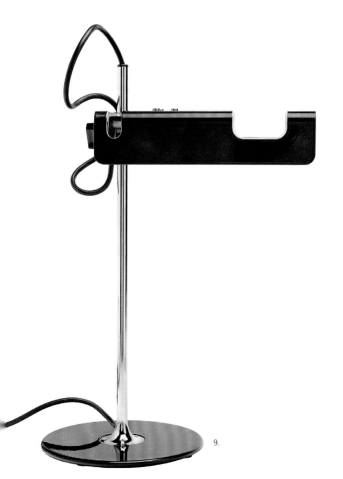

9.

10.

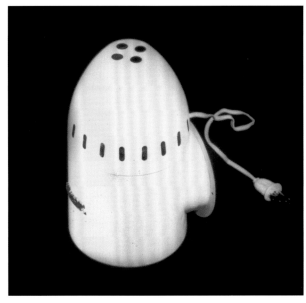

11.

12.

13.

14.

15.

Ufficio Tecnico Fiat
13. **ALLOY WHEELS**
alloy wheels
Cromodora
IX. COMPASSO D'ORO 1967

Claudio Conte, Leonardo Fiori
14. **SISTEMA P 63**
prefabricated components
Prefabbricati Pasotti
photo cscdo Archive
X. COMPASSO D'ORO 1970

Studio MID
15. **TRE SECOLI DI CALCOLO AUTOMATICO**
research
IBM
XI. COMPASSO D'ORO 1979

16.

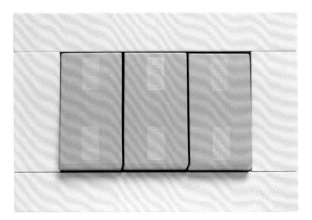

17.

18.

Marco Zanuso
16. **FALSE CEILINGS FOR OPEN SPACE**
false ceilings for open space
Steiner Karl
photo CSCDO Archive
XI. COMPASSO D'ORO 1979

**Andries Van Onck
con Hiroko Takeda**
17. **HABITAT**
switches and sockets
Ave interruttori
XI. COMPASSO D'ORO 1979

Ufficio Tecnico Secco
18. **SC 312 SECCOLOR**
monoblock window frame
Industrie Secco spa
photo CSCDO Archive
XII. COMPASSO D'ORO 1981

Carla Venosta
19. **TECNIKO**
integrated metal false ceilings
Termisol spa
photo CSCDO Archive
XII. COMPASSO D'ORO 1981

Rodolfo Bonetto
20. **WIZ**
multipurpose mechanical and electric power plant
Wizco
photo CSCDO Archive
XII. COMPASSO D'ORO 1981

19.

20.

**Sergio Colbertaldo,
Paolo Rizzatto**
21. **D7**
ceiling and wall lamp
Luceplan spa
XII. COMPASSO D'ORO 1981

Sergio Pininfarina
22. **RESEARCH FOR
AERODYNAMIC SHAPE**
research
Pininfarina con CNR Consiglio
Nazionale delle Ricerche
XI. COMPASSO D'ORO 1979

**Beppe Benenti,
Walter Olmi**
23. **ELDEC**
underwater instrument
Benenti e Olmi
XII. COMPASSO D'ORO 1981

Enzio Manzini
24. **LA MATERIA
DELL'INVENZIONE**
book
Arcadia edizione srl
XIV. COMPASSO D'ORO 1987

Gianpietro Tonetti
25. **BOOMERANG**
drawers for pharmacy
Icas srl
XIV. COMPASSO D'ORO 1987

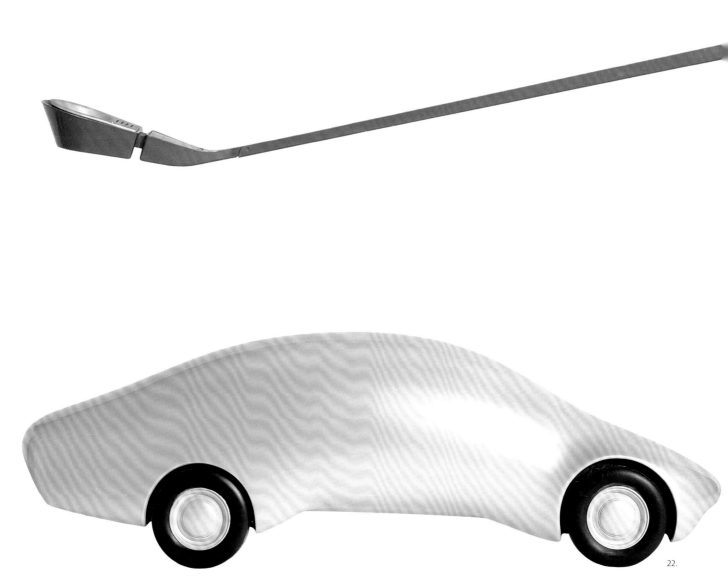

22.

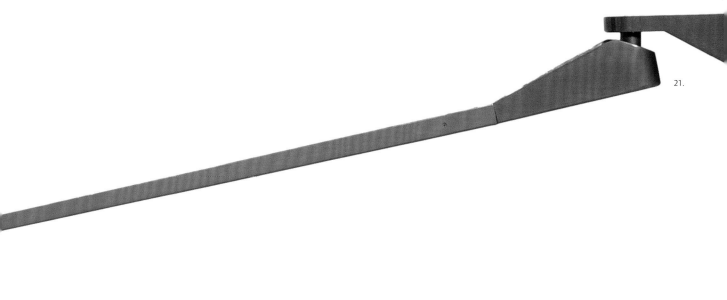

21.

23.

24.

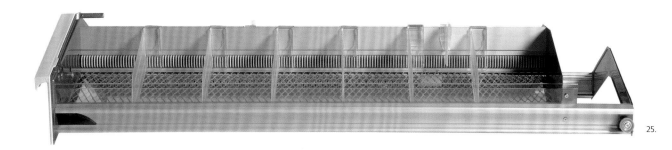

25.

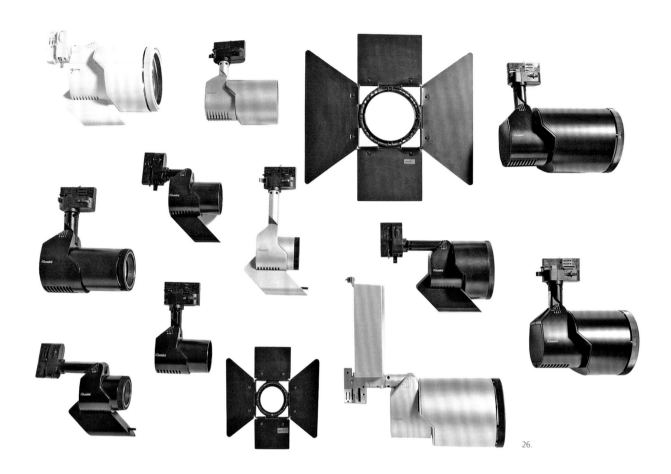

26.

27.

28.

Bruno Gecchelin
26. **SHUTTLE**
range of spotlights
iGuzzini Illuminazione spa
XV. COMPASSO D'ORO 1989

Pierluigi Spadolini
27. **MPL MODULO PLURIUSO**
prefabricated house
Edil Pro spa Gruppo iri-Italstat
XIV. COMPASSO D'ORO 1987

Gino Gamberini
28. **MURA**
seating system for lecture rooms
Pagnoni & C. srl
photo cscdo Archive
XV. COMPASSO D'ORO 1989

Giuseppe Zecca with Direzione Sviluppo Ticino
29. **SERIE LIVING**
electric devices
Bassani Ticino spa
XV. COMPASSO D'ORO 1989

Design Group Italia
30. **SACE MEGAMAX F**
industrial circuit breaker
ABB Sace spa
photo cscdo Archive
XVI. COMPASSO D'ORO 1991

Bruno Gecchelin
31. **AGH 171 NEW**
chiller - heater
Riello Condizionatori
photo cscdo Archive
XVI. COMPASSO D'ORO 1991

Paolo Rizzatto, Alberto Meda
32. **LOLA**
floor lamp
Luceplan spa
XV. COMPASSO D'ORO 1989

29.

30.

31.

32.

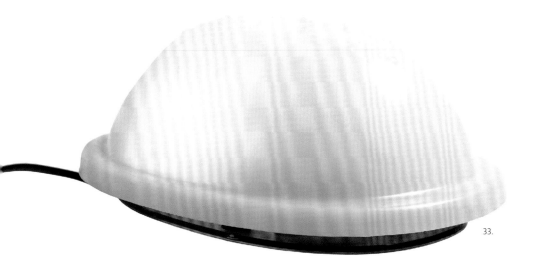

33.

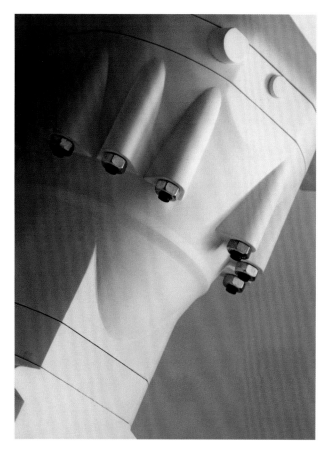

34.

Marc Sadler
33. **DROP 2**
wall lamp
Arteluce - Divisione FLOS spa
XVII. COMPASSO D'ORO 1994

Richard Sapper
34. **PONTI 180/182**
*modular system for fixed arms
for shovel*
Hurth axle
photo cscdo Archive
XVI. COMPASSO D'ORO 1991

**Promotor Facoltà
del Design/Politecnico
di Milano, with 17 research
units from 12 Italian
Universities Politecnico
di Milano, Politecnico
di Torino, Università degli
Studi di Brescia, Università
degli Studi "Gabriele
D'Annunzio" di Chieti,
Università degli Studi
di Firenze, Università degli
Studi di Genova, Università
degli Studi di Napoli
"Federico II", II Università
degli Studi di Napoli,
Università degli Studi
di Palermo, I Università
degli Studi di Roma
"La Sapienza", Università
degli Studi di Reggio
Calabria, Istituto
di Architettura di Venezia.
National coordinator
Ezio Manzini 1998-2000**
35. **SDI - SISTEMA DESIGN
ITALIA, RICERCA DI SCENARIO**
research
Ministro della ricerca
Scientifica e Tecnologica
photo cscdo Archive
XIV. COMPASSO D'ORO 2001

Paolo Targetti
36. **MONDIAL F1**
lighting modular system
Targetti Sankey spa
XVIII. COMPASSO D'ORO 1998

Marc Sadler
37. **TITE** and **MITE**
suspension and floor lamps
Foscarini Murano srl
XIX. COMPASSO D'ORO 2001

SDI | Sistema Design Italia

35.

36.

37.

38.

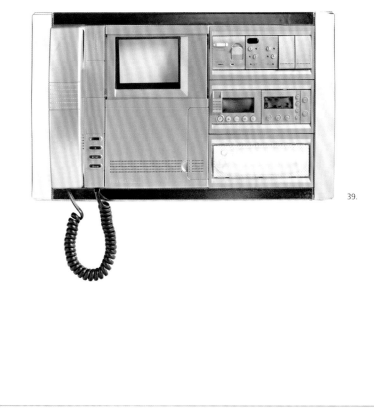

39.

Fausto Colombo,
Lorenzo Forges Davanzati
38. **BOMA**
bus shelter
Consorzio Arredo Urbano
XXI. COMPASSO D'ORO 2004

Giuseppe Zecca con
Direzione My Home
39. **SVILUPPO PRODOTTI**
BTICINO
home automation system
BTicino spa
XIX. COMPASSO D'ORO 2001

Zagato
40. **EUROTRAM PER MILANO**
public transport system
(rendering)
Bombardier Transportation
Italy spa
XIX. COMPASSO D'ORO 2001

Brembo Technical
Department
41. **BRAKING SYSTEM**
carbon ceramic disc brake
calliper
Brembo spa
XX. COMPASSO D'ORO 2004

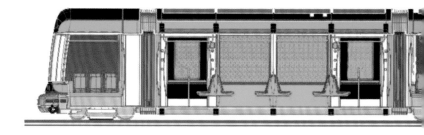

41.

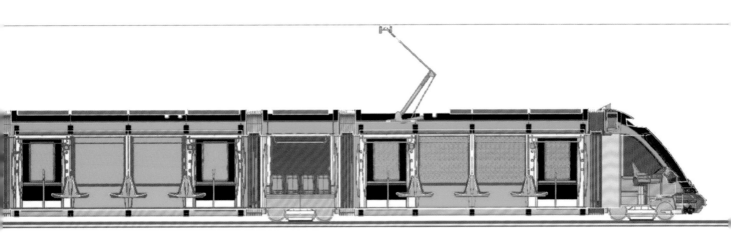

40.

42.

43.

4

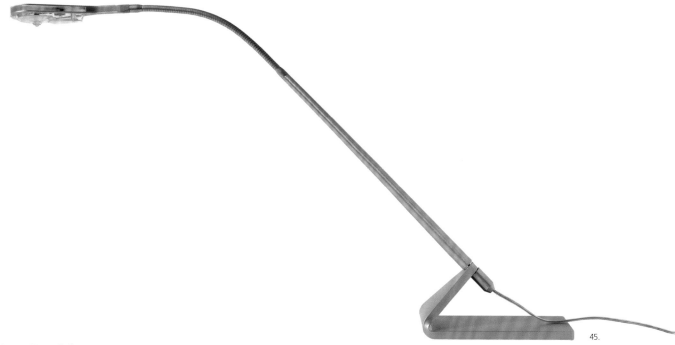

45.

Isao Hosoe, Peter Solomon
42. **ONDA**
lighting system
Luxit spa (già Luxo Italiana)
photo CSCDO Archive
XX. COMPASSO D'ORO 2004

Eoos Design con Ugolini Design
43. **KUBE**
community seating
Matteograssi spa
XX. COMPASSO D'ORO 2004

Toyo Ito
44. **STAND HORM**
stand design
Horm srl
photo CSCDO Archive
XXI. COMPASSO D'ORO 2008

Alberto Meda, Paolo Rizzatto
45. **MIX**
luminaire
Luceplan spa
XXI. COMPASSO D'ORO 2008

Pininfarina
46. **NIDO**
concept car
Pininfarina
photo CSCDO Archive
XXI. COMPASSO D'ORO 2008

46.

ETTORE SOTTSASS, CALCULATOR ELEA, OLIVETTI
COMPASSO D'ORO 1959

It was probably Enrico Fermi, on his last visit to Italy in 1950, who gave Olivetti the idea of entering the electronics market. Only nine years later, Olivetti launched the world's first fully transistorised electronic calculator.

Within that short space of time and using exceptional foresight, Olivetti had opened a research centre in the US, started investigating the semiconductors sector and set up an electronics division, run by Adriano Olivetti's young son, Roberto. Managing the division was an equally young and brilliant Italo-Chinese engineer, Mario Tchou. Not without a certain amount of courage, Adriano Olivetti gave the assignment to design this innovative machine to yet another young man, Ettore Sottsass.

Little more than an experimental object at the time, the electronic calculator had no real identity of its own, and it was Sottsass who took on the challenge to give it shape and sense: "Designing an electronic calculator [...] does not simply mean giving shape and meaning to the plastic appearance of a machine, [...] it means giving shape to organisms [...] that never have specific features but that take on different ones according to their size and the tasks they have to perform."

Being an architect, Sottsass started from the archetype of a domestic container such as the cupboard. This gave ready access to the electronic components and made mass production easy. Formally, Sottsass chose aluminium: "In metal they ended up looking like any old office cupboard; and you could not do wood. So I thought of black metal structures, enclosed with six- or seven-millimetre aluminium strips [...] a sort of silver architecture that was really mysterious [...] rather nasty and totally incomprehensible."

The height of the various units was restricted to 140 centimetres so that the employees could see one another, like among the household furniture: "In other words, the idea was to turn the machine into a piece of furniture, or rather into a house you live in performing a specific job that is hard, modern and dignified, but that is nevertheless a job still done by people."

The first Elea 9003 calculator was bought in 1959 by Conte Marzotto who installed it in the offices at his Valdagno factory. In the same year, the Olivetti Elea 9003 won the Compasso d'Oro.

Although, for complex reasons, Olivetti sold its electronic division to General Electric in 1964, the fruits of this experience continued to germinate through time. In 1969 Olivetti launched the first programmable desk computer (the P-101 designed by Mario Bellini), and Federico Faggin, considered the "father" of the microchip, began exploring new possibilities at Olivetti. E.M.

BENETTON, WHOLE-PIECE DYEING SYSTEM FOR KNITWEAR

The idea is apparently quite simple. Instead of producing knitwear from dyed yarn, it is produced from raw yarn and dyed later as a finished garment. This intuition was the essence of the Benetton siblings' success, thus giving rise to one of the most important industrial groups in the varied galaxy which we could call "made in Italy".

In 1960, Benetton produced in all about 800 sweaters, while after introducing the new system in 1962 production jumped to 10,000 garments, an exponential growth made possible by their intuition. Working with raw materials means rationalising the whole process: purchases are simplified, shops are kept stocked without accumulating stock in warehouses, orders are completed within very tight deadlines, costs are contained and the whole service improved.

Soon afterwards, the group introduced single brand shops designed by Afra and Tobia Scarpa and later came the involvement of Oliviero Toscani who endowed the Benetton Group with a finely honed, aggressive and successful image.

Currently the group runs very different activities internationally; from fashion it has moved on to motorways, mass retail and restaurant chains involving a turnover of over 11 billion euro. All this began with coloured sweaters produced by creative and efficient entrepreneurial intelligence, an example of authentic industrial design. E.M.

AFRA E TOBIA SCARPA, DIVANO CORONADO, C&B

On the face of it, Coronado was a modern sofa, although certainly not a revolutionary one. While it was devoid of the overstuffed look that in the mid 1960s characterised most upholstered furniture, Afra and Tobia Scarpa did not abandon the comforting and reassuring classical look. But then the two designers were never as extreme as some Italian designers and remained within their moderately modernist style. Coronado had a simple shape that, while it did not exactly charm design writers, assured it an extraordinary sales success.

However, the industrial design of the upholstery was really innovative. It was designed as components that could be assembled through a few simple steps. This rational supposition enabled a constant reworking of the design; the early version had a wooden frame which was quickly changed to an entirely metal frame in the second version. Taking advantage of ongoing research in expanding foam, the firm produced a third version that was completely original and uniquely built.

Instead of wrapping the metal and pre-stressed steel frame in soft foam sheets, the frame was inserted inside the mould. The polyurethane was cold cured directly around it forming a moulded finished element; a revolution merging traditional upholstery procedures with industrial automation for the first time.

Not even the Bayer technicians who had provided the initial synthetic resins were able to explain the cold foaming secret and the factory came under close scrutiny by many of the Bayer engineers and chemists.

With Coronado, Italian furniture design really went industrial and Brianza stood out as one of Italy's most successful furniture making districts. E.M.

PININFARINA-CNR, STUDY INTO AERODYNAMIC SHAPE
COMPASSO D'ORO 1979

Battista Farina, known as Pinin, had had a feeling for aerodynamics since 1912 when he designed a barely suggested conjunction between the bonnet and the then still-flat windscreen for the legendary Fiat Tipo Zero.
During the 1930s, his intuition took the shape of a sinuous and streamlined racing car and, although not yet subjected to wind tunnel tests, it was exceptionally swift and efficient.
Immediately after the war, however, these experiments began to affect the lines of more normal automobiles. No longer just the racing cars, but virtually ordinary road vehicles. In 1947, Pinin Farina designed the bodywork of the Cisitalia, a particularly sporty type of coupé known as a Berlinetta whose outline seemed to have been drawn without ever taking the pencil off the paper. With the design of the 1957 Lancia Florida, aerodynamics became a form deriving from elegance. The smoothness of volume was replaced by taut lines and large areas of glass, entrusting the reduced front sections with the greatest diffusion of aerodynamics. At the same time, Enzo Ferrari engaged him to design his race-winning automobiles, which had now caught the attention of the whole world. His ideas in this field constituted the basic principles upon which the modern car was founded. A success sanctioned by a change of name: in 1961, the president of the Italian Republic, Giovanni Gronchi, in consideration of his huge contribution to society and industry, authorised the engineer's name to be legally changed to Pininfarina.
As the years went by, aerodynamics stopped being a case of intuition and aeronautical research and wind tunnel tests were introduced to the world of the automobile as well. Pininfarina, however, saw aerodynamics not as a solution in itself but as a starting point. When, in 1976, the CNR engaged him to run an advanced research programme for a vehicle with a low air penetration co-efficient, the result was not an automobile, but a production of experiences. It was only the increase in fuel costs and worrying levels of pollution that forced aerodynamics to become an exact science. It is remarkable if we think that the cars on the roads today still feature the lines of those studies carried out by Pininfarina thirty-five years ago. E.M.

GRAN SASSO LABORATORY INFN

In 1979, Antonio Zichichi, at the time working as an experimental physicist at CERN in Geneva and professor at the University of Bologna, thought of establishing a huge underground laboratory dedicated to the study of subatomic particles.
The project was supported by the pioneering research of the American physicist Raymond Davis who had realised that in order to isolate and study particles produced by solar activity a filter that would substantially block cosmic rays was needed, so as to simplify the detection of particles such as neutrinos or the search for dark matter.
Italy, with its prestigious tradition in physics could not lag behind. Zichichi sought out the site under the Apennines, where the mass of the mountain and the chemical and physical composition of the rocks offered ideal conditions, namely next to the Gran Sasso tunnel, along the planned route of the Rome-Aquila-Teramo motorway. The government headed by Amintore Fanfani approved the project and work started in 1982 together with the work on the motorway.
Entrusted to INFN (National Institute for Nuclear Physics), the laboratory began operating in 1987.
An imposing engineering work, the laboratory has three 100 x 18 x 20 m chambers plus related service areas and is the biggest underground research facility in the world. Here a sort of sophisticated camera is installed, that in 2006 managed for the first time to capture a still of the elusive neutrinos, showing all the "events of neutrinos oscillation" and measuring all the particles produced by the interaction extremely accurately.
Currently, 750 researchers from twenty-two different countries work in this cutting edge facility and conduct experiments coordinated by an international scientific committee. E.M.

MASSIMO MARCHIORI AND THE HYPER SEARCH ALGORITHM

When the World Wide Web was starting out, it needed a directory to help navigate through the world of virtual information. Initially, search engines were approximate – able to identify a page but not the relationship between the page and the rest of the Web.
The situation changed dramatically with the arrival of a young mathematician from Padua: Massimo Marchiori: "It was 1996 and at a conference in Santa Clara, California, I presented Hyper Search, my project for a search engine that would really work." His idea had germinated in Italy but the rigid bureaucracy of the Italian universities had paid it scarce attention. In Santa Clara, however, one of the future inventors of Google, Larry Page, was in the audience. He was bowled over by Marchiori's idea. He trailed him throughout the conference, going over all the details and the mathematical formulas perfected by Marchiori. At the end, as they said goodbye, he promised he would try and develop the project. And this he did, with his partner Sergey Brin, assisted by funding promptly granted by Stanford University.
On September 27, 1998, Page and Brin started the Google company, today considered the world's most successful business.
Despite the fact that the two founders of Google did not forget to mention the Italian mathematician's contribution, Marchiori was not given a Chair in Italy and he moved to Boston's prestigious MIT, one of the internet's birthplaces. Afterwards, though, he decided to return to his Italian university. Marchiori is associate professor at the University of Padua, where he graduated and began his research. Dedication and the wish to contribute to the future of his own country have prevailed over riches and fame. E.M.

GINO COLOMBINI, KS 1481 JUICER, KARTELL
COMPASSO D'ORO 1959

Speed and comfort are the most dramatic effects of postwar Italian modernisation; speed of transportation, a new dynamism in work and daily life, comfortable homes and new appliances to simplify and lighten housework. Both these trends mean practicality. The ideal of practicality is evident in the spread of light, brightly coloured, resistant plastic. In Italy in the 1950s and 1960s, plastic was synonymous with Moplen® and Meraklon®, the commercial names of isotactic polypropylene, a new synthetic material produced and patented in the Montedison Laboratories in 1954.

Synthesised for the first time by Giulio Natta, who was later awarded the Nobel Prize in 1963, this extraordinarily adaptable material ensured Italy an unforeseen leading role on a global scale in chemistry, and was fundamental in helping to consolidate the fledgling national industry.

The sudden availability of relatively low cost materials which fitted perfectly with modern production processes but had not been fully explored designwise, inspired designers. By using plastic material technique and typology, Italian design actually grew and became well known.

A pupil of Giulio Natta at the Politecnico di Milano, Giulio Castelli was among the first to believe in the possibilities of synthetic materials. When he founded Kartell in 1949, he began working with semi-finished rubber products from Pirelli. But in the early 1950s he approached polypropylene and polyethylene, and, after two years spent studying the situation and the needs of the Italian market, he started producing home accessories. Gino Colombini was the director of the technical office of Kartell; the small KS 1481 juicer is just one of around 200 objects which Colombini designed in only nine years, thus redesigning the domestic environment by introducing cheerful colours and original functions.

Thanks to the low investment needed to work plastics, Kartell entered the field of lighting in 1958 and interior design in 1962.

The turnover of Kartell went from 100 million in 1950 to 650 million in 1962, with a new strategy that delegated the production to outside companies, only keeping in-house the development of the product: market analysis, design of products and moulds, and advertising and commercial distribution. E.M.

RICCARDO MORANDI, POLCEVERA VIADUCT, GENOA

The Polcevera viaduct, designed by the engineer Riccardo Morandi, was inaugurated in 1967. It enabled the Autostrada dei Fiori to cross over the Polcevera Valley, and the western outskirts of the city of Genoa. It was a particularly dense urban area, with the Polcevera river coming down through it. There were also several railways to be crossed, and in all the design required a careful study of the base pillars of the viaduct that is over 1000 metres long with eleven bays, some of which spanning more than 200 metres. Besides all this, the still near-experimental use of the technique of pre-compressed reinforced concrete, a building technique carried out in Italy by engineers working in an exceptional development and research environment, made the viaduct an extraordinary work of engineering for the time.

Morandi's Polcevera viaduct is the culmination of group work of an extremely high level engineering school that also produced other top professionals such as Sergio Musumeci, Aldo Favini, Silvano Zorzi and Massimo Majowiecki. Throughout 20th-century Italy, this lasting phenomenon produced extraordinarily high levels of engineering of which Pierlugi Nervi was perhaps the most famous exponent, but not uniquely so.

These were engineers who were not only capable of innovation in construction systems, but also of handling the business and management aspects of construction; they were real partners of a system of great construction companies which were amongst the most important in the world. E.M.

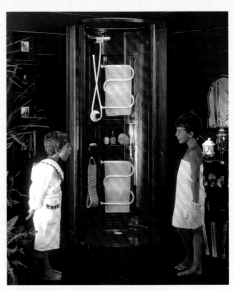

FABIO LENCI, TONDA SHOWER, TEUCO

In 1969, Joe Colombo was asked by Bayer to create an experimental installation for a fair in Cologne that would bring the possibilities of the plastic materials the German chemical giant produced into the public eye.

Colombo created an apartment, which was mainly composed of three large fitted capsules: the Central-Living block, made of two matching parts (one on the ground and one suspended) which housed a seating area, bookcases, audio, video and lighting systems; the Kitchen-Box was in a small module that housed a fully equipped kitchen blending into an eating area; the Night-Cell included a wardrobe-sleeping area with a bathroom cell.

It was an idea of a house squeezed into these functional units, whose design became more interesting as the complexity of living functions increased. Typically, the bathroom cell was a solid, enveloping moulded plastic form. It was a waterproof, sealed unit with a controlled microclimate, totally given over to water and cleanliness.

While Joe Colombo's projects may have been a bit too futuristic and complex they did, however, respond to a real need for change in the kitchen and bathroom areas of homes. Just three years later, Teuco, then a new firm which produced bathroom fixtures, presented a shower on the market which was quite novel from various points of view. The shower, designed by Fabio Lenci, was a small transparent acrylic capsule. It made use of the plastic working techniques that had been developed by the Guzzini family, owners of Teuco, to create a high-performance element that was both functional and beautiful.

Perfectly circular, this shower was an independent and self-sufficent unit which housed a variety of accessories that would make personal hygiene fun and relaxing. Tonda was the ancestor of all bathroom improvements during the last twenty years, the first of many future developments, which, over the years, have included hydromassage tubs and nozzles, sauna or steam functions, chromotherapy and ambience music. Perhaps hygiene has not particularly improved, but washing has certainly become easier and more fun. E.M.

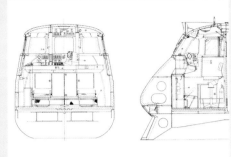

PENDOLINO TILTING TRAIN, FIAT

Although the oldest of the modern means of transport, trains are still perhaps the most efficient way of travelling middle distances.

A modern electric train reaches high speeds, does not pollute, stops in the heart of the town and provides a comfortable ride for passengers.

To offer all its advantages, the system needs to be able to bear the speed of the fast trains, however. The main problem is the railway track which only allows high speeds along straight stretches, or at least where the curves are limited. High speed trains travel on special lines which require viaducts and tunnels in order to overcome the unevenness of the landscape. With a densely-populated and geographically complex country like Italy, it is not only extremely expensive to build high speed track but the environmental impact is also considerable.

Faced with this situation, made worse by the extremely dated railway lines, built mostly at the turn of the last century, railway designer Francesco Di Majo decided it would be useful to rethink the engineering of the train itself. To counterbalance the centrifugal force that would normally cause the coaches to derail around a tight bend, engineer Di Majo imagined how the axis of the train might be tilted to lean into the curve, like a motorcycle.

In 1965, he set his hunches down on paper. Using gyroscopes and hydraulic jacks he found a way of making the train follow the curves of the track without losing speed around the bends. Developed and perfected by Fiat Ferroviaria Savigliano, the system was patented in 1975 under the name "Pendolino".

The first trains of this type were adopted by the Italian State Railways as early as 1976, reducing travelling time by 25%-30%. By the 1990s, trains of this type were already covering the 632 kilometres between Rome and Milan in a mere four hours.

The Pendolino was a worldwide success for Italian railway engineering and it was adopted in Germany, France, Spain, Switzerland, Britain and Portugal.

When Fiat sold the Ferroviaria Savigliano to the French Alstom, in 2000, the portfolio of orders amounted to 900 million euro, much of which was related to the Pendolino. E.M.

Pendolino Fiat ETR 401, 1975 - Archivio Storico FIAT

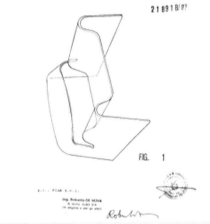

21 891 B/87

FIG. 1

GHOST ARMCHAIR, CINI BOERI, FIAM

Transliteration signifies transcribing the letters from one alphabet to another, without worrying about the meaning of the text, but taking care to keep the original order of the characters. In terms of shape, something similar can be achieved by creating or "rewriting" an existing model of something using different materials.

Cini Boeri takes all the most easily recognisable features of the traditional armchair: (its ample size, softly rounded forms, swelling profiles), then shifts it all into a dry, ethereal and almost two-dimensional context. Almost a piece of technological virtuosity, Ghost is magic in a thick, curved piece of glass.

Modernist rigour by now outmoded, this Italian design focuses on the semantic value of the object, uniting form and illusion and no longer thinking of form as a derivative of function.

It remains, however, a concrete project that uses technology and matter. A design that promotes research and pushes technology into uncharted waters. E.M.

Technical drawing attached to patent, MICA, UIBM, fasc. 50655

BREMBO DISC BRAKES
COMPASSO D'ORO 2004

Every car driver knows that disc brakes are a guarantee of safety. Usually, though, we only think about them when we buy a new car and look through the standard features in search of the classic words "disc brakes on all four wheels". From then on, unpleasant surprises aside, we do not think about the brakes any longer except when the car is up for its motor safety test.

If, however, we are dealing with racing cars, things are somewhat different. The brakes are under constant scrutiny. Efficient braking reduces deceleration time, leaving more leeway for speed.

With the introduction of futuristic materials such as carbon, disc brakes once again became the focus of experimentation and research. With the high technology involved, their performance can determine the outcome of a Formula 1 championship and become a subject of lively discussion among racing fans.

Suppliers to many racing car teams – Ferrari first of all – Brembo is one of the leading companies in the typically Italian precision mechanics sector. Its braking system, using callipers and carbon ceramic discs, is an example of high technology designed to provide maximum performance.

When technology reaches a point of uncompromising self-expression it is not infrequently accompanied by an implicit elegance that derives from the perfect balance between optimum functioning and technical performance. E.M.

Leisure Time

Leisure time is the opposite of working time, it offers physical and intellectual alternatives that are actual paedagogical, political, and psychological alternatives.
UMBERTO ECO

Leisure time is by no means a modern invention. However, the idea that everyone is entitled to a share of leisure time is certainly modern.

The upper classes, the wealthy and the Church have always enjoyed the privilege of leisure time, upon condition that others worked for them, at worst as slaves or at least from the ranks of the poor. It was only with the advent of machinery that production increased to the extent that everyone had access to personal leisure time.

Time has therefore been made available by modern progress and technology. In any society, besides illustrating its vices and virtues, objects intended for leisure use are an accurate indicator of its progress. Such objects represent our direct involvement in sports, travel and moments of pure recreation. Still others show us as mere paying spectators of any one of the myriad opportunities for entertainment offered by our contemporary entertainment-oriented society.

Araldo Sassone
1. **ITALIA**
jacket for fishermen
Contex spa
photo cscdo Archive
I. COMPASSO D'ORO 1954

Bruno Munari
2. **ZIZI**
foam rubber toy
Pigomma srl
I. COMPASSO D'ORO 1954

Attilio Mario Franchi
3. **MOD. 48AL**
automatic shotgun
Luigi Franchi spa
photo cscdo Archive
I. COMPASSO D'ORO 1954

4.

5.

6.

Enrico Freyrie
4. **UNIVERSAL**
water skis
F.lli Freyrie
II. COMPASSO D'ORO 1955

Egon Pfeiffer
5. **ORIGINAL VEREX**
vacuum bottles
Società Industriale Chimica
Dewas
II. COMPASSO D'ORO 1955

Carlo Alinari
6. **ATLANTIC**
sea fishing reel
L'Alcedo di E. Rolandi
III. COMPASSO D'ORO 1956

7.

8.

9.

Cesarino Benso Priarollo
7. **SLALOM SECURIT**
ski boot
La Dolomite
IV. COMPASSO D'ORO 1957

Natale Beretta
8. **SUEDE CALF LEATHER BAG**
bag
Artisan leatherwork
by Natale Beretta
III. COMPASSO D'ORO 1956

Stelio Frati
9. **FALCO F.8.L.**
light passenger aircraft
Aviamilano Costruzione
Aeronautiche
photo cscdo Archive
VI. COMPASSO D'ORO 1960

Danilo Cattadori
10. **FLYING DUTCHMAN**
sailing boat
Alpa
photo cscdo Archive
10. VI. COMPASSO D'ORO 1960

11.

1

13

14.

15.

Mario Germani
11. **BACKPACKING TENT**
backpacking tent
Ettore Moretti spa
photo cscdo Archive
VI. COMPASSO D'ORO 1960

Roberto Menghi
12. **GUSCIO**
holiday shacks
ICS
photo cscdo Archive
IX. COMPASSO D'ORO 1967

Ugo Zagato
13. **ABARTH ZAGATO 1000**
car
Carrozzeria La Zagato srl
photo cscdo Archive
VI. COMPASSO D'ORO 1960

Ufficio tecnico La Dolomite
14. **4S**
ski boot
La Dolomite spa
IX. COMPASSO D'ORO 1967

Peppe Di Giuli
15. **ASTOLFO**
rocking horse
Studio Giochi srl
XI. COMPASSO D'ORO 1979

Carlo Ferrarin, Livio Sonzio
16. **CALIF A21SJ**
motor glider
Caproni Vizzola
photo CSCDO Archive
XI. COMPASSO D'ORO 1979

Franco Quiringhetti
17. **TRANSAHARIAN**
research for cab
Fiat V.I. Iveco Image
photo CSCDO Archive
XII. COMPASSO D'ORO 1981

Enrico Contreas
18. **MATTIA ESSE**
catamaran
Mattia & Cecco srl
photo CSCDO Archive
XII. COMPASSO D'ORO 1981

Italo Cammarata
19. **TENDER**
moped
Quasar
XIII. COMPASSO D'ORO 1984

18.

19.

20.

21.

22.

**Peppe Di Giuli
with Ufficio Progettazione
Comune di Terni**
20. **STREET FURNITURE**
street furniture
Comune di Terni
photo cscdo Archive
XIV. COMPASSO D'ORO 1987

**A. Caringola, G. Corretti,
M. Prampolini**
21. **BONSAI PRUNING SHEARS**
tools
ISIA
photo cscdo Archive
XIV. COMPASSO D'ORO 1987

**V. Di Dato, P. Zanotto
with Nautilus Associati**
22. **AFS 101**
mountain climbing boot
Asolo spa
XIV. COMPASSO D'ORO 1987

**Renata Fusi, Silvana Rosti,
Paolo Zanotto**
23. **DETECTOR**
goggles
Briko srl
XVI. COMPASSO D'ORO 1991

**Antonio Colombo, Paolo
Erzegovesi**
24. **LASER NUOVA EVOLUZIONE**
racing bicycle
Cinelli spa
XVI. COMPASSO D'ORO 1991

23.

24.

**Richard Sapper,
Francis Ferrarin**
25. **ZOOMBIKE**
folding city bicycle
Elettromontaggi srl
XVIII. COMPASSO D'ORO 1998

Bruno Giardino
26. **LH 500**
snow plough
Leintner spa
XIII. COMPASSO D'ORO 1994

Design Continuum Italia
27. **SCORPIO 270**
folding camp stove
Campingaz
XIX. COMPASSO D'ORO 2001

**Ufficio Progetti
Campagnolo**
28. **VELOCE**
bicycle accessories
Campagnolo srl
XVII. COMPASSO D'ORO 1994

**Centro Stile Dainese, Aldo
Drudi**
29. **T-AGE SUIT**
suit for motorcyclists
Dainese
XIX. COMPASSO D'ORO 2001

25.

26.

27.

28.

29.

30.

Guido Canali (layout design), Lucia Fornari Schianchi (idea and coordination)
30. **PARMIGIANINO E IL MANIERISMO EUROPEO**
exhibition
Galleria Nazionale di Parma–Palazzo della Pilotta
XX. COMPASSO D'ORO 2004

Giovanni Anceschi, Valeria Bucchetti, Matteo Bologna
31. **POLDI PEZZOLI MUSEUM MULTIMEDIA ARCHIVE**
multimedia archive
Museo Poldi Pezzoli
IX. COMPASSO D'ORO 1998

Zelig
32. **SOPRINTENDENZA ARCHEOLOGICA DI POMPEI CORPORATE IDENTITY MANUAL**
corporate identity
Soprintendenza Archeologica di Pompei
XX. COMPASSO D'ORO 2004

German Frers (nautical design), Wally con Serena Anibaldi (interior design)
33. **TIKETITOO**
sailing boat
Wally
XX. COMPASSO D'ORO 2004

31.

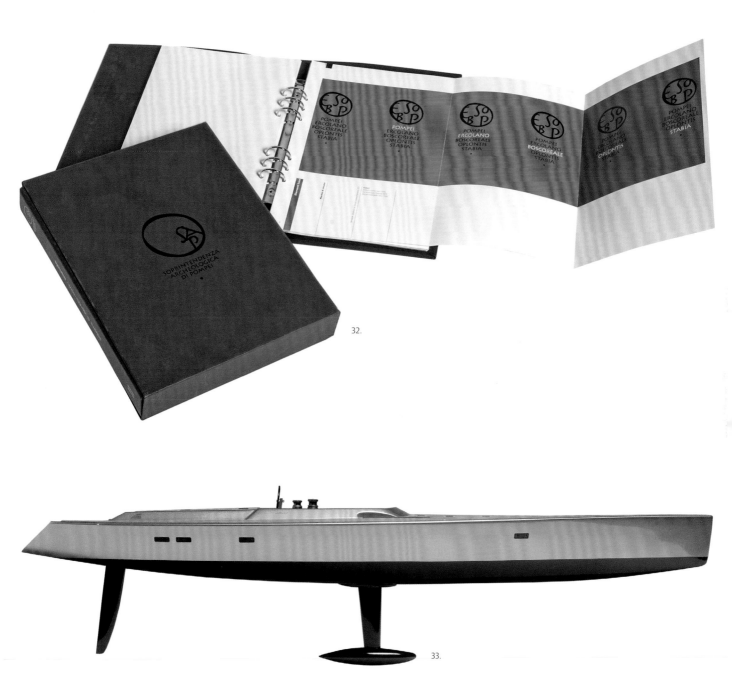

32.

33.

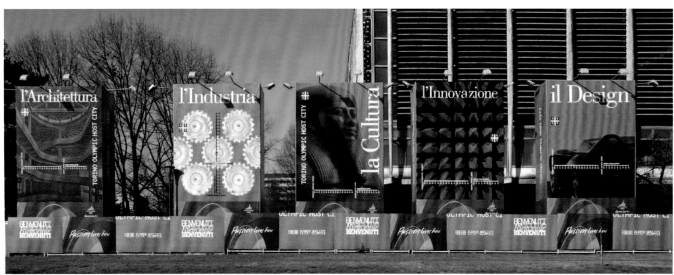

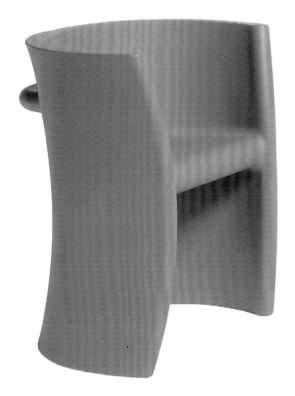

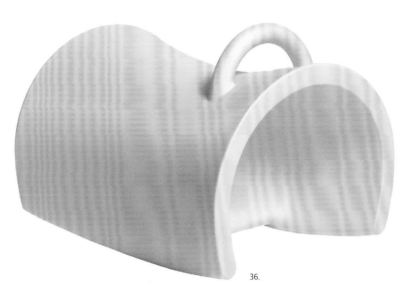

36.

Wally, Lazzarini Pickering Architetti e Farr Yacht Design
34. **SHAKA**
sailing boat
Wally
XXI. COMPASSO D'ORO 2008

Italo Lupi, Ico Migliore, Mara Servetto
35. **LOOK OF THE CITY OLIMPIADI INVERNALI 2006**
Turin urban design
Città di Torino
photo CSCDO Archive
XXI. COMPASSO D'ORO 2008

Eero Aarnio
36. **TRIOLI**
multipurpose children's chair
Magis spa
XXI. COMPASSO D'ORO 2008

CARLO SCARPA, RESTORATION AND SYSTEMISATION OF THE CASTELVECCHIO MUSEUM, VERONA

NATALE BERETTA, ARCATA SUITCASE, BERETTA
COMPASSO D'ORO 1956

The decision to award the Compasso d'Oro to a carefully crafted, fine leather suitcase might at first seem hard to understand, and almost a slight in a country where, at the time, millions of people were leaving their homes with cardboard cases held together by string.

The award was organised by the most luxurious Italian department store, where the leather goods departments was of considerable importance.

One might ask why that particular suitcase; what was special about it, for example? It would have been hard for a jury of architects not to appreciate the structure of the case, with its arc-shaped sides and the way it opened cleverly at the front with a semi-circular zip. The system allowed you to pack logically and gave easy access to the lower layers. Although always described as a suitcase, it is actually a fairly small soft sack. Rather than a case for long trips it is closer in concept to the sports bag, but smarter and more sophisticated. Behind the success of the model lies the fact that a new middle class was discovering free time, a taste for weekends and short breaks away from home. This other side of Italy was quickly learning how to appreciate the pleasures of its improved standard of living. E.M.

Designed by Carlo Scarpa and inaugurated in 1967, the renovation of the Castelvecchio Museum in Verona was in some way both the ending and the highest achievement in an extraordinarily intense and high quality renewal of Italian museums that had lasted nearly twenty years. Just to mention a few: the work on the Castello Sforzesco in Milan by the BBPR (1949-63), the Gardella Pavilion of Contemporary Art (built in 1953 and rebuilt after the odious assault of 1993), the prolific work of Albini in Genoa (Museo di Palazzo Bianco, Palazzo Rosso and the Treasure of San Lorenzo, completed between 1949 and 1956), the Gallery of Modern Art in Turin by Bassi and Boschetti (1959) and Scarpa's projects in Palermo (Palazzo Abatellis, 1954) and Possagno (Gipsoteca Canova, 1957). These restorations were necessary due to war damage, but despite the unfortunate circumstances, they resulted in a general rethinking of the spaces, forms and functions of cultural institutions within Italy's new democratic and republican system. This would not have been possible without a masterly convergence of skills and goals between designers, public authorities and intellectuals who firmly believed in the fundamental and formative role of culture. From a place of storage or mere rhetorical celebration, the museum became an irreplaceable generator of shared values and civil cooperation. No longer a space reserved for the study of a selected few, but an accessible place for opportunities of lifelong learning, the new Italian museums formed a network that spanned the country, collecting both Italy's diverse local heritage and defining the characteristics of a newly desired collective identity. E.M.

Photo P. Perina, AMC Archivio Museo di Castelvecchio

MARIO BELLINI, RECORD PLAYER GA 45 POP, MINERVA

Launched in the USA by Columbia Records in 1948, 45 rpm vinyl records with a single track on each side announced the arrival of individual music consumption on a mass scale.

More and more people started listening to music and gramophones began to get smaller and smaller. By the end of the 1960s they had become light, portable record players.

Before audio cassettes were to pave the way for the worldwide success of the Sony Walkman (launched in 1979) and the arrival in the 1980s of a way of listening to music that was introverted and solitary, the record player was a perfect reflection of the taste and behaviour of a youth movement that moved in groups and seemed unable to bear moments of silence in the permanent soundtrack that defined their identity.

When Mario Bellini designed the GA 45 Pop portable record player, the first thing he did was to reorganise the internal layout of the technical components, exploiting his experience gained working with the far more complex Olivetti office machinery. Once the bulk was reduced, he designed a casing that looked like a handbag. The model was simple, not highly technical-looking, but the colour was captivating. The design consisted of a rigid ABS case with mouth-like opening, geometric holes for the loudspeakers and a lightweight sliding polished steel handle. E.M.

COSTA CLASSICA, COSTA CRUISE LINER

When the two major turbo liners *Michelangelo* and *Raffaello* went out of service in 1973, it marked the end of the great transatlantic crossings.

By now passenger transport by sea was unable to compete with air transport. It was the end of a long and glorious period, during which the great ocean liners of the Italian shipping yards had become the high point of Italian manufacture.

It was above all Gustavo Pulitzer Finali in the early years of World War Two, and Gio Ponti during the 1950s to make these liners showcases for the new Italian style. Involved were not only the finest furnishers but even top Italian artists and interior decorators.

However, at the end of the 1970s few people would have bet on the rebirth of sea travel. And yet the success of the holiday resort as a new type of vacation was to offer the large transatlantic liners a new lease of life.

No longer conceived as luxury floating hotels, or as a pleasant interval between departure and arrival at one's destination, these cruise liners were self-sufficient worlds devoted to enjoyment and leisure time, on a par with the new package holidays and theme parks. No longer intended as a means of discovery but simply a method of getting away, these ships were ideal for those seeking free time, without the need to stimulate the curiosity and saturated by the idea of free time and recreation.

In 1991, Costa Classica brought Italian style back to the cruise liner. Placed in the capable hands of Pier Luigi Cerri, the ship was fitted in such a way that it united elegance of design and important works of art, according to the best Italian tradition.

Costa Classica was the doyenne of a new generation of transatlantic liners. Today, one of the world's major cruise ship companies, Costa Crociere, has a fleet of themed boats catering for a wide range of holidays. The liners travel to multiple destinations, offering seas and landscapes to suit a multitude of tastes. E.M.

RICHARD SAPPER, FRANCIS FERRARIN, FOLDING ZOOMBIKE, ELETTROMONTAGGI SRL
COMPASSO D'ORO 1998

"It is an efficient response to the new requirement of city dwellers to seamlessly combine public transport with an environmentally respectful private transport means when moving about the city. With its adaptability, it signals a new relationship between the city and its inhabitants." This was the motivation with which the jury of the Compasso d'Oro assigned the prize to the bicycle designed by Sapper and Ferrarin.

Besides the recognition of the high standard of this design, it is a hope and a wish that echoed the gradually increasing respect for the environment throughout the country.

As we all know, the habit of carrying a folding bike on the bus or on the tube and of opening it to finish our journey is not yet fashionable. However, over the last few years, bicycles have made a come back as part of a general environmental awareness regarding energy, food and recycling.

Even If these were the values to which the Jury of the Compasso d'Oro wished to award recognition, at the same time the bicycle is a very intelligent and versatile object, very easy to handle and efficient to use. Although probably more suited to leisure time than daily use, it exploits applied engineering and advanced material technology to create minimal size and weight. E.M.

OPENING OF THE SERRAVALLE DESIGNER OUTLET

With the success of the first department stores, which opened in Paris around the mid 19th century, shops and boutiques began to move away from the city streets, to be concentrated in large edifices purpose-built for trade. Modern versions of bazaars and markets, the department stores copied the museum concept, tempting the public – not with works of art but large quantities of goods. Although they were something of a luxury experience, they were nevertheless tempered by the cruder and more functional approach of the supermarket and its rapid mass-consumerism. Nowadays the roles seem to have been reversed and it is the modern shopping malls that imitate the old streets and squares of the town. Indeed, these centres are not simply areas in which to shop but they provide places for the public to meet, pass the time or enjoy the air conditioned climate.

Opened in 2000 at Serravalle Scrivia in the province of Alessandria, the Serravalle Designer Outlet is the largest outlet in Europe. Outlets are special kinds of shopping malls where you can find items, especially famous clothing brands, at discount prices. Indeed, to underline its selective approach, the Serravalle outlet uses the word "designer" as part of its name. The municipality of Serravalle was chosen for its strategic position, with good road connections, more or less equidistant to the three major cities of north-western Italy and close to some of the country's most affluent provinces. Built like a small town, with streets, piazzas and fountains, the Serravalle Outlet resembles a fairytale village not unlike Disneyland or any other amusement park. With shopping now considered as a pastime like any other leisure activity, outlets are at their busiest at the weekends, and, during the sales, Serravalle is often responsible for lengthy traffic jams along the motorway.

Now, ten years since its opening, Serravalle Scrivia has been visited by over 20 million Italians. Statistics may not be an exact science but that is nevertheless one third of the population of Italy. E.M.

ROME OLYMPICS

SLALOM SECURIT SKI BOOTS, LA DOLOMITE
COMPASSO D'ORO 1957

After two unsuccessful candidatures, the first due to the outbreak of war and the second to competition from the Norwegian capital Oslo, the International Olympic Committee awarded the 1956 Winter Olympics to the Italian town of Cortina d'Ampezzo. Of the twenty-five gold medals, Italy came home with only one. This one medal was thanks to Lamberto Dalla Costa and Giacomo Conti, who won the double bob race. To complete the Italian medal table were two silvers won by Eugenio Monti, again in the bob competition. However, the real winner of the 1956 Winter Olympics was Austrian Toni Sailer, who took home all three of the gold medals for the downhill skiing races.

These victories brought skiing as a sport to the Italian masses. No longer was it reserved for an elite of aristocrats or adventurous intellectuals. What senator Agnelli in the 1930s had anticipated when he built a modern ski resort at Sestrière was now a reality.

The 1950s also marked a rapid progress in downhill skiing techniques, which were marked by equally fast changes in the equipment, above all in the skis – faster and more dynamic. To remain in control less flexible boots with safety clamps were needed.

The 1957 Compasso d'Oro jury rewarded technical progress that would meet the needs demanded by the new leisure time available. Not unexpectedly it was the last edition of the prize to be organised by the department store La Rinascente. The Slalom Securit ski boot was made by La Dolomite. Owned by Giuseppe Garbuio, the company founded in 1897 was at the time already a supplier to numerous military sports teams. E.M.

In 1955, after earlier disappointments, the Olympic Games were assigned to Rome. The 1960 Games were particularly important as it was the first time the competitions were broadcast on TV throughout Europe. Italian television (the RAI) was to produce over 100 hours of programmes. The Olympic Games in Rome marked the transition to the type of entertainment that we are all familiar with today.

These were the first Olympics not to produce unapproachable heroes but real public figures who would dominate the headlines and popular imagination. While Cassius Clay and Wilma Rudolph became household faces, Livio Berruti's victory in the 200 metres would be for the Italians the image that symbolised all the emotions of the 1960 Rome Olympics.

But the thirteen gold medals won by the Italian athletes were not the only consequences of this important event: Rome was finally transformed into a modern metropolis. Although the sports facilities were examples of superb architecture and great engineering, what still surprises us today is the concentration of public works built and completed in such a short time on a limited budget and with farsighted vision for the city of the future.

In addition to the stadiums, gymnasiums and the exceptional Palazzetto dello Sport by Pierluigi Nervi, the great ring road (Grande Raccordo Anulare) was completed, Fiumicino airport opened, underpasses and fast track roads along the Tiber constructed; corso Francia and the new via Olimpica were terminated, and road conditions were overhauled on an almost regional scale.

One example for all is the construction of the Olympic Village, which offered a chance for urban renewal, architectural experimentation and careful management since, after the Games had finished, the properties were assigned to the families of employees in the public sector. E.M.

AMBROSIANO AND GIANCARLO ZANATTA, MOON BOOT, TECNICA

Although the Zanatta Brothers owned a firm that produced ski boots, in 1970 they decided to launch a casual after-ski boot on the market, inspired by the shapes of the space suits that the astronauts wore when they landed on the moon in the summer of 1969.

While the successes of the "Valanga Azzurra" [Italian Avalanche] pushed sales higher in the technical skiwear sector, where Italy became the absolute leader at the time, on the other hand, Moon Boots were the epitome of mass winter holidays. Simple, cheerful, and cheap, Moon Boots were the result of a small technological invention that produced a shoe from just three parts: sole, synthetic outer shell, and lining and laces. Practical and unisex, Moon Boots could be worn on either foot and just a few sizes fit everyone.

Colourful and decorated with a large printed text on the uppers, Moon Boots are not only a lucky entrepreneurial intuition but one of the first instances in which design dictated a fashion trend. E.M.

**BRONZI DI RIACE EXHIBITION,
PALAZZO DEL QUIRINALE, ROME**

Like most Mediterranean countries, summer in Italy is generally the season of free time and holidays. At the end of the 1970s, though, the traditional mass holiday period of twenty-eight days of idleness throughout the month of August – deck-chairs, sun umbrellas and half board on one of the Italian rivieras – began to be influenced by new and more sophisticated needs. Promoted by all the magazines that observed the daily habits, culture and social behaviour of the Italians and publicised on the front covers of the major illustrated weeklies, the concept of the smart holiday began to take root. No longer an opportunity just for rest and leisure, holidays became first of all a chance for freedom and release. It was a time to cultivate the interests that months of work had thwarted. While certain intellectuals happily revealed their favourite spots, others indicated, tourist-guide style, the haunts of writers and artists of the past. Suddenly, appearing cultured became a sign of social distinction and the media asked itself every summer what the Italians would be reading on the beach, almost as if we had suddenly become a nation of avid readers (recent statistics show that 62% of Italians still read less than one book a year).

It is perhaps in this context that the exemplary event of the Bronzi di Riace, two magnificent Greek statues dating from 450 BCE, found in the Ionian Sea in 1972, can be explained. After several years of restoration at Florence's Opificio delle Pietre Dure, they were exhibited first in Florence and then, in the summer of 1981, at the President of the Republic's Quirinale Palace in Rome. After which, they were returned to Reggio Calabria.

The second exhibition was an exceptional success. Despite the torrid Roman summer, visitors queued for hours to get even a brief look at these magnificent bronze statues.

When they were returned to the specially-built museum in Reggio Calabria, though, they were virtually forgotten by the public. The absence, especially of foreign visitors, prompted suggestions that they be moved to a more accessible site.

It is the perfect metaphor of the idea of culture equated to a consumer item. Something to be acquired in comfort and that does not require effort. E.M.

The Riace bronzes, June 29, 1981 - Archivio Storico della Presidenza della Repubblica (ASPR), Archivio Fotografico

MASSIMO VITALI, PHOTOS OF ITALIAN BEACHES

War reporter and chronicler of Italy's *anni di piombo* [years of lead] Massimo Vitali was one of the last eye-witnesses of Germany as it was behind the Iron Curtain. He also recorded its subsequent political and social upheavals. Born in 1944, Vitali documented the end of the 20th century, capturing the events and images of a changing world.

This was a world in which it was becoming increasingly hard to distinguish between truth and the way it is represented or manipulated, however; a fact which urged him in 1995 to turn to a more minimal landscape. He moved away from the portrayal of large-scale collective change towards a contained panorama of more personal types of behaviour.

From the top of a five-metre tripod planted in the water, with his back to the sea and camera facing the beach, Vitali photographed Italians on holiday, with entomological precision. Ruthless yet sympathetic, Vitali portrayed Italians in moments of public intimacy, when the masks of clothes or professions no longer conceal vices and virtues. His photographs were whitened by the heat yet thick with narrative detail.

All of this took place as his subjects calmly went about their everyday leisure time rituals, entirely indifferent to his camera. E.M.

Massimo Vitali
Rosignano 3 Women, 1995
Courtesy of the artist and Brancolini Grimaldi

TURIN WINTER OLYMPICS
COMPASSO D'ORO 2008

The history and character of Turin made it difficult to imagine that the city would be able to organise and hold the Winter Olympic Games of 2006. Despite there being excellent ski runs less than 100 kilometres away from the city centre, there did not seem to be a sufficiently business-like ethos that reached beyond factories and cars, Turin's prime interest. However, both Gianni Agnelli and the city council believed in Turin's possibilities, the former because he saw an opportunity for profit, and the latter because Turin had already been carrying out urban and social renewal programmes that diversified the city's economy with respect to the car industry. This started at the end of the 1980s, and continued, involving investments in university research, culture, museums and art.

Actually, the Olympics were very successful and showed the world a very different city, much more colourful and lively than had been expected.

The achievement was in part due to a communication success linking past and present, Turin's industry together with its glory as the capital of Savoy, its creativity and sobriety.

Set up by the Milanese graphic designer Italo Lupi, and the architects Ico Migliore and Mara Servetto, the coordinated series of images served to highlight a new identity, steeped in history, but with multiple enterprises, dynamic and forward looking. E.M.

La Rinascente, ADI and the Compasso d'Oro

Enrico Morteo

BACKGROUND

When in 1917 Senatore Borletti took over what remained of the Città d'Italia's large chain of stores from the Bocconi brothers, he turned to Gabriele D'Annunzio for a new name for the company. Even though in the middle of the battle of Bainsizza, the poet found the time and inspiration to coin the new name: "My dear friend, I'm writing to you in a great hurry. I'm leaving in half an hour to bomb Grahovo [...] This is the name of the company. I came up with it yesterday evening in the Chiampovan valley: LA RINASCENTE. It's simple, clear, and useful." This was the beginning of the history of the most famous emporia in Italy.

The programme undertaken by Senatore Borletti and his brother-in-law Umberto Brustio, managing director of the company from 1919, was to make La Rinascente the most authoritative reference point for the tastes of the newly developing Italian middle classes, but also to make the most of an opportunity for a modernist renewal of society. On the one hand, "to bring art nearer to life" and, on the other, "to allow the acquisition of criteria of practicality, hygiene and good taste by increasing numbers of the population, and to propose in new forms the most everyday objects for interior decoration and dressing." And so – having entrusted its advertising to the posters of Marcello Dudovich, the refined creator of the most sophisticated illustrations of the time – at the end of the 1920s La Rinascente had already commissioned a collection of modern furnishings from the architect Gio Ponti. Under the name of *Domus Nova*, the new line aimed, in the words of Gio Ponti, at "bringing to the forefront [...] the essential problem of hygiene, comfort, practicability and quality", and, even though quite different from the rationalist rigour of the Bauhaus, it marked a decisive renewal of Italian taste and production.

But it was to be above all in the post-war period that, thanks to its dominant position in the sector of large-scale distribution, La Rinascente found its role as the leader of the evolution of production and communications at a time when a radical reorganisation of the Italian economy and a progressive increase in consumption was underway.

INTRODUCTION

At the end of the 1940s, La Rinascente, following along the lines of what Olivetti had undertaken in 1928, constructed its own internal design office with the aim of supervising image and communications strategies, the building of new stores and service structures and, shortly after, the designing of products with the La Rinascente brand name which could then be made by other firms. For over twenty years, La Rinascente's study office was for Milan a cutting-edge centre for the culture of making projects: it was involved with graphics, design, archi-

1. *PREMIO LA RINASCENTE IL COMPASSO D'ORO PER L'ESTETICA DEL PRODOTTO EXHIBITION CATALOGUE, 1954, COVER*
design by Albe Steiner
14.6 × 14.6 cm
Steiner-DPA-Politecnico Archive, Milan

tecture and communications. Such important designers as Franco Albini, Carlo Pagani, Marco Zanuso, Alberto Rosselli, Bruno Munari, Tomás Maldonado and the tireless Gio Ponti all worked there. And it trained some of the most talented young designers, including Italo Lupi, Mario Bellini, Adries van Onk and Roberto Sambonet, Giorgio Armani. Albe Steiner was asked to coordinate the advertising department, while the design of the new La Rinascente logotype was entrusted to Max Huber in 1950. In 1951, on the occasion of the 9th Milan Triennale, which was based on the theme of *The Form of Usefulness*, La Rinascente presented a model apartment for four people designed by Pagani, as well as a collection of furnishings designed by Albini.

It was in this context that La Rinascente began to develop an idea for organising a show of new products that, under the title of *L'estetica del prodotto*, might highlight the aesthetic and cultural value of all objects for daily use. The show opened in October 1953, and was publicised using a refined image by Albe Steiner.

IL COMPASSO D'ORO

The success of the *L'estetica del prodotto* show convinced Cesare Brustio, the son of Umberto, to launch a prize, not just for the recognition, promotion and cultural qualification of products, but also to stimulate the growth and even the birth of businesses concerned with quality and design.

The uncertainties about the name of the prize seem to have been resolved by Albe Steiner who, during a preparatory meeting, took out of his pocket a Goeringer compass – given to him by the sculptor Jenni Mucchi, the wife of Gabriele Mucchi – a tool often used by sculptors because it did not just outline a perfect circle on a plane but also served to define in space the harmonious proportional relationships of the golden mean, the most classical measure of beauty. They had found their name: Compasso d'Oro, the Golden Compass. Steiner himself designed the prize's logo while Zanuso and Rosselli translated the drawing into an actual compass. The first edition of the prize took place in 1954 at the same time as the 10th Triennale and almost concurrently with the launching of "Stile e Industria", the first Italian magazine wholly devoted to design and which was edited by Alberto Rosselli. During the first edition, fifteen prizes were awarded for various types of product using extremely different materials and types; they ranged from the Olivetti Lettera 22 typewriter to Murano glass vases, objects for sport and leisure, services of plates, chairs, toys, and domestic appliances – in fact all the merchandise that was to be seen in the various departments of La Rinascente. The selection process was severe, with just a few prizes in recognition of high quality and many recommendations in order to encourage further exploration and to consolidate the new professional figure of the designer.

ADI

La Rinascente organized the first four editions of the Compasso d'Oro, but in 1958, the prize passed under the jurisdiction of ADI, the Italian industrial design association, which had been founded in 1956 by some designers (De Carli, Gardella, Magistretti, Munari, Nizzoli, Peressutti, Rosselli and Steiner), two firms (Kartell and Officine Meccaniche Pellizzari) and a critic (Dorfles). Unlike other union-run or cooperative associations, from the very first ADI aimed at being the fulcrum of cultural debate between all the protagonists of industrial design.

Inevitably, in the passage from a management governed by a large chain of stores to one run by professionals and manufacturers, there were various changes, but the original aim of the Compasso d'Oro remained basically unchanged: that of promoting and recognising quality and innovation in Italian research, material culture and design. In the twenty-one editions organised by ADI, the Compasso d'Oro prize was awarded to 276 projects; to these must be added the forty-one Compasso d'Oro prizes in recognition of the careers of the same number of designers, while thirty-six have been awarded to firms or institutions whose overall activity merited the prize. At the same time, during this period ADI promoted Italian design by organizing some 120 exhibitions and numerous study conventions throughout the world. The Compasso d'Oro was awarded at the end of a three-year period of research for choosing the best of Italian design. This work of selection, which involved some 200 people, was undertaken by the 13 ADI delegations throughout Italy and by 12 thematic commissions made up of specialists in various fields of design. After the evaluation of thousands of candidates, at the end of the three years some 360 selected works finally emerged. From these an international jury would choose the projects to be awarded either an honourable mention or the Compasso d'Oro prize. Edition after edition, ADI would gather together a large part of the prize projects and conserve them in a collection supervised by the Fondazione ADI - Compasso d'Oro whose administration board included: the Fondazione Valore Italia; Abet Laminati; IED-Istituto Europeo del Design; the Miroglio Group; POLI.design; Alberto Alessi Anghini; Aldo Bassetti; Carlo Forcolini; and Rodrigo Rodriquez. Today the collection has been recognized as one of national interest and has been placed under the aegis of the Ministry of Cultural Heritage and Activities.

2. ***ESTETICA DEL PRODOTTO*** **EXHIBITION POSTER, LA RINASCENTE, MILAN, 19-31 OCTOBER 1953**
design Albe Steiner
70 × 70 cm
silkscreen print
Steiner-DPA-Politecnico
Archive, Milan

2.

Un coltello, un abito, un bicchiere, un ferro da stiro, hanno la loro dignità non solo nel prezzo o nella funzione, ma anche nella linea; sono manifestazioni di un unico stile nel quale la perfetta funzionalità del prodotto moderno trova la sua esaltazione come forma raggiunta.

La Rinascente, che queste enunciazioni pone a se stessa, vuole, con la piccola selezione dei suoi articoli di vendita raccolta nella Mostra dell'Estetica nel prodotto, affiancarsi a tutti coloro, industriali, progettisti, pubblicisti, uomini di gusto, che hanno operato e operano per l'affermazione degli stessi principi e convinzioni.

È certa, con questo, di compiere un atto da essi apprezzato, perché la sua azione si svolge tra un pubblico di 30.000.000 di persone, pone sui banchi di vendita 35.000 articoli, attinge i suoi prodotti da 15.000 fornitori italiani e stranieri.

L'estetica nel prodotto

19|31
ottobre
1953

Per la prima volta un Grande Magazzino si impegna di affrontare quel "problema sociale" che esprime le sue soluzioni nella maggiore dignità di un prodotto. Dignità come attuazione di un disegno intuito e creato e come forma che libera e dà vita a una illuminata realizzazione dell'utile, del razionale, del ragionato.

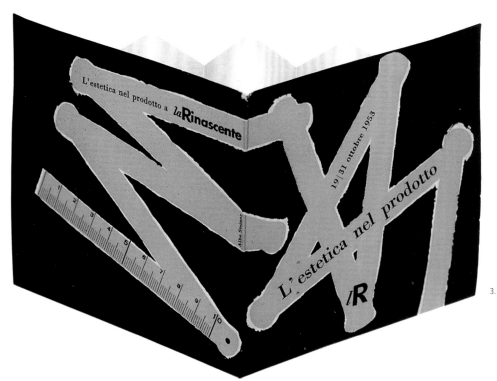

3.

4.

3. *ESTETICA DEL PRODOTTO*
**INVITATION-BROCHURE FOR
THE SHOW, LA RINASCENTE,
MILAN, 19-31 OCTOBER 1953**
10.8 × 22 cm
Lucini print
Steiner-DPA-Politecnico
Archive, Milan

4. *ESTETICA DEL PRODOTTO*
PHOTOGRAPH OF THE SHOW
Steiner-DPA-Politecnico
Archive, Milan

5.

6.

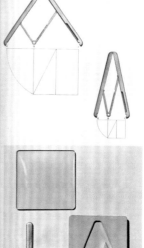

7.

8.

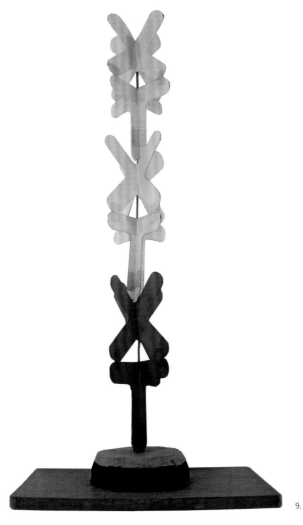

9.

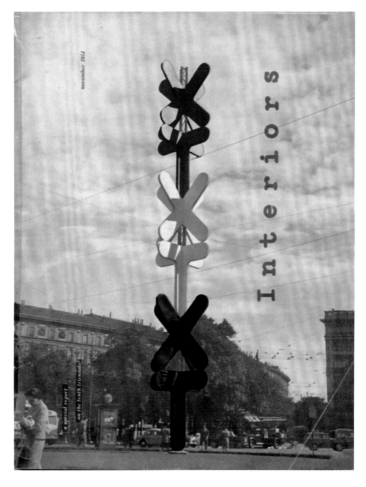

10.

5. LA RINASCENTE, BROCHURE FOR PRESENTING PRODUCTS
design by Albe Steiner,
English version, May 1952
10 × 14.7 cm
Printer A. Lucini & C.

**6. *L'ESTETICA DEL PRODOTTO ALLA RINASCENTE*
IN "DOMUS" N. 290, 1954**
editor Gio Ponti
Library of the Steiner-DPA-Politecnico Archive, Milan

7. "STILE INDUSTRIA" N. 1, 1954, COVER
editor Alberto Rosselli
design for the cover of the first issue by Albe Steiner
Library of the Steiner-DPA-Politecnico Archive, Milan

**8. *UN PREMIO PER L'ESTETICA DEL PRODOTTO*
IN "STILE INDUSTRIA" N. 4, 1955**
editor Alberto Rosselli
Library of the Steiner-DPA-Politecnico Archive, Milan

9. MODEL OF THE TOTEM REALIZED FOR THE X TRIENNIAL
Marco Zanuso head of the design department
totem design by Albe Steiner with Claudio Conte
Steiner-DPA-Politecnico Archive, Milan

10. "INTERIORS" N. 1, 1954, COVER
Library of the Steiner-DPA-Politecnico Archive, Milan

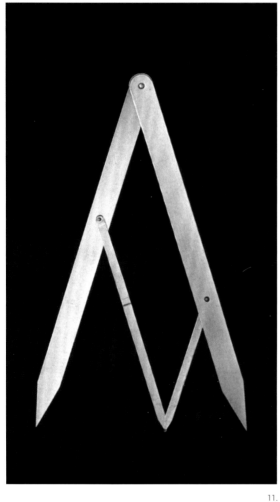

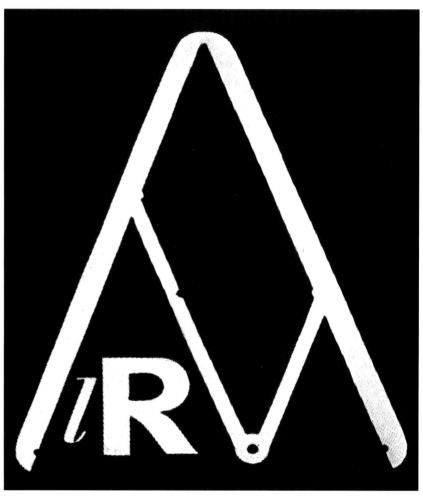

11.

12.

11. **GOERINGER COMPASS**
Private collection

12. **TRADE-MARK FOR THE COMPASSO D'ORO DESIGNED BY ALBE STEINER**
La Rinascente, 50 anni di vita italiana, edited by the public relations department
of La Rinascente, vol. 3, 1968, p. 99, editorial layout and graphics by Roberto Sambonet and Max Huber
Library of the Steiner-DPA-Politecnico Archive, Milan

13. **PRIZE RULES, BROCHURE**
design by Albe Steiner
15 × 15.5 cm, closed
Steiner-DPA-Politecnico Archive, Milan

Regolamento del Premio *la***Rinascente**

1

Estensione del premio

Al premio Compasso d'oro sono invitate a concorrere con i loro prodotti tutte le aziende industriali e artigiane italiane ed i creatori dei modelli, nelle categorie dell'abbigliamento (tessuti, confezioni, accessori), dell'arredamento (mobili, illuminazione, tessuti, accessori), degli articoli casalinghi (mensa, cucina, servizi elettrodomestici), degli articoli da sport, da viaggio, di cancelleria; dei giocattoli e, infine, degli imballi di presentazione.
I partecipanti possono presentare più prodotti, anche nella stessa categoria.

2

Svolgimento della manifestazione

I concorrenti al Compasso d'oro faranno pervenire i loro prodotti alla Segreteria indirizzandoli in Via San Raffaele n. 2, entro le ore 16 del 31 agosto 1954; la ricevuta varrà come iscrizione al concorso; i prodotti verranno presi in carico dalla Segreteria del Premio Compasso d'oro, e, su richiesta dei concorrenti, potranno essere assicurati contro tutti i rischi.
Ogni prodotto dovrà portare chiaramente nome e indirizzo della ditta e del creatore del modello, se la creazione ha un autore.

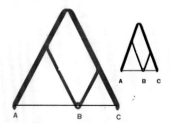

Il compasso per la proporzione aurea, detto il compasso d'oro, è il noto strumento qui raffigurato che divide sempre con la punta intermedia (B) la varia distanza delle punte estreme (A-C) in due tratti tali che il maggiore (A-B) sta al tratto A-C come il minore (B-C) sta al maggiore A-B.

Questo rapporto, individuato da Euclide, dove le parti son dette *media ed estrema ragione* è anche definito *sezione aurea* e nel Rinascimento questa proporzione costante, possibile fra il tutto e una parte e fra le due parti del tutto, fu anche chiamata *divina proporzione*; Leonardo se ne servì per identificare nel suo celebre disegno le proporzioni nel corpo umano; altri architetti, artisti e trattatisti la impiegarono per controllare le proporzioni delle opere loro, sia per ricercare nelle opere più famose i termini delle loro proporzioni.

Regolamento del Premio *la***Rinascente**

1

Estensione del premio

Al premio Compasso d'oro sono invitate a concorrere con i loro prodotti tutte le aziende industriali e artigiane italiane ed i creatori dei modelli, nelle categorie dell'abbigliamento (tessuti, confezioni, accessori), dell'arredamento (mobili, illuminazione, tessuti, accessori), degli articoli casalinghi (mensa, cucina, servizi elettrodomestici), degli articoli da sport, da viaggio, di cancelleria; dei giocattoli e, infine, degli imballi di presentazione.
I partecipanti possono presentare più prodotti, anche nella stessa categoria.

2

Svolgimento della manifestazione

I concorrenti al Compasso d'oro faranno pervenire i loro prodotti alla Segreteria indirizzandoli in Via San Raffaele n. 2, entro le ore 16 del 31 agosto 1954; la ricevuta varrà come iscrizione al concorso; i prodotti verranno presi in carico dalla Segreteria del Premio Compasso d'oro, e, su richiesta dei concorrenti, potranno essere assicurati contro tutti i rischi.
Ogni prodotto dovrà portare chiaramente nome e indirizzo della ditta e del creatore del modello, se la creazione ha un autore.

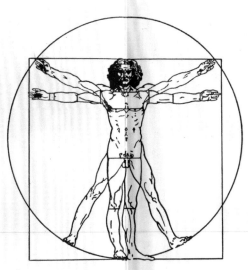

3

Alle pratiche esecutive del Premio Compasso d'oro provvede la Segreteria del Premio alla quale vanno indirizzate le eventuali richieste, mentre un ufficio di Consulenza diretto dall'Arch. Carlo Pagani assisterà i concorrenti, se loro occorressero notizie o chiarimenti tecnici sulle categorie di produzione.

4

La Giuria del Compasso d'oro opererà una selezione generale e le opere ammesse riceveranno un diploma di partecipazione al Concorso per il Compasso d'oro, a riconoscimento del valore del prodotto.

5

Questi prodotti selezionati verranno presentati in una pubblica mostra e saranno oggetto della scelta definitiva della Giuria, per l'assegnazione dei 20 Compassi in oro alle aziende produttrici; delle 20 targhe d'onore, con i premi di 100.000 lire ai creatori di modelli.

6

I prodotti premiati verranno presentati alla X Triennale di Milano con una mostra speciale, un mese prima della chiusura di quella manifestazione, durante la quale verranno con cerimonia solenne conferiti i premi.

IL COMPASSO D'ORO
alla sua fase conclusiva

Oltre 5.000 prodotti sono pervenuti entro il termine stabilito dal bando del concorso alla Segreteria del premio in Via S. Raffaele - Milano.

Si può quindi parlare di successo propagandistico. Il nostro invito alla produzione nazionale perchè inviasse i prodotti migliori da un punto di vista di Industrial Design è stato accolto con molto interesse.

Tutti i settori merceologici considerati sono rappresentati (abbigliamento: tessuti, confezioni, accessori; arredamento: mobili, illuminazione, tessuti, accessori; articoli casalinghi: mensa, cucina, servizi elettrodomestici; articoli da sport, da viaggio, di cancelleria, giocattoli e imballaggi di presentazione). Grandi nomi come Olivetti, Pirelli, Richard Ginori e oscuri nomi di artigiani sono riuniti insieme nell'elenco, come ci si proponeva.

Il Compasso d'oro vuole essere un'azione di propaganda alle attività di estetica del prodotto che in Italia non hanno ancora raggiunto lo sviluppo toccato in molti paesi d'America e d'Europa.

Si vuole dire alla produzione: al nostro pubblico vogliamo non solo offrire i prezzi più accessibili, merce di qualità « civile », ma anche una produzione aggiornata nei gusti, prodotti che si avvalgono di tutte le esperienze della nostra epoca.

In Italia, se si vuole qualche cosa, bisogna saper fare da soli; non si può contare su nessuno. La Rinascente, un'altra volta, ha preso in campo nazionale una iniziativa che in nazioni più organizzate spetta a enti e organizzazioni fuori dal campo economico privato.

Oltre 5.000 articoli ci sono pervenuti, ma a guardarli nel loro insieme si vede come sia preoccupante la mancanza, nella maggior parte della nostra produzione, dei principi cui si ispira l'Industrial Design (per rendersi conto della gravità di questa

Il compasso d'oro è incastrato in una forma di legno rivestita di pelle sulla quale posa una piastra di cristallo. Viene assegnato al prodotto e quindi alla Società produttrice.

La targa di segnalazione d'onore. E' d'argento ed è fissata su una piastra di legno. Viene assegnata al progettista del prodotto cui è stata attribuito il compasso d'oro.

12

deficenza si pensi che, ad esempio, la produzione dei Paesi Scandinavi imposta tutta la propria pubblicità all'estero, collettivamente e singolarmente, su quei principi e si osservi il successo mondiale di quella produzione).

Comunque anche in Italia parecchie ditte, parecchi artigiani lavorano con impegno e serietà e possono benissimo competere con le migliori espressioni straniere; così abbiamo potuto selezionare 200 esemplari da porre in gara per i compassi d'oro. Questi 200 prodotti saranno esposti dal 25 settembre al 10 ottobre al Circolo della Stampa a Milano, in Corso Venezia 16.

In questa sede verranno designati i 20 prodotti premiati, i quali saranno esposti in posizione d'onore alla X Triennale di Milano.

La Giuria

Dott. Aldo Borletti Vice Presidente della Rinascente
Cesare Brustio Vice Direttore Generale della Rinascente
Architetti:
Gio Ponti direttore di « Domus »
Alberto Rosselli direttore di « Stile e Industria »
Marco Zanuso membro della Giunta esecutiva della X Triennale

Nelle due foto:

Uffici e Magazzini in via Carducci a Milano sono stati per più giorni occupati da una massa di prodotti di ogni tipo partecipanti al concorso.

13

14. *IL COMPASSO D'ORO
IN "CRONACHE DE LA
RINASCENTE – UPIM" N. 3, 1954*
list of the jury members
for the first award
Library of the Steiner-DPA-
Politecnico Archive, Milan

15. **"CRONACHE DE LA
RINASCENTE – UPIM" N. 4,
1953, COVER**
Library of the Steiner-DPA-
Politecnico Archive, Milan

15.

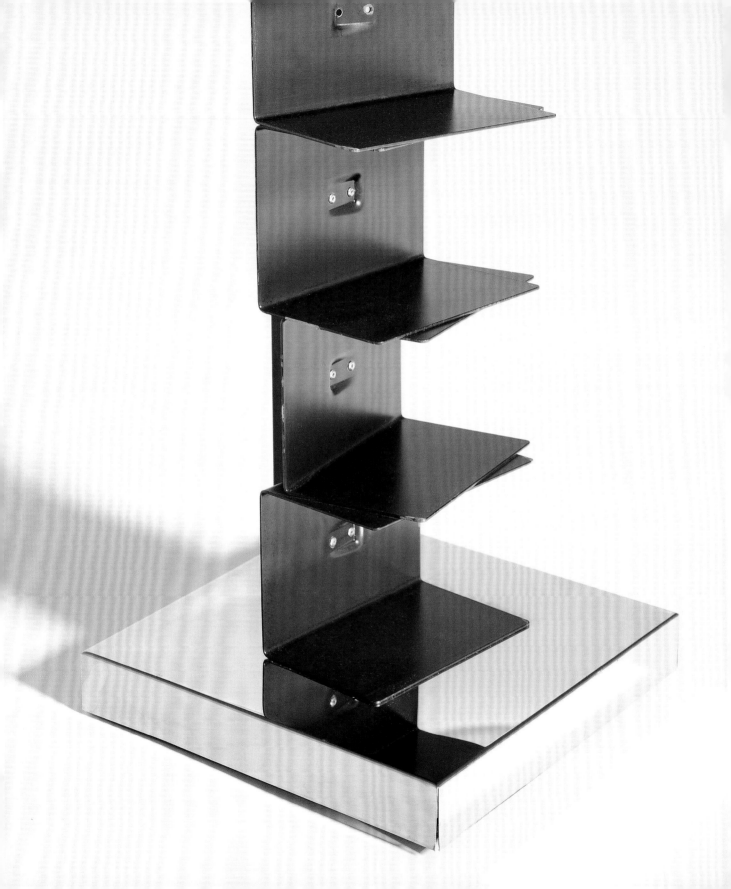

Power to Creativity.
The Objects and Forms
of the Twentieth Century

Alessandra Maria Sette

If we translate the phrase *made in Italy* into Italian it could well be expressed as *modi in Italia*. And if by *modi* we mean expressive modes and languages, well then we open up a rich, multiform and highly stimulating world. If we limit ourselves just to the twentieth century, the period in which we matured, we find that there are many testimonies to art research, to the invention of expressive languages and courageous examples of individual poetics. But there are just as many testimonies to creativity, inventiveness and innovation which, in fields different from that of the visual arts, have also left a deep mark on the macro-category of *modi in Italia*.

The element common to all these experiences is planning, in the sense of studying, analysing and creating. A project is not felt by Italians as a rigid and well-ordered scheme in which to pour a content but, rather, as a space in which to experiment in a creative, free and disciplined manner.

The first to understand and apply a planning method were the Futurists. Their anxiety to renew the world, and the excitement they showed in experiencing at first hand what they were promoting, ran through every area they were concerned with. Art was action and nothing could escape the artist's control; from the traditional languages of painting and sculpture, it was a short step to decorative objects, furnishing, advertising and packaging: in other words to what today we call the applied arts. Balla painted, but he also designed furniture and textiles; he exchanged ideas with illustrators and artisans in that marvellous studio in Rome known as Casa Balla, with the loving help of his daughters and wife. Similarly, in Rovereto Depero painted, drew, invented scenery, advertisements, designed fashion, and created the Casa d'Arte Depero, the first example of a studio workshop; here he did not just work but also exhibited and received clients. And together the two artists wrote the *Ricostruzione futurista dell'universo* manifesto (1915). But perhaps Depero is mainly remembered as the first important artist to interest himself in contaminations between the visual arts and design. In the 1930s Davide Campari asked him to design the bottle for his new drink. With all his artistic sensitivity Depero concentrated on the brilliant, luminous, transparent red of the product: three clean lines gave a form to the liquid. And it was done. Both of them of course were ignorant of the fact that this would become an icon of Italian design, and has remained unchanged over the decades: an example of packaging that is by now completely identified with the firm's brand. Boccioni – one of the most deeply enlightened of the group – painted, sculpted and went to war, and many other masterpieces would have been handed down to us had his life not ended prematurely when he fell from his horse. Prampolini painted and devoted a great deal of energy to the theatre. Thayaht drew, painted and created overalls, the most democratic item of clothing to be invented in modern times.

This versatile approach to the most varied disciplines didn't worry our artists at all. It seems to have been a question of method, an approach to the creative material which, at this time in history, was experienced "horizontally", with few hierarchic distinctions of value. This explains the strong traditional relationship of equality in Italy between the visual arts and applied arts or, if you like, design. The all-important element was creativity.

De Chirico and Morandi answered Futurism with their Metaphysical movement, one that was more self-contained and less interested in the surrounding world, unless as an expression of states of mind. With certain exceptions. The painter Felice Casorati adhered to the movement but also devoted himself to designing furnishings (the best known are those for the industrialist Riccardo Gualino in the 1920s).

Fascism then erupted into Italian political life and even involved the work of artists who, though being subject to the regime, still worked autonomously without reducing their output: on the contrary, they continued to create works of great prestige. For example, just think of Mario Sironi's paintings of city outskirts and townscapes, or even of his vigorously sculptural figures. But Fascism left its deepest mark on architecture. One example among many is the Palazzo della Civiltà Italiana in Rome, a symbolic building for rationalist architecture, the testimonial to a way of designing architecture as a space for living but also as a background for celebrating the regime. Its original content, among other things, is even more relevant today: it was to have housed the show of "Italic genius", a part of the 1942 universal exposition (which never took place). A kind of museum of the *modo italiano* that today we refer to as *made in Italy*. And never as in the period of Fascism did architects and artists work in such close collaboration, without putting aesthetic qualities before functional ones, and vice-versa.

We can state that a typical aspect of *modo italiano* is the continuous and constant changeover between art avant-gardes and design research.

Between the 1940s and 1950s, Burri and Fontana, the former in Rome and the latter in Milan, dominated the art scene with their work on material and space. Sacks and plastic, tearing and cutting, were the distinctive signs of the work of two artists concentrated on condensing the flow of time and space into a single mark: a trace of human existence and an absolute symbol of living.

Here too was art, design, architecture and communication. Throughout his whole career, Fontana designed furnishing for private homes as well as devoting himself enthusiastically to ceramics. In the 1980s Burri designed the poster for the Italia '90 World Cup. Both worked with industrial materials such as plastic and neon tubes, and thus ennobled materials produced for mass consumption.

Law 717 was passed in 1949; this established that 2% of the overall costs for constructing a public building had to be destined for works of art inserted into the project. Even though often ignored, this regulation is important for the significant role it conferred on the artistic component, which was given the same importance as the planning and architectonic aspects.

In the 1950s, Informalism was the most widespread art language, one that had the aim of breaking with traditional expressive schemes. At the same time as Neo-realism, which was nearer in spirit to Roman artists, the Concrete Art Movement (MAC) was established in Milan where it mainly developed . These were two antithetical yet complementary ways of "feeling" and expressing reality. Neo-realism had its most significant results in the cinema; Concrete Art became a movement that catalysed various forms of research. Founded by Dorfles, Monnet, Munari and Soldati, and characterised by works with abstract geometrical forms derived from reality but re-elaborated at a conceptual level, Concrete Art promoted research halfway between art and design and led to shows such as *Materie plastiche in forme concrete*. Its followers propounded a "synthesis of the arts" with the aim of widening the traditional functions of the artist in order to meld together the languages of painting, sculpture and architecture.

That emblematic figure, Bruno Munari, established himself in the fields of both painting and design; so did Joe Colombo, another interpreter of spatial painting who later devoted himself to design.

But for Italy the post-war period was also one of economic expansion, of industrial development, the beginning of the consumer society. It was the moment when wealth was no longer a dream but actually within the reach of all. Italian creativity and inventiveness managed to imagine and build a new society on the ruins of the Second World War, one in which enthusiasm for ideas, often quite simple ones, managed to be translated into concrete fact. Even the limits imposed on our country by peace treaties, instead of damping down this enthusiasm stimulated inventiveness and gave life to solutions which were as simple as they were genial.

The proof of this is the great number of patents for models and inventions registered in the 1950s and 1960s. They not only testify to a particularly fertile moment for Italian creativity but also, once again, to the contaminations between various disciplines. In these precious documents, the projects made a wide use of drawing in order to communicate. Technical and aesthetic aspects were superimposed, allowing us to see, from a historical point of view, documents that offer many levels of social, planning and artistic analysis, all of them equally interesting.

Emblematic of this moment was the creation of the Vespa Piaggio. This originated in 1946 from an idea by Enrico Piaggio, who needed to re-launch his aeronautical firm (which was forbidden by international treaties to make aeroplanes), and by the engineer Corradino D'Ascanio. For a country that needed to be on the move, the two proposed a light vehicle for both men and women, at a low cost and with low consumption.

Historians attribute the birth of the figure of the designer to the Olivetti firm in the 1950s. The unusual industrial policy adopted by the enlightened Adriano Olivetti was that of considering the firm as a centre for social progress which involved not just the workforce but also their families. From this point of view it seemed necessary to create objects that could interpret new values. Marcello Nizzoli was the protagonist of this new aim. As tended to happen in this period, Nizzoli was also the creator of the advertising campaigns for many products, and he thus originated the practice of image coordination.

The initial drive of the 1950s reached its highest point in the following decade. The increase of industrial production, technological development and economic wellbeing were accompanied by other historically important occurrences. For Italy the decade opened with the Rome Olympics, the first media event in Italian history, the first attempt by our city to compete with the world's great capitals.

In 1962, the second Vatican council opened. In 1963 Giulio Natta won the Nobel Prize in Chemistry for his invention of isotactic polypropylene, a material that completely changed world industrial production. In 1965 the Mont Blanc tunnel was inaugurated and this was also the year that the Beatles, already world famous, burst onto the Italian scene. In 1967, the surgeon Barnard effected the first heart transplant. In 1968, while the world was in torn by the war in Vietnam and by student protests, there was an Italy that light-heartedly sang the happy yet vaguely melancholy song *Azzurro*, words and music by Paolo Conte, with Adriano Celentano as its singer. Stanley Kubrick presented his film *2001 A Space Odyssey*, a meditation on the links between humanity, space and time; at the same time man was also preparing to go to the moon where he would land in the hot summer of 1969. The conquest of space, apart from being an extraordinary scientific feat, was metaphorically also the overcoming of all limits by mankind. It was the conclusion, even at a symbolic level, of a decade considered by many to be unrepeatable and, by others, actually "fabulous".

Television, the new means of communication, amplified every event. Collective myths and rites were forged, there was born the hedonism typical of mass society, and the factory of desires and of bogus needs was invented.

In this decade the languages of art and design tended to specialise and follow increasingly autonomous paths without, however, losing sight of each other. These were exceedingly lively years for artistic experimentation and for design research. Design, in particular, an increasingly favoured tool for industrial production in a rapidly expanding market, took on an extremely important role. The protagonists of this period were Ponti, Zanuso, Magistretti, the Castiglioni brothers, Caccia Dominioni, Albini, Mari, Bellini and many others. On the other front, the word "art" was preceded by various qualifying adjectives that indicated its field of inquiry: Programme art, Kinetic art, Op art, Pop art, Objectual art and so on.

Such a well-known personality as Piero Manzoni, who transferred into his art all his resourcefulness, transgression and his will to break down established schemes, was typical of this decade. For his *Corpi d'aria*, Manzoni inflated balloons; he traced out thousands of metres of lines on rolls of paper (*Linee di migliaia di metri*); he canned *Merda d'artista*, and even transformed the whole world into a huge work of art by placing at various points a great overturned base: the *Base del mondo*. In this particular moment the work in itself was not important; what was important was the gesture, the action, the conceptual passage towards the act of making it.

Pop culture began to become known and to gain a reputation through the work of such artists as Rotella, Schifano, Gilardi, Marotta, Boetti and Ceroli. Once more languages began to interweave, be superimposed and enrich each other in turn; the chosen materials were from industry, crafts, the press, plastic or rubber, Plexiglas, fabrics, wood: they were popular, in other words. The works stood halfway between artistic and decorative languages. Design projects were more inclined to be playful, ironic and good-naturedly provocative. Vico Magistretti's Eclisse lamp, the Superonda sectional divan by Archizoom, the Blow inflatable armchair by De Pas D'Urbino Lomazzi and the Pratone lounger by the Gruppo Strum all originated as furniture for a more relaxed, informal and, at times, rule-breaking way of living. Without, however, overlooking modernity. The Castiglioni brothers designed the Allunaggio stool. Another couple of brothers, the Zanattas, launched Moon Boot, an innovative kind of footwear.

Towards the end of the decade and throughout the 1970s, criticism of consumer society had already begun, led, on the one hand, by Arte Povera and, on the other, by radical design. Pistoletto, Merz, Kounellis and Fabro used materials, objects and symbols to create their work and their world.

An object that is emblematic of the influence of Arte Povera is the Sacco armchair, designed by the Gatti Paolini Teodoro trio. Three other designers, De Pas D'Urbino Lomazzi, created the Joe armchair: a large baseball glove which was comfortable and elegant. Achille and Pier Giacomo Castiglioni, referring back to a practice started much earlier by Duchamp, recuperated old industrial objects to invent the Mezzadro stool (although, in fact, it had been designed at the end of the 1950s, it was only produced in the 1970s). Mendini amazed everyone with his Proust armchair: an explosion of colour that played with kitsch and was characterised by a texture inspired by Signac's Divisionist technique.

Just as in the case of the visual arts, Conceptualism began to leave a decisive mark on design. The end of the 1970s saw the return of a surge of optimism that was to remain throughout the 1980s. A mark of this new course was the re-launching of the premio Compasso d'Oro, after a pause of some ten years.

In 1981, the Memphis group, led by the tireless Ettore Sottsass, presented a decidedly original collection: totemic forms, vivacious colours, asymmetries and decorations. In the same years the successful Trans-avant-garde movement originated in Italy a new and painterly figurative expressionism which seemed the perfect rival attraction to Memphis production; both appeared in the wake of the Postmodernist revolution which came to international notice at the end of the 1970s and which involved all art languages. Cucchi, Clemente, Chia, Paladino and De Maria were the Trans-avant-garde's protagonists. Besides aspects of new modernity, both art and design production, with the help of commercial television which had begun to broadcast in Italy, brought to life the "fashion" phenomenon which began to gain ground rapidly and stably among social customs. A beautiful relationship from the 1980s was that between Alessandro Mendini and the Alessi firm. The businessman who ran the firm and who for years had been involved in an ambitious programme for renewing production, asked Mendini to supervise the *Tea and Coffee Piazza* collection in which design, art and architecture met up through the creation of a series of objects designed by various people and related by ideas about a single theme. This was a way of rethinking domestic objects: not just the table, for example, but the whole house; this was to become so deeply rooted as to condition the later production of many other firms in the sector.

It is more difficult to identify movements from the 1990s onwards in which to classify, even if only for convenience, various art products. Individual people, artists and designers, tried to develop their individual poetics alone and autonomously. There were many referential models and many new techniques to try out.

There is no doubt that the World Wide Web has greatly enlarged our horizons and, at the same time, reduced distances; it has also made our world more horizontal and more democratic. Just as society, even the world in fact, has changed so there has been an intermixing of races, cultures and religions. Languages have multiplied; *modi italiani* have approached international modes without surrendering their distinctive marks. The most courageous creators, those who consider globalisation as a resource rather than a levelling-out process, have already expressed a world-beating creativity. The knowledge that there is no longer a single nucleus but that each one of us represents a centre has shaded the confines of groups until they have disappeared. It is still possible to follow trends and fashions, but it is not easy to classify them: Beecroft, so fashionable; Cattelan, sought after by all the great international collectors; Ontani, a refined artist reserved for the élite. Bertozzi and Casoni so good as not to seem true; the less well-known Fabrice De Nola, who looks towards a future that is already underway, and Massimo Catalani who still manages to express pure beauty through a material and robustly substantial painting. So there we are. All these are the warp and weft of a great fabric consisting of *modi italiani* as well as of a lot more. Paradoxically, today it is museums that influence art. These spaces were originally created to contain art, but now the balance has been overturned. In the wake of the evolution of art languages which have completely deconstructed the work of art, its forms, techniques and meanings, architecture too has begun to think of more complex spaces with a far more marked personality. Museums have become the protagonists. They are monuments that are complete in themselves and in which it is the works which have to deal with the imposing architecture.

The container conditions the choice of content. Art has come down from the walls to find a place on the floor or the ceiling; it has enormously increased in size; it needs an exceptional sensibility in order to be installed. In this sense, art works increasingly resemble an architectural manner of studying space, just like a design project or a piece of furniture. So: art, design or architecture? What are we talking about? It is difficult to give an answer today. But this contamination of languages is in no way a debasement. It is, rather, a more complex way of thinking and communicating, one consonant with the twenty-first century's more sophisticated and mature creativity.

Altogether, what this rapid overview of recent history (full of many gaps, which I am quite aware of) wants to show and underline is that, in Italy, the experiences of the art avant-gardes have always been interwoven with our deep-rooted artisan culture in order to give life to the *modo italiano* that everybody applauds us for. Even though with strongly individual characteristics – another typical aspect of being Italian – our creativity has managed to originate an unmistakable style that has often been a driving force for our economy. What always seems relevant is the idea, the *necessity* in fact, to continue with a project in the sense of a creative method. In the words of Bonito Oliva, a "mild project" that might contain in itself a controlled and domesticated aspect side by side with another freer and unpredictable one, one that responds to the uncertainty typical of the present time.

Italia 61

Celebrazione del Centenario dell'Unità d'Italia

Torino Maggio-Ottobre 1961

danilo nubioli

Collecting Italian Art: a Conversation with Massimo and Sonia Cirulli

Alessandra Maria Sette

The collection of the Massimo and Sonia Cirulli archive, devoted to 20th-century art, is a storehouse as unique as it is valuable. It is the result, not only of years of intense work, but above all of a tenacious and never flagging enthusiasm.

Your collection is concentrated on Italian 20th-century art, but with an original slant.
In Italy the twentieth century was an amazingly innovative period from many points of view.
The drive towards modernisation forced rapid changes on society. The speed of these changes altered the perception of time and radically changed ways of thinking, communicating and living.
Modern art had been born. As far as I am concerned the highest expression of this modernity was advertising, cinema, photography, propaganda; you see, I understood that at the time there was no longer the traditional distinction between visual arts, applied arts, industrial design... we could say that art had become total.

How did this enthusiasm of yours begin?
Thirty years ago, and quite by chance, I found myself looked down on by a poster: it wasn't Italian but French. It was a beautiful poster by Toulouse-Lautrec that dominated the room of the L'Escale restaurant in New York. I had recently moved from Italy and, while I was doing a course in Economics at the NYU, I worked in a law office. So I was far from Italy and even further from the art world.
The evocative strength of that work so captured my attention as to impel me to search for information. And so, during my walks around New York, I began to notice certain shops that had escaped my attention before: the various Poster Please, Philip Williams, Poster America, Chisholm Gallery and others which I began to haunt out of straightforward curiosity but also with increasing interest. And then I realised that there were posters from all over Europe as well as America, but not from Italy. This deficiency got me thinking. How was it possible that Italy, the cradle of the arts, hadn't left its mark on this field? After a series of careful searches in the city bookshops, I managed to get hold of a certain amount of material that gave me information about an Italian artistic milieu completely unknown to me but that greatly intrigued me.

Did you begin to frequent the art scene?
In the 1980s, New York was an extremely lively city. And I found myself, as they say, in the right place at the

right time. I got to know Leo Castelli, Warhol, Basquiat and Haring; in musical circles I met maestro James Levine as well as Cindy Lauper, Madonna and Billy Joel. In the field of fashion I met Ralph Lauren. And then actors and photographers. I think that all that energy increased my growing interest and refined my taste, also because many of these people were collectors of the most varied kinds of art. However, what continued to interest me most was graphics: advertising as a form of communication but also as an expression of art. I remember an exhibition at the MOMA about the Russian Constructivists, and one in the Metropolitan about Modernism. The various arts, from posters to painting, from photography to sculpture, acted together in perfect harmony.

When did you begin to collect?
Shortly after I returned to Italy where, together with my wife Sonia, I continued my searches. We managed to get in touch with the descendents of many of the artists of Italian posters, among them Roberto Metlicovitz and the heirs of Dudovich. We became aware at once that the overwhelming majority of posters came from the Ricordi publishing house in Milan. We contacted the director, Eugenio Grassi, during our first large show in the Palazzo delle Esposizioni in Rome, one devoted to Art Nouveau posters. Grassi told us many anecdotes about the life of the publishing house and of those who, like him, during the 1960s had witnessed the destruction of whole storehouses of material. Decades of work was sent to be pulped; without any sense of remorse the industrial archives had been deprived of a great deal of advertising material. Luckily, some of the old employees who were fond of their work had saved something and we, with the help of Eugenio Grassi, managed to trace the heirs and recuperate a certain quantity of works.

Did you have to do a lot of research in order to put this collection together?
This wasn't the traditional relationship between dealer-merchant and collector-investor. We virtually became detectives in order to find where the material was kept. It is true that fortune favours those who dare. The more I came into contact with people, the more of them I came to know, and so I quickly extended my range of contacts and, of course, my opportunities too. Looking back after all these years we are still at times surprised to think how so many meetings, which we thought had happened by chance, revealed themselves to be fundamental and marked a change in our activities. Like that with Micky Wolfson, an extraordinary collector from Miami and a lover of Italian 20th-century art and who collects not just paintings and sculptures, but design objects, applied art and advertising material. Our interest in Italian art was renewed and our horizons were broadened: not just to include advertising posters, but also painting, sculpture, photography, furniture and memorabilia from 1900 to the end of the 1950s and, later, up to the 1980s.

Isn't it rather strange that you learned to appreciate Italian art by way of the USA? And that it was an American collector who stimulated your intuitions and desire for knowledge?
Yes, it is rather. But perhaps that means that a certain art is Italian art because it originates and develops in Italy, but that its values are such as to overcome geographical and cultural boundaries and become the heritage of everyone.

When did your archive come into existence and what does it hold?

The archive began in New York in 1985 and is today considered the major private historical archive of Italian 20th-century art, above all for the art of advertising, communication, and propaganda in all its forms.

The archive consists of various groups whose common denominator is 20th-century Italy. So in it you will find a collection of posters with over 12,000 works that recount the society and behaviour of our country in the last century; there is also an important section devoted to theatre and cinema – from silent films to neorealism – and another large section devoted to propaganda, aviation, transport, travel and the advertising of all kinds of products. We can also boast of a record: the two largest posters in the world, printed by Ricordi in about 1885 and which advertise plays in London at the end of the nineteenth century; they each consist of 58 sheets, equal to a total surface of 42 square metres and a length of 12 metres.

Towards the end of the 1940s, the offset technique simplified the lithographic process and allowed the reproduction of a greater quantity of posters at a lower cost. These were the post-war years and the years of the economic boom when such artists as Bruno Munari, Erberto Carboni and Armando Testa launched on the market such products as the Lambretta, the Vespa, Coca Cola, the RAI television or Invernizzi's Mio processed cheese. There are a great number of these in the archive. We then enlarged the sectors and bought photographs, magazines from the 1930s, 1940s, and 1950s, archives of business histories, and so on.

Our aim was and still is to invest in personalities who are not well-known to the wider public, not just the great 20th-century artists, in order to tell a great Italian story through various kinds of media.

More or less, how many works does the archive contain today?

So far, and this is a testimony to our research, the archive contains over 130,000 works of art which offer a fairly complete panorama of Italy in the last century. There are sculptures by Thayaht, Giovanni Romagnoli, Tedeschi and Ettore Colla cheek by jowl with paintings by Sironi, Previati, Afro, Nomellini and Licini, as well as advertisements by Enrico Prampolini, Lucio Fontana, Armando Testa and Marcello Dudovich; photo-montages by Bruno Munari; ceramics by Gio Ponti; important drawings by Sant'Elia; newspapers, magazines and documents of great historical interest; collections of Futurist books, and the EUR 42 archive with fascinating projects for an interplay of lights and water created by great rationalist architects for the Rome universal fair.

We seem to have reached our aim of offering a multidisciplinary view of the turbulent Italian artistic panorama of the 20th-century, at least in part; this was also because of other collectors in America and Italy who have helped, advised and backed us up over the years; our thoughts go to them above all. Many of them are no longer here, but we are quite certain that they are always by our side to help us tell the marvellous story that is the uniqueness of Italy.

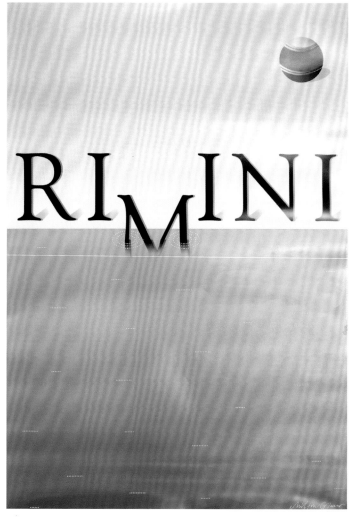

Alberto Burri
ITALIA 90, 1990
offset on paper
100 × 70 cm
Petruzzi Editore - Roma
© Massimo & Sonia Cirulli
Archive, New York

Milton Glaser
RIMINI, 1995
offset on paper
68 × 48.5 cm
© Massimo & Sonia Cirulli
Archive, New York

René Gruau
OCCHIO ALLA FODERA!
FODERE BEMBERG, 1960 C.
offset on paper
140.5 × 100 cm
N. Moneta - Milano - Roma
© Massimo & Sonia Cirulli
Archive, New York

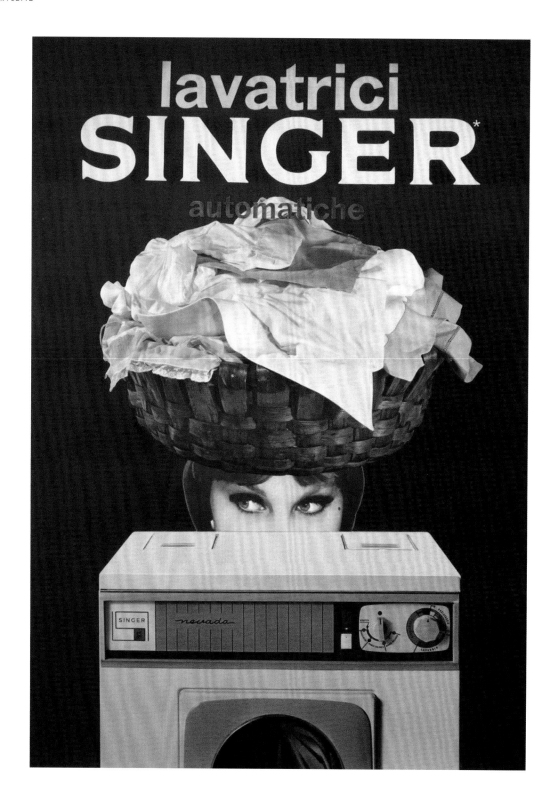

Anonymous
LAVATRICI SINGER
AUTOMATICHE, 1960 C.
offset on paper
137.7 × 97 cm
Ind. Graf. Pietro Vera - Milano
Publiunion Italiana
Advertising
© Massimo & Sonia Cirulli
Archive, New York

Anonymous
CICLI DI CUCITO SINGER,
1960 C.
offset on paper
99 × 68 cm
Ind. Graf. Pietro Vera - Milano
© Massimo & Sonia Cirulli
Archive, New York

Anonymous
SÌ... SINGER, 1970 C.
98 × 67 cm
Ind. Graf. Pietro Vera - Milano
© Massimo & Sonia Cirulli
Archive, New York

Anonymous
LEZIONI GRATUITE SINGER,
1954
offset on paper
139 × 100 cm
Ind. Graf. Pietro Vera - Milano
© Massimo & Sonia Cirulli
Archive, New York

Anonymous
PURA LANA VERGINE,
1965 C.
47.5 × 30.5 cm
© Massimo & Sonia Cirulli
Archive, New York

Anonymous
FINALMENTE UNA PIEGA
CHE RESISTE. CAESAR,
1965 C.
48.7 × 32.2 cm
© Massimo & Sonia Cirulli
Archive, New York

Anonymous
VESTI BENE, 1965 C.
34.5 × 48 cm
© Massimo & Sonia Cirulli
Archive, New York

Anonymous
LA SARTOTECNICA, 1962
offset on paper
97.3 × 57.2 cm
Ind. Graf. Pietro Vera - Milano
© Massimo & Sonia Cirulli
Archive, New York

Anonymous
CONCORSO NAZIONALE
SALMOIRAGHI. LA SARTINA
D'ITALIA, 1950 C.
offset on paper
100 × 70 cm
Ind. Graf. Pietro Vera - Milano
© Massimo & Sonia Cirulli
Archive, New York

Franco Grignani
VESTI BENE, 1965 C.
33 × 23 cm
© Massimo & Sonia Cirulli
Archive, New York

Franco Grignani
VESTI BENE, 1965 C.
33 × 23 cm
© Massimo & Sonia Cirulli
Archive, New York

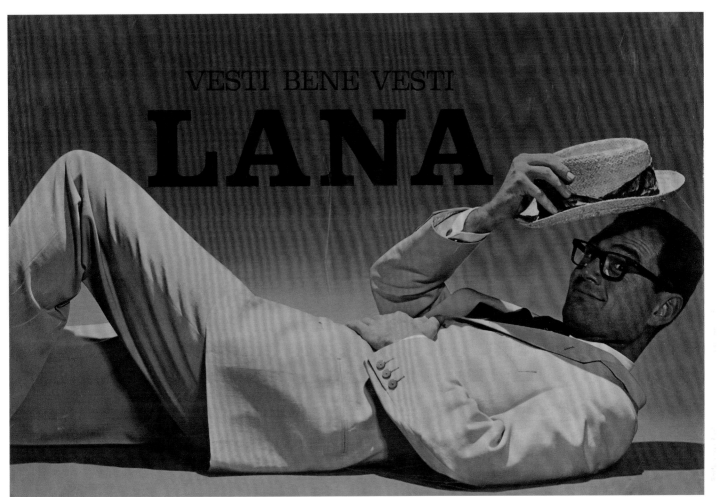

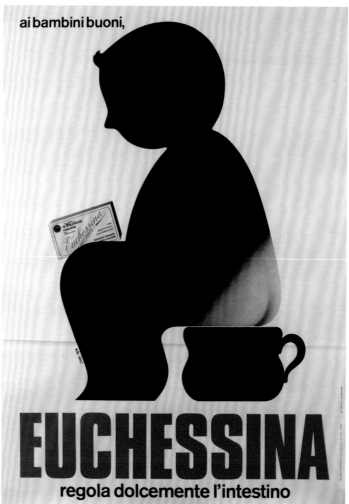

Anonymous
OMO, 1963
offset on paper
138.2 × 99 cm
© Massimo & Sonia Cirulli
Archive, New York

Armando Testa
AI BAMBINI BUONI,
EUCHESSINA, 1960 C.
offset on paper
141 × 100 cm
Ind. Graf. G. Zeppelini & CA.
sas - Milano
© Massimo & Sonia Cirulli
Archive, New York

Romeo Invernizzi
IO SONO CAROLINA,
1965 C.
offset on paper
70 × 97.5 cm
© Massimo & Sonia Cirulli
Archive, New York

Anonymous
MARGARINA GRADINA,
1960 C.
offset on paper
137 × 97.7 cm
Arti Grafiche F.lli Bonetti -
Milano
© Massimo & Sonia Cirulli
Archive, New York

Anonymous
NUTELLA FERRERO.
UNA DELIZIA DA SPALMARE
SUL PANE, 1964
offset on paper
139.5 × 101 cm
Poligrafico Roggero&Tortia -
Torino
© Massimo & Sonia Cirulli
Archive, New York

Propaganda Motta
RITZ CRACKERS, 1955
offset on paper
48.2 × 34.6 cm
Grafiche A. Mariani - Milano
© Massimo & Sonia Cirulli
Archive, New York

Agenzia Clan - Milano
Venturino
GOLIA. LA FRESCA LIQUIRIZIA
PER LA GOLA, 1964
offset on paper
139.5 × 100.5 cm
SISAR - Milano
© Massimo & Sonia Cirulli
Archive, New York

Armando Testa
PERONI NASTRO AZZURRO,
1970 C.
offset on paper
139.5 × 100.5 cm
© Massimo & Sonia Cirulli
Archive, New York

Armando Testa
GODITI UN PAULISTA. SE NO...
CHE VITA È!, 1960 C.
offset on paper
137.5 × 97.5 cm
Ages Arti Grafiche - Torino
© Massimo & Sonia Cirulli
Archive, New York

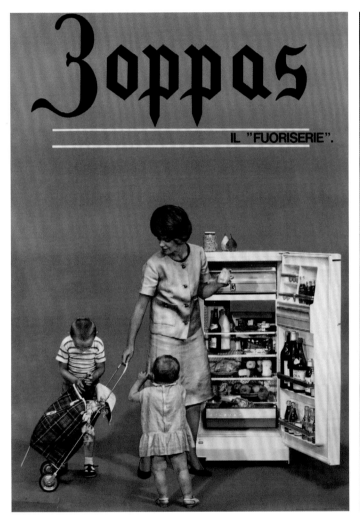

T. Lattuada
LANA E COLORI, 1965 C.
29.5 × 22.3 cm
© Massimo & Sonia Cirulli
Archive, New York

Anonymous
ZOPPAS. IL "FUORISERIE",
1960 C.
offset on paper
139.5 × 98.5 cm
Industrie lito-tipografiche
Mario Ponzio spa - Pavia
© Massimo & Sonia Cirulli
Archive, New York

Anonymous
ELETTRO... ADDOMESTICATI
SAN GIORGIO, 1960 C.
offset on paper
137.8 × 98 cm
Ind. Graf. Pietro Vera - Milano
© Massimo & Sonia Cirulli
Archive, New York

Anonymous
BOXER SUPERMOLLEGGIATO
PIAGGIO, 1970 c.
offset on paper
100 × 68 cm
Giuseppe Lang spa - Genova
© Massimo & Sonia Cirulli
Archive, New York

F. Frigé
ULTRAVOX. NON OCCORRE
GUARDARCI DENTRO...
È UN ULTRAVOX, 1960
offset on paper
98.1 × 137 cm
Ind. Graf. Pietro Vera - Milano
© Massimo & Sonia Cirulli
Archive, New York

FIAT 500L, 1968
138.5 × 100 cm
Centro Grafico IGAP Milano -
Roma - Torino
© Massimo & Sonia Cirulli
Archive, New York

Anonymous
ALFA ROMEO. GIULIA SS, 1970 C.
offset on paper
48.5 × 138.5 cm
Ind. Graf. Pietro Vera - Milano
© Massimo & Sonia Cirulli
Archive, New York

Anonymous
PIÙ CAVALLI NELLA J4 INNOCENTI, 1970 C.
offset on paper
32.5 × 69 cm
Ind. Graf. Pietro Vera - Milano
© Massimo & Sonia Cirulli
Archive, New York

Anonymous
GOMMAPIUMA PIRELLI, 1952
offset on paper
100 × 68.2 cm
Officine Grafiche Ricordi - Milano
Pirelli sapsa
© Massimo & Sonia Cirulli
Archive, New York

Anonymous
ALFA ROMEO GT 1300 JUNIOR. PROMOSSI ALL'ALFA JUNIOR, 1970 C.
offset on paper
68 × 48 cm
Ind. Graf. Pietro Vera - Milano
© Massimo & Sonia Cirulli
Archive, New York

Anonymous
LAMBRETTA INNOCENTI 125 LI. A SEDICI ANNI CI VUOLE UNA LAMBRETTA, 1970 C.
offset on paper
68 × 32.5 cm
Ind. Graf. Pietro Vera - Milano
© Massimo & Sonia Cirulli
Archive, New York

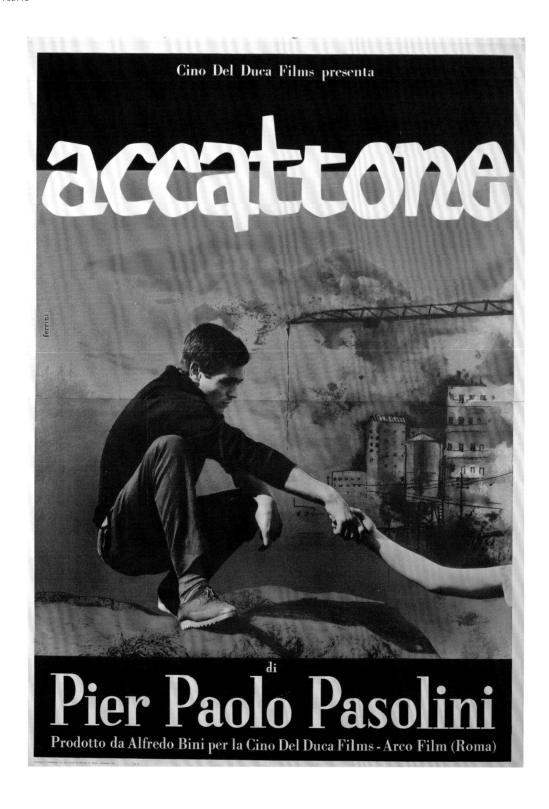

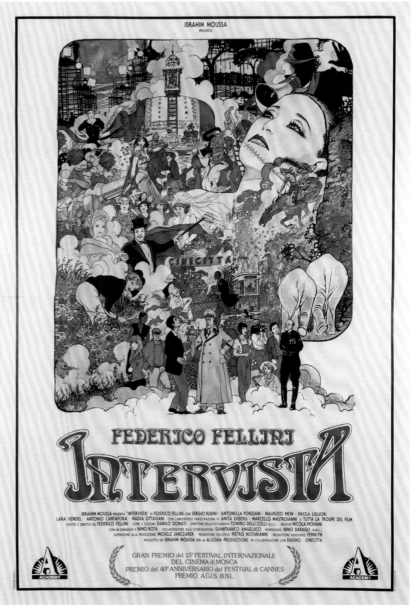

Ferrini
ACCATTONE, 1961
203 × 144.5 cm
Vecchioni&Guadagno, Roma
© Massimo & Sonia Cirulli
Archive, New York

MAMMA ROMA, 1962
69 × 29.5 cm
Vecchioni&Guadagno, Roma
© Massimo & Sonia Cirulli
Archive, New York

Milo Manara
INTERVISTA, 1987
203 × 144.5 cm
Fotocrom Italiana srl Roma
© Massimo & Sonia Cirulli
Archive, New York

IN UN FILM DI

VITTORIO
DE SICA

IERI,
OGGI,
DOMANI

Cinema: an Expressive Form of Art Made in Italy

Lina Job Wertmüller

Cinema made in Italy over the past fifty years… how many images, photographs and unforgettable scenes come to mind. But above all I think of people, the great artists and friends whose careers have represented – and still represent! – Italian art in the world. Federico Fellini, Luchino Visconti, Suso Cecchi d'Amico, Vittorio De Sica, Francesco Rosi, Franco Zeffirelli, Mario Monicelli, Piero Tosi, Danilo Donati, Nino Rota, Ennio Morricone, Marcello Mastroianni, Sophia Loren, Silvana Mangano, Gina Lollobrigida… The list is too long for the few lines available. However, it is sufficient to name these personalities in order to evoke at once the idea of an Italian way of "making cinema". Our films are an expression of what is made in Italy. In Visconti's films we are at once aware of the perfection with which Pierino Tosi made his costumes with their highly refined textiles and matching of colours, and the accuracy with which he recreated a setting. Piero Tosi was a founding father with his art. The costume designers Milena Canonero and Gabriella Pescucci were his pupils and learned their skills as costume designers from him: they even won various Oscars.

Cinema and fashion have often gone hand in hand. To mention Visconti once again, in *Conversation Piece* the elegant furs worn by Silvana Mangano were created by my friends the Fendi sisters, and the diamond brooch came directly from Bulgari. It has often been the case that the impact of cinema has acted as a driving force for a new style or a way of wearing your hair; at other times they have acted in harmony, as when fashion designers themselves are called on to "dress" the characters in a film. This has often happened with Giorgio Armani and Valentino. Perhaps the most outstanding case was seen just a few years ago when a brand name that was a symbol of Italian fashion was listed in the film credits together with Meryl Streep!

But, to remain with the theme of costumes, such great foreign designers as Sandy Powell often make use of textiles made in Italy for their refined historical reconstructions. In Campania, near to Caserta, the fabrics of San Leucio have been produced since the time of the Bourbons, and my husband, Enrico Job, together with Gino Persico, was inspired by them for the costumes for my film *Ferdinando and Carolina*.

Design is another great Italian achievement; it is the new art of everyday life openly scattered around the places we live in, interacting with people's lives and not just as decoration or something to be admired. Since the 1960s, Italian design has conquered the world due to the fact that it is able to wed usefulness to beauty as happens nowhere else. Certain artists, stage designers, architects and costume designers such as Ceroli, Job, Mongiardino, Coltellacci and Tosi, even though not designers in the strictest sense of the word, have in recent years produced extremely interesting work inspired by their fertile imagination. Details of furnishing used for a stage set or a costume for a film or play have since become objects reproduced on an industrial scale.

I have always had the good luck to have worked with splendid composers. Two in particular, as a result of their great sensitivity, have gone beyond the national confines and are appreciated throughout the world. I am, of course, speaking of Nino Rota and Ennio Morricone. I must point out that Ennio composed his first film music for *The Lizards*, which was also my first film too. With Nino, on the other hand, we wrote together all the songs for *Gian Burrasca*, and then he composed the music for *Love and Anarchy*. All together he has been an important part of my life and I love him dearly. Nino is also the only person in the world I have seen compose while asleep. You see, my mother had a weakness for him and, every time he came to our house to work, she prepared delicious meals which were so tasty that, after eating, when it was time for work Nino became rather sleepy: he closed his eyes, his head nodded slightly, but his hands continued to play. Incredible but true! When Francis Ford Coppola asked him to compose the music for *The Godfather*, Ninetto had no wish at all to become involved with American cinema. I remember that as soon as we heard, I and another great friend of mine, Suso Cecchi d'Amico, rushed home to a cupboard where he kept an enormous amount of scores containing all the music he had written. We picked some up and took them to Nino and forced him to accept Coppola's proposal. Some years later he won an Oscar for *The Godfather*... This anecdote shows that often the greatest Italian artists had no great ambitions and yet, despite themselves, they have become international symbols.

Italian creativity is not only to be found in films but also off the set where it is part of the world of stars and divas who, out in public, wear the jewels and clothes of Italian designers. Who can forget the Bulgari emerald and diamond necklace worn by the great Elizabeth Taylor, the violet-eyed star, the gift of her ex-husband Richard Burton while they were shooting *Cleopatra* in the Cinecittà studios? This was in 1963. In the afternoon, after shooting had finished, the two actors would often go to via Condotti for "casual" shopping in the various boutiques dotting the street. Apparently, Burton said, "I introduced Liz to beer, she introduced me to Bulgari!"

Aspects of Italian production are also present in the studios of Cinecittà which have hosted American productions of such immortal films as *Roman Holiday* and *Cleopatra*. Made in Italy is the inventiveness of the special effects by Carlo Rambaldi, someone who with his mechanical genius created *King Kong* for the film directed by Dino De Laurentiis, the *Alien* monster and the unforgettable creature from outer space, Steven Spielberg's *E.T.*

But when I come to think closely about it, I believe that the greatest expression of cinema made in Italy was unleashed by Federico Fellini's infinite creativity. With his unforgettable masterpieces he, more than any other Italian artist, has not just influenced the fashionableness of an object – a pair of glasses, a car, or a hairstyle – but he also represented the era of "la dolce vita": he knew how to capture the whole world through a lifestyle. The cinema has always been a great broadcaster of images and fashion. It is enough to remember a frame from a film by Fellini himself in order to see, in the evocative strength of that image, all Italian creative quality. Cinema has been a great vehicle for spreading design and fashion throughout the world. Certainly, behind Marcello Mastroianni and Anita Ekberg there was the Trevi fountain – but what a great excuse that was for promoting the idea of Italian art around the world. I have always thought that that image would even have pleased Michelangelo.

R. Casaro
UN BORGHESE PICCOLO PICCOLO, 1977
140 × 100 cm
Selestampa, Roma
© Massimo & Sonia Cirulli Archive, New York

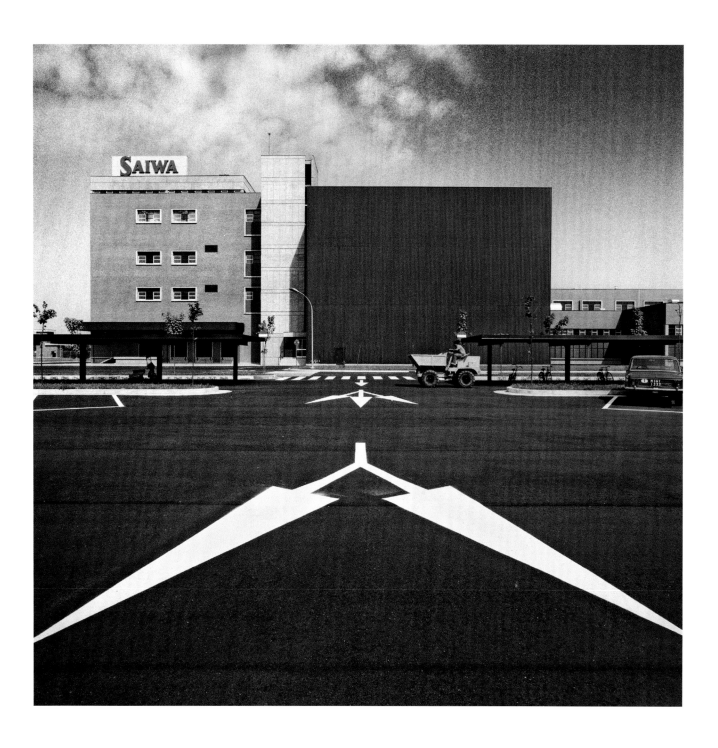

The Background. Why Ugo Mulas?

Enrico Morteo

Whatever critics like to remember, the works by Ugo Mulas do not simply consist of a famous series of reportages about artists and their world. It is quite true that, having arrived in Milan in 1948 to study law, he soon found himself in the milieu of the Giamaica bar, the gravitational centre for the new, dynamic art-life in post-war Milan. And it is also true that, without any training, he began to photograph that very world, one so strange and fascinating and based above all on meetings and friendships. Only later did the Giamaica orbit attract others who were to become his contacts for working with newspapers and magazines.

But the impulse that led Mulas to abandon a possible career as a lawyer and become a professional photographer was not simply the wish to record the fugitive world of creativity; it was, rather, the need to understand and capture the opportunities and contradictions of the society around him, one which was rapidly changing the shape of things and relationships.

In the 1950s and 1960s Milan was one of the most important epicentres of genuine social and anthropological change, a change that transformed Italy just as deeply as the rapidity with which it gained a new and unknown modern dimension. A scene of the irrepressible clash between past and future, Milan represented the collision between two worlds until then separated by astronomical chronological and geographical distances: north and south; new riches and old structures; factories and workshops; rural slowness and metropolitan acceleration; comfortable middle-class neighbourhoods and fragile brand-new outskirts; consolidated trades and new professions. Apart from his artist friends, his first subjects also included the areas in Milan where he himself lived: the outskirts; the station's entrance hall where at times he was forced to take shelter; the night and its denizens. Even though inevitably there is to be found in these images a neorealistic vein analogous to that of Italian cinema in the same years, what is really striking is Mulas's point of view. However much he was attracted by photojournalism, he was never a cynical hunter of the fleeting moments of which he was a more or less chance spectator. His shots, which portray ordinary and everyday scenes, are made special by Mulas's ability to be present and receptive. It was his sense of *being there* that allowed him to be receptive to the relationships that link people to places and, above all, of relationships that in some way involved himself. Mulas never hid himself but underlined his status as a photographer; he never robbed gestures and emotions from others without their being aware of it; instead, he tried to be a participant: this might consist of children throwing snowballs and looking in surprise at the camera, or a dustman's awareness of being part of an image. But without a doubt this artist had a special empathetic relationship, a highly formative one that allowed him to create a particular attitude

Ugo Mulas
SAIWA
The Locate Triulzi factory
1969

and a precise language for himself. Originating from his curiosity about the discussions agitating the art world regarding the ways and means of representation, his friendships with artists allowed him involve himself with them and almost be their accomplice. And yet, by presenting himself as a photographer, Mulas soon assumed a position of respectful distance, something that allowed him to record not just artists, but his relationship with their milieu and emotional context. In order to do so Mulas had an unthreatening approach, and he often used a hand-held camera without artificial lighting. The angles of his shots respected the gestures of the artists and the formal layout of the work; they hovered over what was about to happen and captured hints, situations, spaces and the working materials. Above all, what Mulas captures with his series of images is the mental process that the artist was following in his imagination in order to construct the work. To use a metaphor, we could say that Mulas was in a position of a participating listener and that he chose for himself the role of a witness and, at times, of a critic.

His detachment had certain basic consequences: on the one hand, it was this very detachment that allowed him to develop the autonomous form of his viewpoint and way of looking; on the other, that detachment is precisely where his field of action, his critical and thoughtful contribution, is to be found; at the same time, it was his awareness of this distance that defined him as a professional who made a trade of photography and made his images a record. If the camera became the working tool for a photographer who often defined himself as an artisan of images, photography was to become the area for testing and making sense, for understanding reality. In his conquest of this balanced way of looking, this authentic space for his thoughts, Mulas went beyond his brief neorealist period and laid the basis for a language with which to deal with his first professional engagements. It was in this brief period that he allowed his photographs to capture views of that rapidly changing Italy that he came into contact with. The prototype of a young, flexible and adventurous professional, Mulas accepted all kinds of engagements which, by alternating his favourite reportage with commercial photography, led him to come to grips with extremely different situations and people: factories and fashion journals; industrialists and designers; workers and models. A world that Mulas did not view from the outside but of which he was both a protagonist and a witness. But then, Milanese society at the time was a receptive one where artists and professionals could, without problems, mix with industrialists and intellectuals, and where graphic artists and architects, by working for industry, had the possibility of exchanging ideas with businessmen and photographers. A society where you communicated by meeting and talking together and not through the filter of marketing and advertising offices. These were the photographs that make Mulas's work crucial for those who want to re-examine the Italy of the economic boom with all its contradictions and receptiveness. Mulas's images were not limited to description but, rather, were part of the birth of a new Italian language by shaping forms that re-launched or even created a repertoire of fashion and of work aesthetics: the sense of objects and the faces of people, city areas and advertising campaigns.

Mulas himself did not underestimate his commissioned works and he suggested that this was a genuine aspect of photography. In fact, in one respect the unabashed aim of these images required a greater care in studying the angle of the shot, in posing the model, in choosing the setting or scenery; in another it was the opportunity to avoid the most obvious clichés of commercial communications.

Among these first works were the fashion services for "Novità" magazine. Mulas avoided easy clichés and refused to deal with children, love, eroticism and politics, in order to play, instead, with contrast; on the one hand he chose as his backgrounds those places where the sense of form modified by the present and a perception of the landscape were most evident. They might be new places for holidaying or for enjoying free time or, more often, the unstable scenario of the city: desolate outskirts where fragments of nature still survived among factories and pylons, or the new buildings growing in the centre of Milan. One particular fashion service was emblematic: he set it on the balcony of a newly constructed condominium. The photos are built up on three successive planes: in the foreground is the model with her dress in sharp relief; in the background is the outline of the Pirellone, the famous skyscraper designed by Gio Ponti; the space between is with the roofs of old blocks of flats, still blackened by the war and evidently about to give way to newer and more modern buildings.

But it wasn't only with the angle of his photos that Mulas reshuffled expectations. In 1962, Olivetti commissioned him to undertake a reportage about the work in its factories. This was a fairly usual request from this Ivrea-based business which, determined to construct a modern cultural image of itself to reflect and explain the modernity of its products, had already requested similar services from Henri Cartier-Bresson, Fulvio Roiter and Gianni Berengo Gardin. Mulas decided to aim his camera mainly at the women employees. If this time the scenery could only be that of assembly lines, offices, the canteen and the facades of the factories, Mulas employed a way of looking that he had used for his fashion services. What Mulas photographed was the delicate collision between work and femininity. Mulas's women workers were both sharp and seductive, strong and frivolous: the new protagonists of a changing society. His lens could capture a look, and also the care taken over a hairstyle, the whiteness of a collar peaking over a black work-shirt, the detail of an ankle, the brazenness of an autonomous economic and social conquest. Mulas was to create similar contaminations between art, architecture and industry. Again in 1962, he was busy photographing various sculptors who, on a visit to take part in the Spoleto Festival, had been invited to create their works in various Italsider workshops. David Smith in particular chose an old factory in Volpi that had been abandoned for some time. During two days there together with Smith, Mulas did nothing other than show the artist against the background of this piece of industrial architecture. He did not attempt portraits or close-ups but, rather, he acted as though the interior was a landscape and the artist's works were a natural evolution of it. When Italsider then commissioned him to do a reportage on its factories in Genoa, Mulas did nothing other than continue this kind of work. In a telluric and mineral manner, Mulas sniffed out the signs of human presence, he captured the force of their traces and revealed their beauty. In his photos, metal sheets, bobbins, girders running off the rolling mills, and metal-working machinery all became genuine works of art created by the labour of the workers and the machinery. But Mulas did not simply limit himself to the perimeter of the factory: by enlarging his view he saw how industry was pressing against the fabric of the city, almost a metaphor for muscular and expanding modernity. And, walking around the port of Genoa, he investigated points of dissension, revealed the friction between the imposition of the new and the dignified ebb of the old. In a similar manner, when Saiwa asked him to photograph a new factory, Mulas worked as though he had been invited by "Domus", a magazine for which he had begun to photograph architecture. Rather than

Ugo Mulas
LAMBDA CHAIR
Gavina 1959,
designer, Marco Zanuso
Milan, 1965

limiting himself to recording, department by department, the various working places and giving an idea of the overall volume of the building, Mulas used his shots to underline the specificity of industrial architecture and to intensify the relationship between windows and blind walls, to bring materials and structures into relief and to highlight the presence of the equipment and machinery. And not just that. If he related the movement of the production-line to the labour of the workers, in the same way he related the factory to the outside world: not so much to the horizon line as to the cars and trucks that, strategically placed in order to close off the composition of a frame, contemporaneously evoked the constant movement of people, products and raw materials. Only then did he allowed himself some freedom and focussed on the car-park signs as though they were a graphic work by Jannis Kounellis.

This was a mechanism for linguistic dislocation that was to be seen again in all his work over the years: when he undertook a series of publicity shots for Pirelli tyres, even though leaving the tread in the foreground, he had also shot a fashion-and-style service; if he photographed Arnaldo Pomodoro's jewellery, given that he could not put them on the arms of the people who bought them, he would insist on them being worn by a nude model whose body, however, became a stylized sculpture in chiaroscuro.

And not just jewels: there were many products photographed as though they were works of art, or joyously experienced as though they were the setting for a fashion service. Design and designers were captured in their studio while installing a show and posed among their projects.

But the objects and designers were not the last link in the chain: what Mulas was actually photographing was everything that followed and preceded the object: the factories, advertising, the Triennial exhibitions, the houses where the objects were to find a home, the towns and the people living in them and who worked with their new customs, joys and neuroses.

I do not believe that Mulas can be defined as a landscapist. And yet, if we look closely, each of his photos is in fact a landscape. It might be a face or an emotion, a street or a factory, a work of art or a studio, an object or a house. These are not stories but brief poems in which we can find, in their forms and things, the sense of an Italy on the very brink of contemporaneity.

Ugo Mulas
BUILDING SITE
Milan, 1962

Ugo Mulas
ITALSIDER
Genoa, 1963

Ugo Mulas
ITALSIDER
Genoa, 1963

Ugo Mulas
IDEAL STANDARD
Genoa, 1964

Ugo Mulas
IDEAL STANDARD
Genoa, 1964

Ugo Mulas
OLIVETTI
Electric power station, Elea
Ivrea, 1964

Ugo Mulas
CHURCH
*The church of San Giovanni
Battista, architect, Giovanni
Michelucci, Campi di Bisenzio*
Florence, 1964

Ugo Mulas
OLIVETTI
Electric power station
Ivrea, 1964

Ugo Mulas
ENZO MARI
1967

Ugo Mulas
XIII TRIENNIAL
Tempo libero: Esposizione Internazionale delle arti decorative e industriali moderne e dell'architettura moderna moderna (International exhibition of modern decorative and industrial arts and architecture)
Milan, 1964

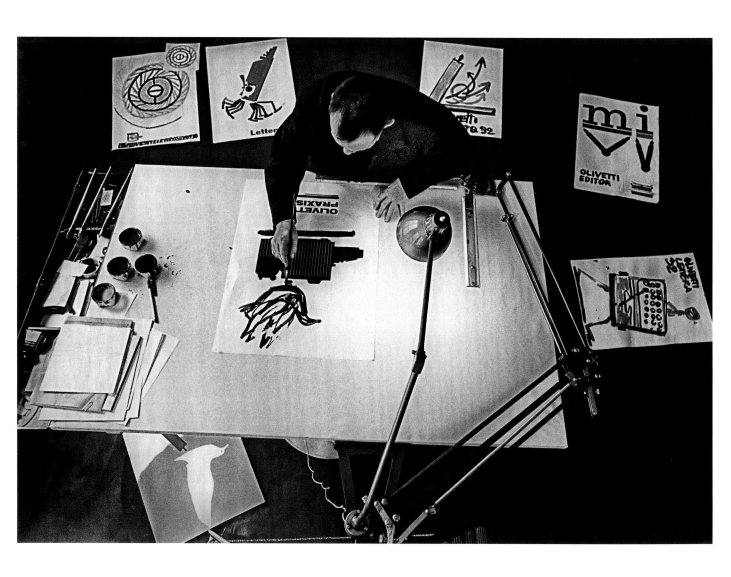

Ugo Mulas
GIOVANNI PINTORI
1966

Ugo Mulas
MARCO ZANUSO
1967

Ugo Mulas
**ACHILLE AND PIER GIACOMO
CASTIGLIONI**
1967

Ugo Mulas
VICO MAGISTRETTI
1968

Ugo Mulas
KARTELL PAVILION
Joe Colombo, Anna Castelli,
Alberto Rosselli, Gino
Colombini, Salone del Mobile,
Fiera Campionaria (Furniture
hall, the Milan trade fair)
Milan, 1969

Ugo Mulas
THE B&B ITALIA PAVILION
Salone del Mobile,
Fiera Campionaria (Furniture
hall, the Milan trade fair)
Milan, 1969

Ugo Mulas
**ETTORE SOTTSASS
AND FERNANDA PIVANO
FOR "UOMO VOGUE"**
1967-1968

Ugo Mulas
**LUCIO FONTANA FOR "UOMO
VOGUE"**
1967-1968

Stories

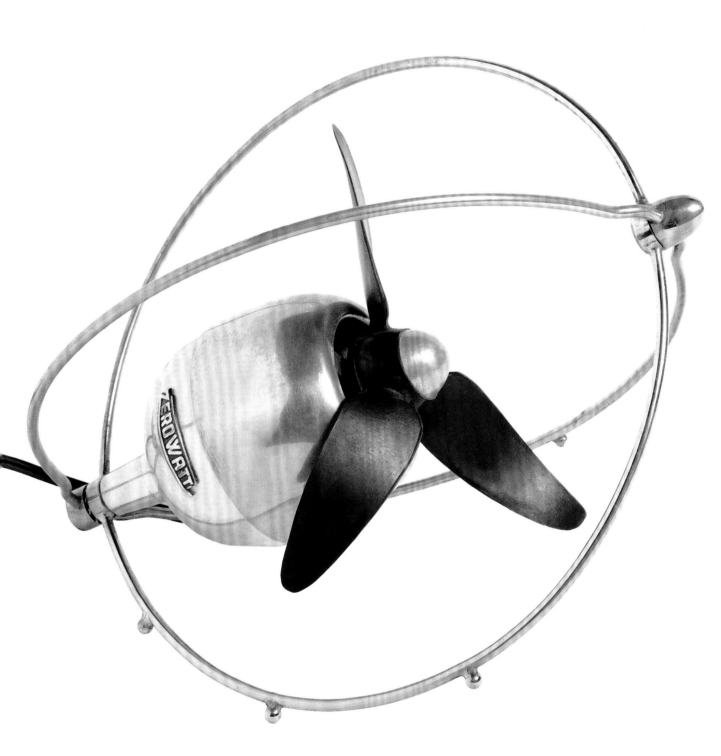

Half a Century of Design for Recounting the Future

Luisa Bocchietto

The *Italian Uniqueness* show, organised by the Fondazione Valore Italia together with ADI and the Fondazione ADI, underlines the role and significance that the high-quality design and production of the fifty years since 1961 has had on our national identity and on the promotion of the image of Italy throughout the world.

We can be proud of the fact that, for this official event celebrating the hundred and fifty years of Italian unity, the Ministry of Economic Development has, through the Fondazione Valore Italia, pinpointed the historical collection of the premio Compasso d'Oro ADI as the most qualified tangible testimony for explaining our recent history through design.

Simply with the works awarded the prize and now exhibited together for the first time (after the patient re-systemisation of the historical collection supervised by ADI and the Fondazione ADI) it is now possible to show the public a wider evolution of taste and customs, technological innovation, the wide-scale discovery of free time, the complexity of economic relationships and the growth of the manufacturing industry: in other words, it is now possible to describe the changes that have come about.

These changes happened between the post-war period and today, together with our country's transformation from an agricultural civilisation to an industrial one; so it is not by chance that industrial design itself, because it is an economic and cultural process tied to new generalised forms of production and communication, has become a paradigm for this evolution.

Industrial design originated in Italy in the 1950s after the settling down of the post-war economic and political scenarios, when society found itself having to build a new identity and to invent products adapted to the fast growth of consumption.

Industrial production became a democratic tool for spreading wealth through the distribution of accessible products that could improve the quality of life; at the same time, they led to a common sense of aesthetic quality.

All this happened rather late in the day, but was similar to what had happened in Germany in the 1920s with the culture promoted by the Bauhaus and the new materials used for an industrial production for the masses, or in America a decade later with the revolution in productive aesthetics characterised by "streamlining".

As is always the case with cultural phenomena that come about in a certain historical moment when external conditions present favourable changes – changes originated further back in time in the minds of certain enlightened protagonists – so too in Italy there were hints of what our industrial design would become.

These anticipatory signs date from the 1930s in Turin where Riccardo Gualino, a visionary businessman, was the first to introduce the serial production of furniture. Gualino had asked FIP (Fabbrica Italiana Pianoforti) to construct the first industrialised furniture, designed by the architect Giuseppe Pagano, necessary for furnishing his new offices. These absolutely modern furnishings, though aesthetically in line with what was being produced abroad, had their own special identity and were rigorously constructed in local materials. It was Pagano himself who, having moved to Milan before dying prematurely as a war victim in a concentration camp, had sparked off a cultural debate – centred on the Monza and Milan triennial fairs, institutions at the heart of the development of furniture design – that was to be successfully resolved in later years.

It was only after the war, however, that the history of Italian design developed in a widespread and highly appreciated way; from the very beginning this history was linked to ADI, the Italian industrial design association, which had been established in that period. Since then ADI,

through its promotion of the Compasso d'Oro prize, has actively contributed to the evolution of design and its place in history. A few businessmen, architects and intellectuals had gathered together in Milan in 1954, stimulated by a competition for the production of new objects of everyday use promoted by the La Rinascente chain of large stores. The prize-competition, which was to be given the name premio Compasso d'Oro and had achieved a completely unexpected success, became the means for the diffusion of new industrial aesthetics and was to be placed in the hands of ADI: this was founded two years later, in 1956, as the result of that meeting between businessmen and designers interested in continuing with the promotion of such aesthetics.

The young industrial society of the time needed new products to undertake new functions. The *material culture* of design was developed around the projects for these unusual products: an interactive coexistence of functional forms, and an aesthetic and ethical vision of society orderly involved in the creative challenge of a different way for producing, creating and consuming. This initial imprinting of Italian design was to remain a basic characteristic, a commitment that was not just aesthetic and economic but also social. Consumer society, with its new rhythms and myths, was being established in these years. In our country this culture could not be separated from our way of living and was rooted in our manufacturing tradition; our particular Italian lifestyle helped construct the concept of products made in Italy, one that was to have no equivalent in other countries. Elsewhere the phenomenon of industrial growth was getting underway at the same time. However, Italian-made production contained within itself a quite particular atmosphere that alluded to food, taste, the climate, the fascination of places, artisan know-how, the joys of living and beauty in general. This vague yet evocative brand was then, over the years, transferred to the whole country with a positive result for all

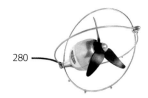

its productive activities and for the image of our exports: it created a permanent halo of quality around our products.

Fashion, design, food, monuments and beauty represent our "natural resources", our own deposits of petrol, and become our distinctive trademark throughout the world.

This happened then and still continues now, due to the labour and fatigue of many people, despite organisational deficiencies that remain an endemic hindrance. Often we speak of the "Italian miracle" in order to explain how, contrary to any possible logic, certain things in Italy come about even when there are not the objective assumptions for expecting them.

This creative capacity – organised with little or scarce external planning, with great uncertainty about checks and regulations and a lack of specific financial support – has given rise to particularly attentive and thus strategic firms and to extraordinary products made by enlightened entrepreneurs and designers.

Strategic design is an essential part of this characteristic Italian vision, and it is extraneous to the idea of design developed in other countries as a component of marketing, facilitated by the economic growth of more structured systems. In our country permanent difficulties have led to the development of a critical attitude, one continually stimulated toward innovation in order to maintain a level of competitiveness that is not guaranteed by other systems.

The endless research into forms, the continual self-criticism of the system – a self-criticism that is knowingly nurtured and which is often accompanied by a political kind of thinking about the very meaning of production – has forced Italian design never to be wholly and only subject to the productive aspect, and to keep alive its subversive content. This content emerges in the iconic products of Italian design, initially originated to give an answer to new needs but then to express a more

strongly critical, or at least ironic, vision of the new consumer society: just think, for example, of the Mezzadro lounger by Achille and Pier Giacomo Castiglioni, or the sack armchair by Gatti, Paolini and Teodoro, produced by Zanotta. This specific aspect of Italian design was underlined in the 1972 exhibition *Italy: The New Domestic Landscape* held at the MOMA, New York, and that sanctioned at an international level the plural identity of Italian design with respect to an international vision based on the development of relationships between form and function.

The subversive content of Italian design was, then, superimposed on that traditional research into the duality of form/function which had characterised design's initial growth. Even such great masters as Marco Zanuso, Vico Magistretti and Achille Castiglioni had anticipated this cultural gap by finding their reference points in early twentieth-century art movements (Futurism, ready-mades, Dadaism) or by introducing such new materials as plastic or by having a new approach to technology and colour which were to be the bases of an independent aesthetic research recognized as peculiarly Italian.

Surface decoration and a return to history were to be the themes rediscovered by movements in the 1980s (Memphis, Postmodernism) and that introduced other critical elements into the norms of industrial production. It is significant that certain of these "subversions" originated from the very receptiveness of such enlightened entrepreneurs as Olivetti, first, and then Alessi, who allowed their designers (Ettore Sottsass for the former and Alessandro Mendini for the latter) freedom in giving rein to their intellectual research, which was not necessarily aimed at production or marketing. Great stimuli for design and its vitality originated from this less mercantile and more speculative approach.

Many commentators insist that Italian design is dead. They do so sys-

tematically. Well, we know that apocalyptic headlines always make their effect. But often it is not noticed just how much over the past few years the design that we consider by now to be part of our heritage, even design by international stars, owes to the great receptiveness of Italian firms. On the other hand, despite a situation of economic growth which is eroding competitiveness, for Italy design continues to be an important driving force for the economy. This is because of the extraordinary strength of businessmen, designers, graphic artists and experts who work competitively and enthusiastically.

ADI itself, a voluntary association for the promotion of Italian design, which does not receive contributions and has been bailed out by the state for over fifty years, is a small Italian miracle. In a country where, unfortunately, there rules a mental division between individual interests and collective ones, ADI has for many years gathered together designers, businesses, distributors, critics and schools with an ideal aim that fires them all: to recognise and give value to the quality of one's own work. Perhaps it is precisely because it is so deeply tied to this group of ideal and, at the same time, concrete values of *material culture* that our industrial design has managed to represent an interest so widely shared and undertaken for such a long time despite the limitations imposed on us. The direct involvement of those who give their utmost for the overall good while ignoring their own interests, is not currently mirrored by the open divisions and inability to structure the country at a public level. In Italy there has always been a kind of irritation in the face of established power. Perhaps this attitude, which today is a reductive one, is the atavist heredity of the divisions and bullying undergone in the past, of the succession of too many outside powers which periodically we have had to respond and adapt to. It was as though the motives for life and survival had become detached from the system's motivations which must have

seemed to individuals as being completely extraneous to reality. But in an unplanned way this component of resistance, this force for the affirmation of life must, despite everything, have also become the basis of our creativity.

Riccardo Sarfatti is warmly remembered as someone with an enthusiasm for politics, business flair and a vision of design (often irreconcilably in conflict with each other). When he said that "knowing how to make do with little" was the characteristic of planning and designing in Italy – a hint that Enrico Morteo has developed in a masterly fashion in the section of the show called "Rigore del poco" – he was expressing one of the vital components of our way of coming to grips with the design of things. Italy is not a country rich in ready-to-be-used extractable resources; it is a country that transforms and that has a great creative capacity. Beauty and the ability to create it, to recognise and recount it: this is our heredity. And this capacity has led to an exceptional sensibility, to works of art and even to whole cities that are masterpieces in themselves. This sensibility has produced a widespread and yet almost unconscious taste in people: the tendency to confer on each individual thing – food, clothes, furnishing and cars, utensils and systems – the same hallmark of elegance and of skill in the use of techniques and innovation, a hallmark which appears quite natural.

The capacities of the individuals scattered over our territory, and the quality of our products, must today be integrated in a desire to create a system.

Rogers' programmatic slogan in the 1950s, "From spoons to cities", which sums up the whole of design's drive towards the construction of a better world, is still profoundly true for the overall approach of those who designed and yet were ignored in the "political" years. Many architects have become designers because of their frustration in not seeing their skills appreciated. In France there exists a "Law

for Architecture" which states, as a principle, that architecture is a possession that must be encouraged for the community as a whole; in Italy there is a "Law for Public Works" which levels out skills and qualities on the basis of economic parameters, a hostage to contractors. Architects, unwelcome in such an system, have built the success of Italian design by applying design to spoons, since it was impossible to apply it to towns. In part this has been the fortune of small private firms throughout our land which have grown while battling against each other. This fight for survival must end. This is not intended to be a clichéd argument but, rather, a heartfelt call to our institutions. The ideas that are emerging on the occasion of the festivities for the hundred and fiftieth anniversary of Italian unification ought to force us to act for urgent change. More than words, we must construct the country's system. What lies outside our private sphere should not be invisible or, even worse, a view of the public as an enemy. Italy has been made, it was once said, and now we must make the Italians; but the Italians have made themselves by their own efforts, in a creative and at times disorderly manner: now what is necessary is an organisational act for giving a driving role to institutions.

The Italians, those for whom every day is a challenge, do not hold back in their efforts and they follow their ideals with enthusiasm; they are far better than the media allows us to think, better than is represented by parties with their superseded shows: if it were not like this there would be no fashion, design, products and other less visible high-quality factors made in Italy. Our presence in Rome has a precise meaning for Italian design: it expresses the wish of designers and businesses to be in closer contact with institutions. For ADI it means making available the work of these past fifty years as a contribution to a history that will tell the future about our qualities. Our history demonstrates our belief that everything is possible in a new way.

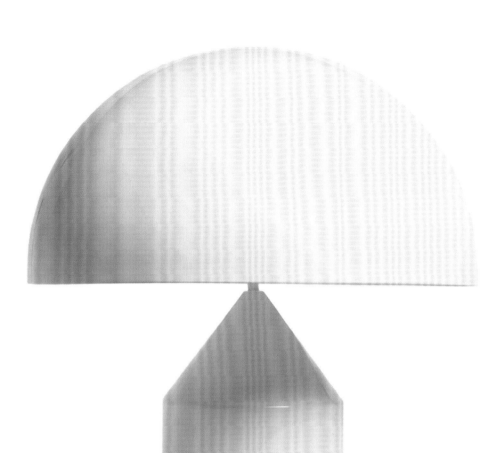

Creativity, Business and Territory as Mythopoeic Narration

Umberto Croppi

Enterprise is a beginning: it means doing something that is not yet there, shattering a limit. But for that very reason enterprise at once becomes a challenge; it takes on the meaning of surmounting, of victory: there is always something agonistic in the idea we have of enterprise. *Sport* and *exploration* too are agonistic, but enterprise is also, par excellence, *warlike*. And yet those who face such undertakings are occasionally called champions, adventurers, discoverers and heroes. There is only one case in which the definition of the author of an undertaking has an intimate relationship with its name: the "entrepreneur". This is the person who originates the network of social, juridical and emotional relationships that creates a group of people who collaborate together to produce forms, objects and ideas. An entrepreneur can be, and often is, a champion, adventurer and hero too. But the enterprise we are dealing with is modern and came about together with new technologies, with the economics of scale, with speed: enterprise is the very symbol of the 20th century, and its visionary quality is underlined by the close link it has established with art: painting, music, poetry, theatre, fashion. Not just Futurist art, which placed technological and industrial force at the heart of its poetics, but all modern art which is built on the fascination, symbols and material relations which derive from enterprise.

It is all too easy to say that the aim of enterprise is profit. But is that to be taken for granted? Is it true? Even if it were true, we would understand very little about the reasons that lead someone to expose himself in such an open and risky way. Profit can be gained in many other ways and often the entrepreneur does not even need it. Nor can it explain the continuation of an enterprise even when faced with open adversity, difficulties and plots from within or without. In no way would it explain the continuation of an enterprise's fame at the end of its life cycle.

Certainly, balancing accounts is one of the elements that allow an enterprise to last (though not even for ever, as we know) but deep down we can glimpse, to paraphrase Sombart, the metaphysics of enterprise. A certain immaterial something that goes beyond its mechanical and accountancy relationships and which is the real essence and soul of the firm-enterprise, something that protects it as far as possible from contingences that would make it precarious and unstable. If the aim really were only and exclusively profit, an enterprise would no longer be such once it was profitable because, according to Gentile, it is "due to our strength that we manage to create a way of being which, without our strength, would never have been: to create a new person in ourselves. This is the only profit a man can speak of: a profit that is his cause."

Or we might ask with Adriano Olivetti: "Can industry have aims? And if so are these simply to be found in the profit index? Isn't there, quite apart from an apparent rhythm, something more fascinating – an aim, a vocation – even in factory life?"

And the person who asked himself this question was a man, an entrepreneur, whose proclaimed utopia did not refer to a small structure but to a firm with 36,000 employees. "In factory life". With this phrase Olivetti also reminds us of other immaterial aspects that are part of the overall idea of business, a business that has its own collective personality. Once again, it is an artistic expression that gives us an idea of this, one to be found in what has been increasingly accepted as a literary genre: factory literature such as Antonio Pennacchi's *Fulgorcavi* or *Ansaldo* by Vincenzo Guerrazzi, working authors who describe the work environment as a coherent, pulsating universe, factories as a living organism.

So an enterprise's identity can be constructed through an imaginary process, a production of symbols that determines its perception and is able to give it a personality that is far more consistent than a purely juridical one. The "spirit" of enterprise as Taiichi Ohno (the inventor of "Just in time") defined it when speaking about "his" Toyota.

And it is exactly a mythical construction: in the sense of both the capacity to establish itself as a myth and as teleology, the convergence point, not just of material interests, but also of drives, expectations and needs that go beyond the production of goods or the acquisition of means of subsistence.

The link between the "myth" and enterprise is deep and fundamental. As Mircea Eliade has written, "The 'myth' is the narration of a beginning; it is the enterprise with which the superhuman establishes how humanity is and how it must be; it is sacredness that erupts into the world and lays down the norms of action". Modernity, however, has taught humanity the importance of autonomy, the need to create norms for oneself: having escaped from the gods, enterprise has become an unexpected and unprecedented human action.

Like every other myth, that of enterprise is made up of many different elements: the product, publicity, its influence on behaviour. It develops on many levels and in many directions; it becomes metalanguage, metaphor and the producer of metaphors. Fashion designers, designers, industrial barons, photographers etc. are associated with that of the originator and become a part of the pantheon of this little universe.

As the authors of a heroic enterprise they and the "creator" become objects of attention, curiosity and inquiry into their own private life; they become models to imitate (or execrate), demigods existing in a parallel reality detached from everyday life.

Because myths are tales, narrative is their form, and so an enterprise uses their narrative tools: the factory museum, archives, publicity and communications themselves are all structured in order to narrate it; its products are nothing more than the bricks for building the story. And, of course, it confers rites on itself: anniversaries, meetings, celebrations of its foundation date. "We can understand nothing unless it evokes one of our memories (Luc Benoist)."

Myths confer sacredness and intangibility; they do not die together with the enterprise because a community exists to perpetuate them. Humanity is a symbolic animal which remembers and plans. And so it becomes a model, an element that is taken over by the community both in order to construct its own identity on it and as an end in itself. Places, in turn, *signify* the enterprise which, like a semiological system, no longer simply communicates its own being but also begins to be the "value for..."

Richard Florida has spoken of "the quality of place", the "power of place", in his well-known essay on the rise of the "new creative class", and sums up its basic components as "what there is", "who there is", and "what happens there".

What would Fiat have been without Turin? Without the great industrial buildings that, together with the mass of immigrants, remodelled the city? Without its colours, climate, city perspectives? Or Olivetti without Ivrea or Ferrari, Versace, or Barilla without Italy?

Once again it was this American researcher who coined the idea of the "dense market" made up of factors that are not strictly mercantile. But what is it that makes the market dense if not the mythical relationship established between the creative protagonists, the protagonists of the enterprise and the environmental influences that they derive from the territory? Density, efficacy and perceptibility: these are the immaterial aspects that "realise" an enterprise when juridical relationships (and profit) might remain abstractions.

In this world time is no longer cyclic, as it was for the ancients, nor finalised as it was for Christians and Marxists; it is increasingly a question of velocity, fragmentation, instantaneity. And then the progressive shift from words to writing and images determines a superimposition of languages and, therefore, simultaneous and fragmented cognition, to quote Roland Barthes.

What reconnects the fragments and guarantees "duration" is the territory itself. The myth has a past and future only in relationship to the context which historicises it. It projects the context backwards for the possibilities it has inherited, and forwards as the creator of new possibilities. And, finally, it establishes context and allows it to exist, even after its own death.

And in the eyes of the foreign public, products made in Italy have the aspect of a myth. But whereas abroad it is perceived as the quintessence of beauty, goodness and elegance for Italians it is considered an integral part of our way of being, thinking and making. This knowledge of making has been handed down to us from a rich past of art history, cultural episodes that have left an indelible mark on the world and have become one with a territory that is in itself a work of art. At times we ask ourselves what Italy is useful for.

Is it a bridge between Africa and Europe? A port for sailors without a compass? A place for high quality products? The land beneath our feet? Our home?

It is all this. And more. It is the practical demonstration that contemporary myths are as complex as contemporary society. Products made in Italy are the outcome of a combination of a generous territory, lively creativity, controlled anarchy and intuitive sensibility. They are a productive model in which enterprise never loses sight of immaterial values linked to humanity, emotions, fascination and tradition. A productive model in which creative and planning activity is placed on the same level as mechanised or manual work.

Made in Italy is a way of looking at the things of life. And it is for this that it is transformed in the eyes of the world into an ideal model to be followed. And Italy is useful for this too.

The Transformations of Work in Italy

Giorgio Bigatti

It is increasingly difficult to talk about work in Italy today. We find ourselves face-to-face with an evanescent and elusive situation which is constantly evolving. To start with, the creative aspect of work has dimmed: as regards its numbers, workers are still a consistent mass, but on closer analysis they risk seeming a sum of individuals with few unifying elements. It wasn't like this once. If carried out in a factory, work was first of all toil and sweat; added to this were noise, tension, conflict, solidarity and, at times, pride in craftsmanship. But it was first and foremost a socialising experience. Factories or, rather, Fordist factories, are by now a sad shadow of what they once were – at least if they haven't disappeared after a lifespan that was, if not inglorious, brief. An example is Mirafiori, a factory symbolising Italian industrialism and which in the 1970s, according to an estimate by Giuseppe Berta, gave work to some 55,000 workers and other employees: it is now a tenth of the size. So where did these nearly 50,000 jobs go? Some years ago, after having predicted the end of history, it became fashionable to speak about the end of labour. These were seductive slogans. But they were deceitful. Change is history's only constant. Of course, a certain way of organising work had come to an end: not work in itself, even though in Italy today, as in most of the West, work seems a mirage to many people. Flexibility, precariousness and short-term work are the most frequently heard words when talking about work conditions; these now have a negative sense with respect to the recent past when, on the contrary, it meant stability and social security above all: basically, the prospect of a better standard of living. But apart from all this we must not forget that the break with the Fordist "steel cage" model has offered many people (not all!) new subjective spaces in their relationship with life-time and work-time which has created new professional figures and new areas of values. A trend rather unthinkingly identified with the end of working class solidarity and, at the other extreme, with the emergence of new social groups: *knowledge workers* with exclusive roles and talents, as well as that heterogeneous group of professional figures who make up what Richard Florida has called the creative class.

In the following pages only brief hints can be made to all this beams of light that do not claim to illuminate an extremely complex process but which offer thoughts useful for understanding what this show is about.

THE FACTORY AND WORK: RECONSTRUCTION AND DEVELOPMENT

The post-war Italian economy, characterised by the small size of its businesses, its high-quality craftsmanship, and its ability to unite aesthetics to industrial output, seemed to have set out on a path of development aimed at destroying this particularity – which once was considered the mark of being behind the times – in order to come into line with other industrial countries. And it is that very short twenty-year period, 1951-1971, that we should start from.

In the dramatic epilogue to the Fascist regime, with the country divided and occupied by the warring nations and with stalled institutional and civil structures, the great industries began to have a relevance that went beyond their economic role. During the war, as is natural in such circumstances, large industries were reinforced, as is confirmed by the increased occupation in auxiliary businesses which had risen from 728,000 employees in 1939 to about 1,200,000 some four years later. With the founding of Mirafiori in 1939, the workers at the Fiat plant increased from 36,000 to 55,000; no less significant increases were established in many other firms such as Alfa Romeo, which went from 3,500 to 13,400 workers; Isotta Fraschini, from 3,000 to 7,000; Officine Reggiane, from 2,000 to 10,000; Ansaldo, from 12,400 to 27,500; and the Breda group, from 8,500 to over 35,000. So-

cially, the increasing importance of large industrial groups formed a counterpoint to the progressive paralysis of economic activity due to the difficulties in supplying combustibles and raw materials. These groups played a determining role in guaranteeing food supplies to a large part of the population through the organisation of refectories, canteen, and war allotments as well as other services; above all, they became one of the organisational nodes of the Resistance movement. These factors were still to be felt in the immediate post-war period when the standstill of the old industrial managing classes, waiting to answer for their relationship with Fascism, coincided with the reinforcement of workers' organisations and their mortgage on business management. This was only a brief period which was cut short by the end of the collaboration of the left with the government and then its definitive defeat at the 1948 elections, which opened the way to a grand reckoning in the factories with a wave of mass dismissals of the surplus of workers, a legacy from the war.

In just a few years Italy changed face as well as changing from an agricultural country to an industrial one: not very different to what had already "happened in other countries with an older industrial civilisation" but with more "difficulties and disorder", as Giorgio Bocca wrote in the "Giorno" newspaper in 1962. The by-now usual name of "the economic miracle" underlines the explosive and unexpected aspect of this transformation, even though in fact it was the outcome of many previous factors and of specific contingencies. Much was due the Marshall Plan's help and the importation of technologies and organisational capacities which arrived from the other side of the ocean. But no less decisive was the peoples' wish to leave behind them decades of hardship and poverty, as well as the lengthy accumulation of experience and competence that, in a century of industrial history, had accumulated in part of the country: what Vittorio

Valletta called the "mechanical granary". In other words, as seems clear today, the origins of that great cycle of growth were various endogenous factors linked to the economic and social history and characteristics of the country (see, for example, the affairs of state businesses) and exogenous factors linked to international political decisions and Italy's membership of the Atlantic Alliance.

In that feverish period, the partnership between the old manufacturing traditions of northeastern Italy and the new techniques for managing and organising work imported from America allowed businesses unexpected areas of development. An inevitably brief summary of the miracle factories has to include Piaggio and Innocenti with their scooters which fostered a widespread desire for mobility; Fiat, whose economical cars offered a tangible sign of recently acquired wealth and were a prelude to the more general consumer revolution; Olivetti, which made quality the distinctive mark of a company which was not afraid to up-stage the world by challenging the giants of the sector on their own ground; of the domestic appliance industry set up by Livio Zanussi in Pordenone, a witness to the expansion of industries which were beginning to find the old "triangle" too restrictive. Nor should we leave out of account public enterprises which were then going through a glorious period, upheld by the faith in the modernising potential of industry by such businessmen as Oscar Sinigaglia and Enrico Mattei.

In order to understand the real sense of the economic miracle we must not limit ourselves to the "usual suspects". No less important than the growth of large businesses was the consolidation of small and even tiny businesses. As regards employment, from 1951 to 1961 the growth rate for firms with over 100 employees was 8%, while that of firms with from six to fifty employees was over 70%, and this not so much because of an increase in the size of the firms as for the increase in their number. Behind each of these "little firms" with just a few employees and, usually, with very modest equipment, were families and nuclei of "tiny, small and medium-sized middle-class industries". This indicates that in this period the country was undergoing an amazing process of mobility: not just a horizontal one, from the country to the town, but also a vertical one of an upward social movement towards wealth.

THE FORDIST PARADIGM

By bringing into effect the productive ideas he had proposed to the industrial constituent assembly, Valletta, president of Fiat from 1946 to 1966, turned Mirafiori into a paradigm of mass production by trusting in the strength of the numbers contained in his programme: 16,000 workers in 1953; 18,000 in 1956; 32,000 in 1962. About halfway through the 1950s, Fiat arrived at the Fordist structure it had been aiming at for some time but that, for one reason or another, it had never completely been able to achieve. In order to do so, it had been necessary to regain full practicability in the various departments, eliminate the residual margins of autonomy in the execution of the works, and rebuild the hierarchical structure which had been questioned in the months immediately preceding the reconstruction. This was a difficult task that involved the management in an action of opposition to the workers' organisations, one that also was not above a discrete use of salary-raising as well as capillary repression; in some cases – and Fiat was exemplary in this – this arrived at sackings and a kind of harassment that could not be justified even in the cold war period (the so-called "isolation sections" well described in the firm's official histories). Assembly lines were set up for the various models, while modern transfer machines imported from America permitted the automation of the different assembly phases which allowed a rigorous

compartmentalisation of the various tasks. This was a setup that was never to be forgotten by those who experienced it. "It was terrifying, this factory never ended, these assembly lines that shot across all over the place, bits of cars sped over your head, ran along beside you, cut off your escape… and all that noise", as Giovanni Falcone wrote of his first day in Fiat in May 1968; he was a worker who then went on to become a militant union member. "A hell of noise and heat", Ottieri wrote in 1951 after having visited the departments of Alfa Romeo. The results of this massive investment in reorganising the firm and the work were soon to be seen. In 1955, the 600 was launched, the first really cheap Italian car; it cost 590,000 lire and some 2,695,000 were produced before 1970. Even more amazing results were achieved by another car designed by that mechanical genius, the engineer Dante Giacosa: the new 500 of which 3,678,000 were to be produced. So when, in 1963, over a million cars had been produced per annum, something that would have been unthinkable just a few years earlier, it was welcomed with great satisfaction but without any sense of surprise. In this period the use of assembly lines, the symbol of the degradation and monotony of work, was extended to all those products which could amortise their costs: scooters, typewriters, radios, television sets, record players and the whole range of domestic appliances: and this list is certainly far from complete. Of course, all this, pushed ahead by an unstoppable demand, meant an intensification of work. The compression of time, cheaper piece-work, "and the continual pressure of the management on the employees to impose an even faster working rhythm", as the Alfa Romeo hands were to complain in 1954, exacted a very heavy toll on the life and health of the employees. But despite this, the factory offered the prospect of betterment for thousands of former peasants newly arrived in the towns. This is confirmed, even through the distorted perspective of the extremely negative view taken of the changes underway by the "white papers" prepared by the FIOM's internal commissions. These, while condemning the progressive degradation of work-tasks, the intense exploitation, the approach to work and the entry into the firm of a new generation of workers mainly from southern Italy, could not help being impressed by the extraordinariness of the processes underway, processes which, what is more, gave lie to many current ideas about the backwardness of Italian capitalism.

But, as though worn down by a process that had outrun itself, as the 1960s went ahead Italian industry seemed to lose steam, as can be seen by the difficulties and failures to establish itself in the technological sectors. The large industrial companies that had seemed to be the key to breaking down the old barriers to growth, were suddenly seen to be fragile. The miracle exhausted its propulsive force and, even though slowing down, it had set off a ferment that would be reproduced on a larger scale and would make the country one of the greatest scenes of industry; its fading away marked the end of a period that is now definitively consigned to history.

FROM FEARS OF DECLINE TO SIGNS OF CHANGE

Today all this is only a distant memory. And the more the present seems uncertain, the more the past is considered as something reassuring. The post-war problems of the living conditions of such a large part of the population, and the bitterness of ideological and social contrasts, have been metabolised and now we admire and are nostalgic about the period, above all with regard to its liveliness, planning and concern about the future. However, even if for some decades now the country has not grown or has grown more slowly than other OECD countries, Italy remains an important manufacturing centre and products made in Italy are still a sign of our success. Factories and

work, though, have taken on a different form. The large Fordist businesses have imploded under the weight of their inflexibility and rising costs, because the permissive condition of low working costs was undermined by the great battles fought from the late 1960s onwards. This is mirrored, on the other hand, by the renewed liveliness of the constellation of small firms: their dissemination has been the basis of growth in the areas of the northeastern Italy and they have often even become industrial districts. In recent years, particularly in the provinces with the oldest industrialisation in the northeast, there have come to the fore many medium-sized firms mainly aimed at international markets. In any case, the communities' life no longer runs to the sound of factory sirens as happened in the past. From this point of view the situation in Milan seems paradigmatic. The old industrial outskirts have given way to a new vibrant, multifaceted situation influenced by the city's increasing service sectors. And the place of one of the great work-cathedrals, Pirelli, has been taken over by a new town of knowledge workers trained by universities and research centres. While, to limit ourselves to another well-known example, to the south of the industrial area that extended from around the port of Genoa and the coordinates of which were centred on via Tortona and via Stendhal, there has been created one of the most fashionable areas of the city, one which is internationally famous in the worlds of art, fashion and design.

The post-Fordist development has various aspects, all equally elusive. In some of the old textile areas the crisis has led to a molecular kind of capitalism which, even if in a miniaturised form, has maintained some of their old manufacturing practices: in Turin the decline of Fiat has in part been counterbalanced by automotive growth; such other industrial centres as Sesto San Giovanni seem to have firmly set out on a conversion to service industries. The large factories built at the

beginning of the last century either no longer exist or, at most, just manage to survive while waiting to be demolished or reconverted into more money-spinning buildings. But this is not only a question of equipment and machinery. The workers disappeared together with the factories or, perhaps more simply, they have another profile. In any case, they have lost both their voice and their visibility.

To many the eclipse of factory work has opened up the possibility of a life that is new and that was unthinkable in the old world; for others it has meant a loss of identity and reference points. Fragmentation and individualism are the hallmarks of a present that obliges us to rethink the hierarchies inherited from the "work century" and try to find new parameters for defining the stratifications of a society that has suddenly become opaque. The very process of accumulating riches no longer seems to happen in well-defined places such as those erstwhile factories, the rhythm of which punctuated individual and community existence and conditioned behaviour, expectations and desires.

The great concentrations of work places have been dispersed. The homogeneity of the working class has been replaced by groups of figures who cannot always be identified in executive work categories: the integration of functions caused by the externalisation of working and services means that today whole areas, and not just in subsidiary services, have been subcontracted to third parties. The small firms which, even at the beginning of the 1970s, still seemed to be the heritage of Italian slowness in catching up with more robust economies, have revealed themselves to be an amazing resource for an increasingly molecular capitalism, one capable of flexibly moulding its structures to the needs of the market and the possibilities offered by new digital technologies and synthetic materials. Work often remains boring and these firms have not always been up to scratch, as we dis-

cover from news items about noxious conditions and accidents; but today they are mostly situated in places that no longer have many of the characteristics of the old factories, even if they are in fact miniature factories. We can make no generalisations about a situation consisting of thousands of small factories; but if we want to map out an ideal type of industrial work, then we can say that a less rigid organisation of work has replaced an obsessive control of time, that the silence of numerically controlled machines or the hum of PCs has replaced the scream of metal and the noise of machinery, that rarefaction has taken the place of density, and clear hierarchical demarcation lines have been replaced by tasks where it is not always easy to distinguish between planning and managerial functions and executive ones, though we find the former in its purest and most impersonal form in certain new situations such as call-centres. As Aris Accornero points out, in post-Fordism there is still a lot of the old Fordism: "It is enough to think of most call-centres or the Carrefour stores, or else of the fact that fatigue is being reduced but accidents are not."

Of course, in the face of the growing aggression of those developing countries grouped together under the acronym BRICS, and in that of the greater innovative trends of other economies, we must ask ourselves if the current productive system is able to ensure the development of a community of 60 million individuals and their growing need for services and comfort. Certain data seem to confirm the worries of those who, like Luciano Gallino, underline the risks implicit in the disappearance of large businesses in key sectors. The country is not growing because it is being crushed by the increasing weight of its contradictions. Unemployment among the young has reached dramatic levels and the younger generation's relationship with work tends to be increasingly uncertain and chancy. However, to represent things in these terms, which undoubtedly contain a part of the truth and are indubitably worrying, risks not being much help for understanding and interpreting the country's economic vitality. Medium-sized businesses have emerged from the plethora of small firms aiming at international markets; above all, recent research into the competitiveness of Italian industry has clearly shown that size is becoming less and less the key to an understanding of an industrial organisation developed along horizontal lines, lines leading to sophisticated networks of relations within which productive functions and service functions are difficult to tell apart. This is an extremely lively situation, one able to follow the crest of the wave and to resist the impact of the crisis. Even if today we look at the future with growing preoccupation, there is well-founded reason to believe that the end of history and labour is still a distant prospect, even if the dynamics and modes of organisation will be profoundly different to those we inherited from the last century.

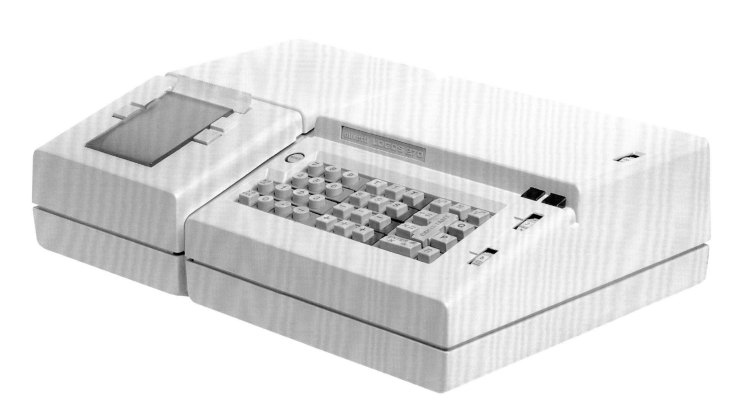

The Context
of Innovation

Nicola Zanardi

Come inventare? [How to Invent] is the name of a useful book published in 1925 by the engineer Giambrocono who worked in the international patents office in Naples.

Grammatica della fantasia ovvero Introduzione all'arte di inventare storie [The Grammar of Imagination or an Introduction to the Art of Inventing Stories] is a book written in 1973 by Gianni Rodari that was far more popular and famous than its predecessor.

Much of Italian production linked to innovation and creativity was concentrated, even in terms of time, between these apparently distant watersheds.

The engineer's popular books include other titles on the theme of invention, even including *Ciò che bisogna ancora disegnare* [What Still Needs to Be Designed], which was written in Naples, a city whose adoptive citizen, Benedetto Croce, was an Italian reference point. It is a learned and lively city, knowledgeable in the art of making-do and other strategies, of social defence which are often and wrongly identified with the commedia dell'arte figure of Pulcinello. Naples at the time was itself a reference point for united Italy and made a great contribution with its intellectuals and leaders in know-how. A few years ago, Roberto Saviano in his most famous book, amazed many people when he underlined the Neapolitan talent for creating fashion; this a quality, and not just a manual one, that goes back centuries but has been buried under clichés and forgotten by Italians and, perhaps, even by Neapolitans themselves.

The first key to Italian design in the "brief century" is autarchy, generated by economic backwardness and a genetic lack of resources increased by the sanctions against Italy after its invasion of Ethiopia in 1935. And because in our country we make a virtue out of necessity, the concept of autarchy became a genuine economic strategy with an official government statement on March 23, 1936.

The scarcity of resources, from raw materials to tools, was the pre-condition of a development that, immediately after the war, was organised both at an individual and a collective level.

The second key was the young age of Italians. Two world wars in the first half of the century had left all humanity, and not just Italy, with a young world, full of hopes, expectations and the desire to reconstruct a new planet in its own image. However, our country stands out, on the one hand, for its sharper individualist vocation and, on the other, for a sense of sharing and community that are the subtle thread running through the period.

Our well-known technical and manual ability (of the workers) was united to often isolated figures whose genius and knowledge would make this ability become the protagonist of sectors lying outside its history and DNA such as chemistry, the steel industry, domestic appliances and various areas of light industry.

It was in this period that a kind of industrial humanism, one that has recently been evoked once more, sowed seeds that, above all in the 1950s and early 1960s, were to mature to capitalise on and increase the skills of the workers and impart a vision to businessmen, or at least some of them.

Rodari's book is a small instruction booklet for how to invent stories for children and/or to help them to invent stories for themselves; according to the author, "it was also written for those who believe that it is necessary for imagination to have its rightful place in education". It was published more or less at the end of twenty years in which the highest concentration of inventiveness (or creativity or talent) in the history of modern Italy, and of innovation and its direct applications, had passed from the planning stage to that of realisation.

It was no accident that the author felt a need to train the new generations and formalise a kind of method, even if with the discretion and minimalism typical of his sensibility, as though the post-war spirit had been finally exhausted.

By mentioning Gianni Rodari I do not intend to go beyond my subject but to expand into other disciplines different from that flood of talent, widespread abilities and applied intelligence – not yet a culture in an academic sense – which from the post-war period onwards increased in quality and quantity. And if design was considered for some time as a subspecies of architecture – and some great architects were undoubtedly genuine masters – it is equally true that a generation of multidisciplinary figures gave form and content to industrial needs ranging from publishing to all kinds of manufacturing; we need only mention Bruno Munari, Silvio Ceccato, Albe Steiner, Roberto Sambonet and Italo Lupi as examples.

The system of design based on Milan, for example, grouped together many kinds of knowledge and cultures. The masters of design dealt with the "thinking hands" of artisans; the area around Milan produced what the city projected and promoted, in a kind of soft fade-out from one sector to another with blurred outlines where it is not always possible to distinguish designers from producers, or prototype-makers and woodworkers from assemblers. The whole world was attracted to this mixture; some were business experts at times looking only for a single part of the process, others were attracted by the unique shop window that is the Milan furniture fair.

One heavyweight figure stands out in the panorama of patented innovations and the grammar of imagination: Adriano Olivetti. Although usually considered an industrialist, Olivetti theorised and put into practice an idea of the community which involved the all the various components and protagonists of an industrial chain, one which was already linked to people in the academic system with great gifts for applications. This was the most interesting example

of Italian-made production that attempted to offer an active role to those with ability and talent and, generally, to all those who work, respecting their inclinations, dignity and knowledge.

Olivetti's experimental approach was applied as much to his buildings as to organisational models, to the concept of a factory as the recipient for profit, one where investments, remuneration and services for the workers and the territory came before the dividends for the shareholders. A business without innovative capacity does not exist and innovative capacity does not exist without a vision of industry that makes a profit to be used according the principles just outlined. In his most important book, *La città dell'uomo* [The City of Man], Olivetti started from universal concepts: beauty, love, truth and justice are the bases for progress. And throughout history these elements have remained the most lively testimony to the sustainability of civilisation. A sustainability that is, above all, the handing down of knowledge, even more than physical assets, to the following generations.

The advance from typewriters to electronics began just after the war. Differently from the American system, where military expenses were the real driving force for progress, the Olivetti company was rooted in the civilian world, one deeply interwoven with academic knowledge and with an *ante litteram* global vision.

The person who suggested studying electronics closely was the Nobel Prize winner Enrico Fermi, who had learned much from his experiences in America. In his last trips to Italy before his death in Chicago, Fermi backed this innovative strategy, one that was unusual for Italy, and indicated – and actually wrote – the path towards electronic calculators. This was a proposal apparently far beyond the reach of Italian industry but one which, however, found in Olivetti a fertile and attentive humus: with his many and varied collaborators he had the bases for constructing an Italian road to innovation characterised by many interconnected disciplines and vision, by planning and many integrated cultures, with techniques and talents also derived from deep-rooted and refined artisan skills. It should not be overlooked that, in the midst of so many engineers, Adriano Olivetti's closest collaborator was the literary critic Geno Pampaloni, that relationships with the personnel were entrusted to such writers as Paolo Volponi and Ottiero Ottieri, and that such poets and writers as Giovanni Giudici and Franco Fortini worked in the communications office. Humanists and engineers, writers and a variety of professional figures were the terrain in which the first Italian calculator originated. In 1952, Adriano's brother Dino Olivetti managed an electronics research centre in Connecticut, and by 1954 the Olivetti Corporation was on the lookout throughout the world for people with talent. Among these the most well-known was to be Mario Tchou, a Sino-Italian who was convinced to come back to Italy to direct the firm's newly created electronics division in Ivrea.

The Elea 9003 also originated from the extremely courageous choice to abandon valves and replace them with transistors. This decision was backed up by the creation of a new company for producing semiconductor circuits. Together with Telelettra and Fairchild, Olivetti founded the Società Generale Semiconduttori SGS, the first European industry for integrated circuits and today a world leader, though now sadly American-owned. The name of the Elea calculator (*elaboratore elettronico automatico*, or automatic electric elaborator) was also inspired by the name of an ancient Greek colony in Cilento, in the province of Salerno. The school of Elea, and its inspiring spirit Parmenides, had a deeply rational philosophy, one that matched the first calculator that could undertake operations for various users at the same time and that was designed for industrial production. And the person who actually gave shape to this object was Ettore Sottsass

Junior, an architect and designer who was to remain a leader in the field of innovation until his death a few years ago. For many this was the first calculator in the world. Certainly it was one of the first, and undoubtedly the first completely transistorised computer to be marketed commercially.

The multidisciplinary approach, which was adopted by many others over the years, not least by Edgar Morin with his "Well-made Head", was to be found again in the large and well-equipped Borgolombardo laboratory near Milan where there worked side by side mathematicians, physicists, philosophers and various others, obviously not all of them Italian. It was to have two thousand employees with a biodiversity of thought that today we find in the great world groups who are making the history of info-sciences. When Olivetti died of a heart attack in 1960, a series of never fully clarified events, and the absence of an industrial policy, meant that the company ended up in the hands of an Italian public-private group which, in 1964, sold off the electronics sector to General Electric. In fact, the group's scientific research was not considered of interest by its shareholders.

However, Italian biodiversity was to give us a second part of this story of men and innovation with the first personal computer in the world. In 1964, an ex-collaborator of Mario Tchou, Pier Giorgio Perotto, who worked at the Turin Polytechnic with a group interested in aerodynamics, went back to work for what remained of the Olivetti company which had gone back to its mechanical roots, as insisted on by the shareholders. Helped by a select group of visionaries, and fostered by Roberto Olivetti, Perotti elaborated a project for a machine that could satisfy the needs for the great calculating potential that had emerged from aerodynamic studies.

Once again the heterogenesis of the aims led to a brilliant product: Programma 101, the first programmable desktop computer in the world. Nicknamed the Perottina, it was designed by Mario Bellini, another young Italian designer who is still working today with international success. The model was extremely popular in America, above all in academic circles and in those of high-level craftsmanship. It was only later that its potential would also be grasped by the small and medium-sized industries system. The American press defined it as the first, authentic personal computer in the world. A success confirmed by the 45,000 pieces sold. In 1967, Hewlett-Packard gave nine hundred thousand dollars compensation to Olivetti after having copied the patent on which the P-101 was based for some of its machines. And all this ten years before the two Steves, Jobs and Wozniac, created Apple, great design objects and, above all, interfaces made for mankind. If Olivetti represents the acme of Italian excellence, the result of vision and application, there are certainly other examples of industries based on a synthesis of progress and culture.

Even the RAI, at the time the driving force behind the promotion of literacy in Italy, had enormous talent working for it, ranging from the 63 group to stubborn independents. However, the centre of gravity for research and innovation was to be found in the study offices in La Rinascente, Pirelli and Eni. The provinces became the starting point for arriving in Rome, cosmopolitan and down-to-earth, refined and artistically fruitful, or else in Milan, a centre that put in order and demonstrated a system of skills with a catchment area covering most of northern Italy.

Design, in the Italian sense, originated from scarcity, from resourcefulness, but also from working together, from the territory, from a world that created in harmony. Today open-source models teach us that to cooperate is to compete. This is not unlike the territories (now called districts) of the past.

This approach to work sees the breakdown of barriers between

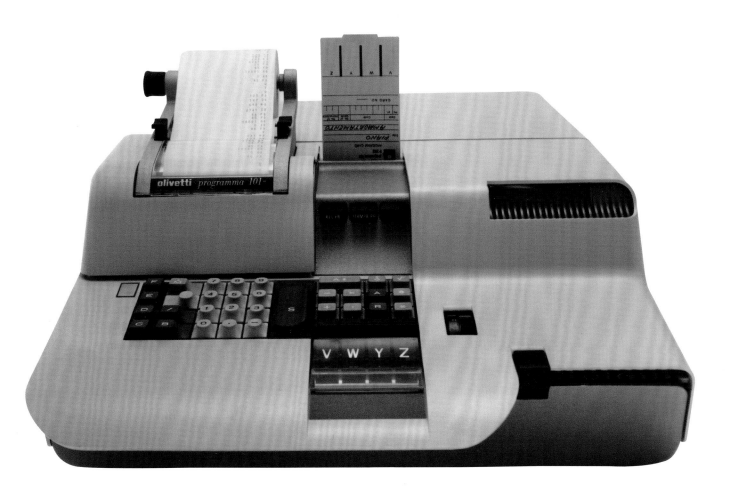

knowledge and know-how, between basic research and its application, between pure and applied art. This is a scenario that Bruno Munari, a great creator, has theorised in many unusual and fascinating books.

Knowing how to do something, a real immaterial value, becomes the impulse for applications and products by coming into contact with academic knowledge in a kind of Italian laboratory that today would have little to fear from areas of digital knowledge and production.

Robert Putnam, in *Making Democracy Work*, says that the social and civil capital of the area between the river Po and the Alps has a long history stretching back to the Italy of city-states. Here I have no space for analysing today's districts and territories for which there already exists a competent and extensive literature, but only for considering how to combine the ingredients that I listed earlier, together with others, in a perspective view.

Innovation in the third millennium means doing three things: metabolising the quality and quantity of various areas of knowledge; putting them in order and making a selection; and above all applying them more or less creatively. Are we able to do this? Are we able to dominate and channel that impetuous river of knowledge that the bio, info and nano sciences increase daily in forms that are far more accessible to us all than in the past?

Potentially, yes. We have all the cultural and cognitive characteristics for governing at least a part of the whole process. This is not an admission of weakness: to cover the niches in a global world means a lot in itself.

Italian planning and, above all, applicative ability exists and is part of Italy's DNA, as we have seen. In 2008, a famous American sociologist, Richard Sennett, published his book *The Craftsman* in which he placed at the centre of the productive world people and their skills, and he asked himself how the connections between the mind-hand-desire-reason can function.

In all these years our country, or at least certain areas of it, has become a leader in, for example, contracting, i.e. the ability to set up and realise projects or parts of projects that require dedicated skills and, at the same time, a great deal of flexibility. From hotels to skyscrapers, from furnishing to assembling. Who if not our artisans, from Friuli down to Sicily, and who are increasingly specialised and technologically prepared, can work to schedule and deliver the quality requested in these sectors? In Monfalcone we are building the largest ships in the world, and our advantage does not just derive from the necessary infrastructures but also from the skills of over a thousand people ranging from technicians to artisans and specialised professionals who simplify the high quality work produced by the country. These contents, industrial humanism's genuine software, are all too often taken for granted.

And then there are models that are the outcome of local visions and have, at the same time, a global character. For example, the Terra Madre and Eataly projects are the latest way of managing activities that are difficult to establish in such categories as Slow Food. Are they a movement, an association, a community, or a network of networks? Terra Madre evaluates the know-how and skill of thousands of modest farm and agricultural workers throughout the world. This is, deep down, one of the possible answers to the "long tail theory" of Chris Anderson, the founder of "Wired". Those working on a small scale can live. They must have a content and visibility in the world. And today such a hypothesis is possible, as is its verification, thanks to the web. You are more likely to find your own niche among a billion people online than with your neighbours.

Eataly, on the other hand, is a way of interpreting business where a

recuperation of our high quality food heritage and biodiversity has been established while keeping prices accessible. For this reason it at once became popular with the market, at all levels, as well as with institutions. Various large towns and cities have set aside areas and specific places for it. This is an example of an Italian-made business that insists on the excellence of Italian food and is already to be found in Tokyo and New York: a synthesis of projects that underlines the contemporaneity of an Italy with deep roots and sustainable talent.

There are sectors in which our innovation continues to have a predominant role throughout the world. Tool mechanics, for example. Or robotics. Then there are others that seem immaterial but which in fact have great potential. A welfare model for one of the two oldest populations in the world forces us to redesign the whole process for what once was called "old age pensioners". A society that finds it difficult to increase, with the growing side-effect of inequality, has more and more need to design social services worthy of its civilisation.

Planning and innovation, even for service models and not just products, will be basic to the third or non-profit sector, a crucial sector for the beginning of the millennium in mature countries and economies.

In a society of knowledge one of its central assets is to connect up professionalism and applicative segments. The other is to have the necessary flexibility for allowing a migration of experience. Design competences, for example, will be increasingly shifted, even systematically so, into public and public/private fields. Health-care models, for example, will be formed to ensure efficiency and efficacy so as to follow people through the diagnostic and preventative stages even before there is any necessity for a cure. Technologies will have a central role but their management, often in real time, still has to be planned, at least outside health centres which are increasingly spe-

cialised in important operations but where convalescence is only for the shortest necessary time.

Planning and innovation are closely intertwined. And they consist of many areas of competence. Humanistic studies, so little considered in the 1980s and 1990s, are coming back into consideration in the very decade of science. Will there be a discipline that will drive the next decade? There doesn't seem to be one on the horizon. Bridging (the creation of bridges between one discipline and another) or direction (today in the uncertain hands of politicians) are still not considered multidisciplinary subjects with specifics to be created ad hoc. To put together areas of knowledge and competence without a specific home base is the real challenge. In the 1990s, the world went mad for "containers" and it wasn't by chance that we had superstars who were often asked to provide a content. At the beginning of the third millennium, the sciences, also thanks to technology, are central and have a pervasive notoriousness, at times coming up against the logics of profit which seem to change constantly. At the crossroads of bio, info and nano sciences we are creating bottlenecks that, in order to be cleared, need many kinds of knowledge but also important decisions and choices. Perhaps ethics might become the genuine raw material of a project for the third millennium. We are on the threshold of utopias which, however, have always had something in common with projects.

Italian Domesticity

Franco La Cecla

Two brilliant Swedish anthropologists, Billy Ehn and Orvar Löfgren, have devoted a book to *The Secret World of Doing Nothing* (University of California Press, 2010). The book is subdivided into three parts: "Waiting", "Routines" and "Daydreaming". The theory of the two anthropologists – the second of the two is the author of a magnificent *History of Holidays* published a few years ago in Italy by Bruno Mondadori – is that a genuine civilisation is distinguished by its capacity to invent ways of doing nothing in order to make life, not a continual race towards something, but a way of feeling and experiencing the present. The book is full of anecdotes, stories and tales of normal and less normal people, but something you would expect from two anthropologists is missing. They do not say that there are cultures which, more than others, are able to exploit this "dolce far niente". So it does not offer a comparative approach, which is a pity because had they done so it would have helped us to understand, for example, why the expression "dolce far niente" is written in Italian in most languages. "Dolce far niente" is the way in which Italians are still seen by both a large part of the English-speaking world and by French speakers, as an ineradicable characteristic of our culture. To loaf about, kill time, loiter, lounge around and dawdle over various pastimes; but there is also jawing, hanging around bars, "taking your own time". Paul Feyerabend, the great Viennese philosopher of science who deeply loved Italian culture, gave his autobiography the title *Killing Time*. So let's try to explain what the two Swedes do not mention: there are cultures, and the Italian culture is one of them, that are better than others at creating a system of approaches, taking time slowly, managing everyday space, and relating dreams and wakefulness that create a domesticated world that makes life bearable and even pleasant. Another anthropologist, Mary Douglas, asked in a 1991 essay (*The Idea of Home: a Kind of Space*, in "Social Research", 58,

n. 1, pp. 288-307) what it is that defines a home. It is not, she suggests, a building with four walls, but an internal order of rules, habits and rhythms. The domestic sphere is above all a series of routines based on silent agreements, and of unconscious thoughts about the way in which "we do things here". Whoever is a part of it learns to survive on waking up or during a stressful morning, to conserve food in the fridge, look after the linen and much, much more.

This kind of domesticity has been, and still is in part, a typically Italian experience. A know-how that consists of invading areas that are public rather than private with our own domesticity. This is why Italians invented a way of colonising space that has made them distinguishable everywhere: that way of allowing the private to seep into the public sphere that is represented by placing chairs outside the front door, the display of merchandise by the greengrocer, the use of the pavements, streets and squares as though they were life's domestic setting. This, for example, is what we find in the "Little Italies", those neighbourhoods where Italian immigration took root from the end of the 19th century until the 1970s. But it is the same noisy, vivacious colonisation that we still find in streets and alleyways, in uproar and rumpus, in doorways and avenues, and which is lost when Italian towns aim at having a European look. Here, though, we have to make things clear: the Italian domesticity that invades public space does so not because we mean "private" in the British sense of "privacy", an activity defined by privation. Italian domesticity is a system of habits, of ways of doing, of waiting, of the practice of doing and not doing, all of which are a form of representation or, rather, of self-representation. Italians conceive of theatre and daily life not as being separate but as a space-time continuum that starts at the kitchen table and ends with the workplace or the town square. Unless we grasp this attitude we miss a great deal of Italian domestic culture and, with it, the ability to "make a home" that marks out our taste, from the construction of objects for everyday life to that of manners and fashions, clothes, postures, ways of appearing and ways of being comfortable.

In many Mediterranean cultures, habits are a form of ascetic practice. Islam, for example, defines them in this way; but even in the Mediterranean Judeo-Christian world we find its own athletics and ethics. Without habits there is no normal life, a "holy" life, because habits mark out time and subject it to the civilisation of being. This is what Peter Sloterdijk says in his very intelligent book *You Must Change your Life*. Sloterdijk states quite clearly that all religions, but also all beliefs, are based on the idea that mankind's body and soul are malleable and that, in order to improve, they must be subjected to repetitive practices because only in this way can they adopt as "natural" something that at first was not. All savoir faire, the capacity to do things, the arts of living, nonchalance and self-control, all the elegance of posture, all the aesthetics of daily life are "practices" that are adopted for athletic and ascetic exercise. Routines are a way of transforming the nebulous magma of everyday life into a rhythm, a game of draughts or chess with life.

In all this, Italian popular history, the history of how people have created the space that we call Italy, is exemplary. To describe the way in which we have learnt over the centuries, and relearn in personal life, how to "feel" the present is to purge "dolce far niente" of its senselessness. (and then why purge it, given that senselessness is part of a deep, aesthetic, relativist judgement about the value of things?)

What kind of taste and comfort is needed to leave home, to slowly enjoy the existence of the bar round the corner, the quips exchanged with the newspaper seller, a walk over to the greengrocer or charcuterie, an activity that it would be blasphemous to call shopping (in

fact we are dealing with something far more efficacious: we are dealing with a reaffirmation of the values of the social intercourse which lies at the heart of commercial exchanges)? What capacity for waiting do we need to enjoy the difficulties of waiting for buses or trams that are forever late, traffic jams, commuters' waiting? And yet all these moments are "profitable" because they create a micro-environment in which to enjoy being there, to enjoy being there just like others "in the same boat". Even waiting in a queue at the post office, the doctor's, or the bank can be the occasion for an art of living in the world, in a culture where a remark, a comment, the prevalence of the present over the future, over the "end", are occasions for daily comedy that recall all the Goldonis and De Filippos of Italian history. Of course, it is obvious that I am only looking at the positive side of things: there are so many negative sides and, obviously, this capacity to adapt is the same one that allows Italians to put up with the many abuses of power and the arrogance and haughtiness of the corrupt. But what I am interested in bringing to light is that this "Italian domesticity" is the source of an aesthetic of the everyday. Italian "dolce far niente" is a beautiful "doing nothing", the ability, that is, to appreciate the beauty of the suspension of time in the normal rhythm of occupying the space next door, the balcony, the street corner, the distance to the underground station. This aesthetic manages to "colonise" urban space and transform it into a habitable place where it is possible to have a consistency, to make a home and remain there. As soon as we find ourselves in another culture, we Italians become conscious of what we are missing: that treatment of everyday space as something that is not only annoyance and defence, a closure inside the cage of our own body and an avoidance of others: Italian civil space is a domestic one; there is no fear of that rarefaction typical of the public spaces in American towns or in the French suburbs. This is

why it is a tragedy and a scandal that architects and administrators have not given an answer to this Italian attitude but have forced the Italians to live in neighbourhoods seen in glossy English and American magazines and aped from the 1970s onwards. In Paris, an Italian is amazed that the people on the streets do not know how to let others pass by, that they do not have the adaptability to walk without bumping into you, that fish-like approach that makes even urban traffic in Italy different to that of other cities in the world. Italians keep each other company in any case, even if at times the company is neither looked for nor wanted. And they keep company with their chatter, quips, questions and answers, sly glances, and the switch between Italian and dialect (to even consider reinstating dialects as exclusive local language does a disservice to Italian intelligence, which has always played on and with the comic effects of slipping between one and the other). I believe that there is nothing more representative of Italian domesticity's ability to "chatter" than its difference from French conversation, its noting down with comments, hesitations, its ability to say nothing while using words as a veil to acoustically separate the physical space of people. That sound of various people who talk and laugh, that repetition of such interjections as "so, right, exactly, in fact, well then, altogether, however, on the other hand…"
This is why the space of a neighbourhood or a village, those four streets that are the fulcrum of a life of relationships, is so pleasurable – as long as it is not claimed that this is everything: this is when it becomes dangerous provincialism. But provincialism is an aberration of domesticity, a withdrawal into itself, a loss of elasticity and sharpness. This habit develops capacities that are not, however, only reserved for the "in-crowd" and the clan. The interesting thing about Italian domesticity is that it is used to assimilate, to welcome the unfamiliar, and turn strangers into potential confidants: perhaps nothing is more in-

dicative of this capacity than the play of glances, halfway between curiosity and receptiveness, that you still find in Italian everyday life. You "look", you look a lot, but with the idea of exchanging looks, not with a smile – which anglophone cultures might consider as a pacifying gesture – but with a look which answers with equal curiosity.

This power of assimilation has made the Italian presence abroad highly acceptable and today could make the arrival of foreigners in Italy something for teaching others about our domesticity. Various Mediterranean peoples know this well; Tunisians and Moroccans know it, but so do the Filipinos and Sri Lankans, who have taken on our ways (just walk around the local markets or our souks in Palermo, Naples or Bari).

In Banana Yoshimoto's novel, *Kitchen*, she tells the story of a girl on her own – we are not told why she is on her own – who finds acceptance and security in the hum and buzz of the fridge a way to be accepted and defended: she finds a domestic space that allows her to interpret her own loneliness. Of course, Italian culture is not the only one to have built a system of domesticity. Japan is an eloquent example: even with all the chaos of modernity and the post-war changes of the Japanese cities, the domestic space that overflows into semi-public space has remained intact with the system of roji gardens, and the alleys behind the houses and skyscrapers that increase the density of the spreading neighbourhood spaces. And today, after the great tsunami, it is this capacity to inhabit and re-inhabit that gives us the hope that Japan will not rise again as a mere shadow of itself but will find the composition of its social space once again. I mention this in order to point out that Italy does not have a monopoly on domesticity, but that domesticity is a different kind of globalisation. It is the repetition of the universal values of domesticity, it is what makes a film by Ozu or Naruse remind us of a film by De Sica or a play by De Filippo.

So let's get back to the triad defined by the two Swedish anthropologists: waiting, routines and daydreaming. The third of these is perhaps the most elusive, and if there is one that defines our country's creative crisis it is this. Italians have stopped being dreamers and have become gross materialists and, like all gross materialists, they become losers when faced by reality because this is certainly not made from material. It is a place for ideas, imaginings, of thinking and moving ahead. We are among the countries with the greatest number of patents, a country where the most isolated artisan or some distant pensioner has applied themselves to the invention of scooters, pumps, glues, funnels, gears, and solutions to other problems with the same doggedness as people who go to the tobacconist to buy a scratch card. Perhaps the Italy of the devious and guileful has destroyed the Italy of the creative minds. What need is there for brains in a country where only guile and cunning are rewarded? And yet using your wits is the same as what elsewhere I have called "concentration".

"Concentration" is not only a question of wits being applied to a precise situation. It is, instead, the kind of knowledge of a context that comes about only after being familiarised at length with the context; even more, it is the kind of thing that is shaped by a relationship to a very particular spatial context. As was well understood by Salvatore Settis who, in his latest book about the ruinous flooding of Italy with concrete, *Paesaggio costituzione cemento. La battaglia per l'ambiente contro il degrado civile* (Turin, Einaudi, 2010), took up the term "concentration". Concentration is the capacity acquired for defining and being defined by remaining and living in a place. Italian domesticity is a corollary of this: it is the subtle pleasure of discovering that the surrounding space is something that can be used as an affective tool to widen your own ability to give meaning to things and, at the same time, to grasp the meaning of the things around you.

It is by starting from here that we can begin again to use the world, an Italian use that is neither vulgar nor uncouth, that readapts popular and intelligent refinement to Italian production. It is in Italian concentration and its ability to make a home in the world, in understating our skill and competence, in an idea sparked off by habit, in the irony of overturning solutions in order to find new ones, in the Italian genius for paradox, in handling that is transformed into a creative gesture: it is in all this that we must search for the future of our country. It is a difficult yet fascinating transition, one from which we hope the new generations might learn more from the geographical or climatic context, from the natural and constructed beauty that surrounds them, than from their parents. But usually this is what the young, if they really *are* young, know how to do.

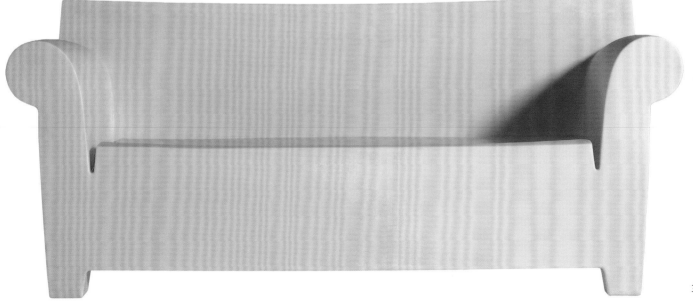

Returning to Nineteen Sixty

Alberto Saibene

Come back, come back to nineteen hundred and sixty!*

In a radio conversation with Francesco Savio, Steno (Stefano Vanzina, father of Carlo and Enrico), albeit rather uncertainly, claimed the paternity of the expression "white telephones" which was used to indicate a certain kind of elegant cinema with an unreal setting – the stories were often set in Hungary – and which absorbed the Italians who dreamt of earning "a thousand lira a month" so as to do "a lot of shopping". And one of the best films of the time was *I grandi magazzini* (*Department Store*, 1939) by Mario Camerini; in this film the new middle classes were taken by the hand and shown, through the adventures of the young Vittorio De Sica, the seven floors of an emporium (modelled on La Rinascente). Here, while extolling the virtues of "first class homemade Italian textiles", the real aim of the director and scriptwriters (amongst whom was Mario Pannunzio) seems to have been to bring our cinema and bourgeoisie up-to-date with models from over the Alps.

With the war still underway, Roberto Rossellini's film *Paisà* (1945) followed the American army as it made its way up the peninsula from Sicily to the north, and showed a poor, rustic, ruined Italy coming up against the victors' material culture: jeeps, chocolate, packets of cigarettes, corned beef, nylons. A revolutionary contagion, one pregnant

---

* This is a tribute to *La pronipote di nonna Speranza* by Paolo Viti Finzi (Milan, Ceschina, 1961) which began like this: "The living room with a balcony, the Burri painting with rags,/ the wall with blue rectangles and a few orange trapezes/ the bristly tinfoil sculpture that wavers lopsidedly at every step/ the many fake Picasso's of his second period/ the baroque print with *cupio dissolvi* between skulls and bones/ rather weedy stools, chairs like hipbaths/ the low crouching armchairs that seem strange toads/ the new and rather audacious books on the brass bookshelves/ Miller... Gênet... Peyrefitte... the bar with the glowing liqueurs/ still and upright like soldiers on parade/ the fat exotic plant with thorns all around it... / My heart, come back, come back to nineteen hundred and sixty!"

with consequences that has never ceased nourishing literary memoirs (Malaparte, Parise, Moravia) and everyday life. If, however, we are obliged to choose a single object to define the post-war period, then this would have to be *Ladri di biciclette* (*Bycicle Thieves*, 1948) by Vittorio De Sica, above all in the scene of the Piazza Umberto market where a whole economy is based on the most widespread and necessary means of transport of the time: bicycles. The Americans went home, but the objects were destined to remain: the jeeps used by Scelba's flying squad in many post-war films; Silvana Mangano's nylon stockings in *Riso amaro* (*Bitter Rice*, 1948) by Giuseppe De Santis; the smuggled American cigarettes – not oysters! – that were a source of earning, according to Totò in Steno's *Totò a colori* (*Toto in Color*, 1952). But it was an American film that revealed a new Italy to the world: Gregory Peck and Audrey Hepburn on a Vespa along the streets of Rome remain unforgettable in Wlliam Wyler's *Roman Holiday* (1953).

And it was around a television store, where the affairs of *Poveri ma belli* (*A Girl in Bikini / Poor, But Handsome*) took place (1956), that Dino Risi revealed a sharp generational change, with youngsters in jeans, on Lambrettas and who danced to early rock and roll in front of their amazed parents. In the late winter of 1957, Richard W. Boogart, an American businessman, wandered around Milan in search of a space of some 7-8,000 square metres where he wanted to open the first Italian supermarket (which would lead to the Italian Supermercati which then became Esselunga), while just in time there arrived in Italian bookshops *The Hidden Persuaders* (1958) by Vance Packard and *The Affluent Society* (1959) by Kenneth Galbraith. A society with peasant roots, one in which saving was a basic value – Titina De Filippo was the pinchpenny landlady in *Totò, Peppino e i fuorilegge* (1956) by Camillo Mastrocinque – and a middle class with a still eighteenth-century system of values and behaviour (there are illuminating cartoons by Novello published at the time in "La Stampa") ruined by a bloodless yet profound revolution that was to transform the (new) town dweller into a consumer.

Even if well-known, the data framing the economic boom are still very impressive. Here are some figures for the 1958-1963 period: 10,000 washing machines produced in 1958, 1,263,000 in 1963; fridges went from an annual production of 370,000 to 1.5 million; car production increased fivefold as the construction of the Autostrada del Sole got underway. National earnings doubled between 1954 and 1964; in the same period three million people moved from the countryside to the city.

This was a change that remixed the geography and history of Italian unity, but above all the change in mentality was so fast that only a means such as film can today allow us to comprehend it. These were the greatest years of Italian cinema: Fellini, Antonioni, Visconti and De Sica together with Germi, Rosi, Risi, Lattuada, Comencini, Pietrangeli and Ferreri were all active, and Olmi, Bertolucci, Pasolini and Montaldo, to name but a few, were the rising generation. An unrepeatable time in which directors, scriptwriters, workers, costume designers, set designers and film editors gave life to a period of collective art and held a mirror (often a deformed one) up to our national life as well as being a means for unifying the language and customs. For an infinity of reasons – not the least that of being seen by two million people – *La dolce vita* (1960) is the most important film of the period and the first sign of an anthropological change in Italy. What characterised the film were the sunglasses worn by many of the protagonists (even at the night), the informal clothing and the Olivetti Lettera 22 typewriter that Mastroianni used while outdoors. One of

the constant factors of life in the via Veneto was life in the open air and the wispered use of plastic for chairs, tables and ashtrays. The setting recreated with the greatest care was the home of Steiner, the intellectual, where he explained the qualities of a painting by Morandi to Marcello Mastroianni. It was Pier Paolo Pasolini who suggested the use of this Bolognese painter in order to make the living room more realistic. Film critics of the time were divided between Fellini and Michelangelo Antonioni who, in *La notte* (1961), mirrored Milan in the windows of the Pirelli skyscraper which was shown more as a design object than as a mere building. The last part of the film, set in a recently built villa in Brianza, shows how the nouveau riche (the very ones that Camilla Cederna skewered in the pages of "L'Espresso") were finally ready to free themselves from the need to legitimate themselves through tradition – in this case an antique piece of furniture that represented their link to nobility – in an age that no longer believed in the past as a value. The birth of mass society and its needs was captured as it was happening by *I mostri* (*15 from Rome / Opiate '67*, 1963) by Dino Risi, a film in which the acquisition of a Fiat 600 was a moment to be shared with the whole family, just as the television set was supplanting the radio (and the piano even earlier) as the centrepiece of middle class families.

Also by Risi were various "seaside" films, such as *Il sorpasso* (*The Easy Life*, 1962) or *L'ombrellone* (*Weekend, Italian Style*, 1965) where we see a whole series of objects (Spiders, plastic toys, portable radios, clothes made from new light materials) that, together with recent buildings, resulted in new kinds of behaviour. A still underrated masterpiece is *Io la conoscevo bene* (*I Knew Her Well*, 1965) by Antonio Pietrangeli, a film in which an aspiring actress (Stefania Sandrelli) is stalked by the Roman demimonde. In the first scene Sandrelli is on the beach in a bikini while she listens to songs on a transistor radio.

Just on the evidence of the images, the director shows how a new generation spoke a different language to those who were only ten years older. Later on we see the girl's parents in their home among the Pistoia mountains which is furnished with the agricultural objects of their everyday life. The effect of the boom has overturned the concept of contemporaneity: those who do not keep up to date are destined to be stuck in the past, on the edges of a society in continual modernisation. A few writers (Arbasino, Ottieri and Volponi) managed to capture this unexpected transformation, but the person who best recounted it was perhaps the writer from Grosseto, Luciano Bianciardi, who in *La vita agra* (1963) showed Milan in the boom years while it was changing before his eyes. Carlo Lizzani's film of the same name (1964) does not reach the same heights as the book, but the life of Ugo Tognazzi who, from a boarding house with a communal bathroom, goes on to rent a home and then to buy one in a "satellite neighbourhood" and with his wife, Giovanna Ralli, buys his furnishings and domestic appliances from La Rinascente, gives an amazing summary of the average Italian of the boom years. In the film, Tognazzi gives up intellectual work in order to join "a centre for mass persuasion", where he studies how to convince people to become consumers.

Already halfway through the 1960s, Italian cinema had begun to change direction. It is indicative that in *Giulietta degli spiriti* (*Juliet of the Spirits*, 1965) Fellini makes use of art nouveau décor in order to distance himself from the present and to confer a dreamlike aspect on the film, while Elio Petri in *La decima vittima* (*The 10th Victim*, 1965), the first Italian sci-fi film (script by Ennio Flaiano), used the ruins of Rome as a contrast to the futurist ambience where Marcello Mastroianni and Ursula Andress wandered in clinging suits among transparent inflatable poufs (reminiscent of the Blow armchairs designed by De Pas, D'Urbino and Lomazzi), foam rubber divans (Bastiano divans designed by Tobia Scarpa), designer armchairs and lamps (the Lambda chair by Zanuso and Sapper; the Taccia lamps by the Castiglioni brothers); on the walls were works of Op and Pop art (a comment on a period of rapid cultural updating). These were the years when children went to bed after the Carosello advertising break which was more educational than aimed at selling individual products. 1968 produced films that were more ideological than significant, with the exception of *Dillinger è morto* (*Dillinger is Dead*, 1969) by Marco Ferreri which, from an anarchical point of view, emptied the wellbeing so laboriously arrived at of its meaning. The film was shot in real locations: Mario Schifano's home with his works hung on the walls, and Ugo Tognazzi's kitchen in Torvajanica stuffed full of every luxury and where the protagonist, Michel Piccoli, prepares elaborate delicacies. The actor's lazy movements were followed around the kitchen, bedroom and living room, where he relaxed and watched TV. The consumer society has saturated every available space, even that of desires, and so the design objects on view (the Eclisse lamp, the Arco etc.) are empty copies of a world that has lost any sense of the future, as is shown by the jokey final scene when the protagonist, like Gauguin, sets out on a sailing boat for Tahiti.

In an episode in the film *Le coppie* (*Man and Wife / The Couples*, 1971), Mario Monicelli entrusts to a 189-litre fridge the function of a secular altar in the basement where Monica Vitti lives, having moved from Sardinia to Turin and who is disoriented by the shift from a subsistence economy to one of abundance. In the same film, there is a scene with Alberto Sordi where two shocked Roman grocers wander around the new and luxurious Costa Smeralda and criticise as "rustic"

(and they were not all that mistaken) the architecture and furnishing by Vietti and Busiri Vici. Class distinctions were still insuperable, as can be seen in *Durante l'estate* (*In the Summertime*, 1971) by Ermanno Olmi in which an illustrator finds himself embarrassed by Joe Colombo's Pop interior design in the house of a nouveau riche school friend. Equally well observed are the design objects (the Brionvega radio by Sapper-Zanuso, the latest hi-fi, and a gigantic armchair that caricatures the rest of the all too fashionable furnishings) in *Indagine su un cittadino al di sopra di ogni sospetto* (*Investigation of a Citizen Above Suspicion*, 1970) by Elio Petri who immersed modern objects in a Caravaggio-like chiaroscuro and furnished Florinda Bolkan's home with allusions to Art Nouveau and a "D'Annunzio style". Stylish design in the 1970s was to be found in many voguish bourgeois homes, but the new middle classes lagged behind: who doesn't remember the gag where Fracchia performs a balancing act on the shaky Sacco armchair offered to him by his nasty boss Gianni Agus? And in other films starring Paolo Villaggio great attention is always paid to status symbols (his office desk covered with pot plants) which the poor "inferiors" always and uselessly long for. The decade, buffeted by the winds of protest and a genuine change in society, had its epilogue in the alienated youngsters in *Ecce bombo* (1978) by Nanni Moretti, and in the inventor Colombo in *Ratataplan* (1979) by Maurizio Nichetti. In the former the objects are humble, often shared or reused; in the latter the risk of technological automation is resolved playfully. This unease, however, was not just limited to young directors, but was also shared by such veterans as Luigi Comencini who in *L'ingorgo* (*Traffic Jam*, 1979) portrayed the paralysis of a whole society, the prisoner of its own cars, objects which in the preceding decade were a symbol of individual liberty. The 1970s or, more in general, a whole epoch, was closed by *La terrazza* (*The Terrace*, 1980) by

Ettore Scola which showed the intellectual left as the victims of the first signs of reaction: the director Tognazzi received phone calls on a primitive cordless phone while sitting on an inflated chair in a swimming pool; together with Mastroianni, a journalist on the verge of a breakdown, he shares lonely periods watching television with a remote control as his only companion; in the meantime a disgraced official from the RAI, Serge Reggiani, loses precious office space when they install new-fangled modular mobile panels.

Television was the symbolic object of the 1980s: the move from black and white to colour and the diffusion of commercial channels multiplied the possibilities for advertising. What's more, after a decade of recession, terrorism and social clashes, there began an era of (presumed) prosperity in which collective needs became individual needs. This was the message conveyed by adverts which began to interrupt films on the television. As had happened in the past, but with more "authorality", various directors began to work for Italian brands: Zeffirelli (Pellicceria Annabella) and Fellini (the inventive advert for Campari in which two commuters on a train change the landscape seen through the window/television with a remote control). And Fellini himself, in *Ginger and Fred* (1985), made a ruthless anthropological study of the new Italians through a criticism of consumer society and in his film reinvented advertising posters and the seductive adverts for food products seen on a television set which was never turned off. In his next film, *La voce della luna* (The Voice of the Moon, 1990), against a background of newly invented village fetes, we are shocked by the excess of all kinds of merchandise with sexual undertones. The decade had begun with a revival of the myth of America, the home of individual freedom. In Marco Risi's *Vado a vivere da solo* (I'm going to Live by Myself, 1982) a twenty-six year old Jerry Calà leaves his

parents' home in order to move into a loft which he furnishes with car seats and posters of Ronald Reagan. We were now ready for *Yuppies. I giovani di successo* (Yuppies, 1986) by Carlo Vanzina where each individual and usually luxurious object defined a life-style. But the imagery of the period was captured above all by thirty-second TV adverts that ranged from Aiazzone's "palissandro furniture" to the future offered by technology, usually with alienating electronic background music ("We could have amazed you with special effects"), or, like the adverts for whisky with "Michele the connoisseur", to settings with bourgeois white divans and crystal tables. There was a sharp division between the "Milan to be drunk", where you were shown shots of contemporary Italy, and the Italy of the Mulino Bianco ads, the most powerful ideology of the time which managed to reconcile nostalgia for a rural past that never existed and the comforts of progress.

Television became an appendix of the Italian homes, either with such drawing-room talk shows as the *Maurizio Costanzo Show* or that of Renzo Arbore who, in *Quelli della notte* (1985), ranged a series of crazy characters around a table while the studio set was filled with objects that, in keeping with the presenter's taste, were gadgets without any kind of function and which, perhaps, were a sly reference to postmodernism.

A radio transmitting news about the end of Communist regimes: this is the background music to Silvio Soldini's *L'aria serena dell'Ovest* (*The Peaceful Air of the West*, 1990). One of its alienated protagonists watches VHS tapes of old tennis matches; many of the scenes take place in middle class kitchens, which are no longer a place for a service but are full of devices for speeding up the preparation of meals. Italy was Gianni Amelio's *Lamerica* (1994), the new America for the thou-

sands of Albanians in search of a land of hope and who had seen our consumerist civilisation thanks to their satellite receivers. This was the last decade in which landline phones were used, by now the victim of petulant single children as in *Caro diario* (Dear Diary, 1993) by Nanni Moretti, a director who wrote the episodic diary of a generation which did not want to grow up and was, therefore, the prisoner of many tiny self-satisfying manias tied to the cultural consumption and objects of modernity which were now becoming vintage (the Vespa on which the splendid forty-year-old travels around Rome). The IT revolution took its first steps: computers clutter office desks, as in Giuseppe Tornatore's *Stanno tutti bene* (*Everybody's Fine*, 1990); the barrier between work and free time had still not been breached, as was to be a characteristic of the 2000s. One of the most attentive observers of customs is Paolo Virzì, a director from Livorno who, in telling the story of the working class in Piombino in his first film, *La bella vita* (*Living it Up*, 1994), records the minimum wellbeing that had been obtained (a fitted kitchen) and, in his next film, *Ferie d'agosto* (*August Vacation*, 1996) shows how Italians at the seaside are now divided by life-styles rather than ideologies. Evidence of a lack of economic wellbeing, instead, is to be found in all the films by Ciprì and Maresco who, starting with *Cinico tv* (from 1991), anatomise with an expressive use of black and white the desolate outskirts of Palermo, populated by television sets, domestic appliances and everything else that has been excluded from the productive cycle.

The money-loving Veneto and its shift from a farming culture to an industrial one are the themes of many films by Carlo Mazzacurati (*La lingua del santo* [*Holy Tongue*], 2000; *La giusta distanza* [*The Right Distance*], 2007) in which we find a syncretism between surroundings and objects (souvenirs of travels in the East, brand new neoclassi-

cism). The comedy of the period, whether set in cities (Ozpetek in Rome, Salvatores in Milan) or in the provinces (Zanasi in Romagna), show the same houses full of objects that all tend to seem the same. These are stories that recount the existential difficulties of the Italian middle classes: wellbeing having been reached (cell phones, technology, a second house), it has to be protected from the threats of interior malaise and from an increasingly global society with which a possible cohabitation has not yet been attained. Even the proletariat in Matteo Garrone's *Gomorra* (*Gomorrah*, 2009) is not untouched by models of widespread lifestyles. And to end, there is Carlo Verdone who, in *Viaggio di nozze* (Honeymoon, 2002), in the episode that recounts the honeymoon of a coerced couple of nouveau riche Romans (Verdone and Gerini) are made by the scriptwriters (Benvenuti and De Bernardi) to express the following thoughts: "Take fashion: once it was us who followed fashion designers to see what we had to wear but now it's them who follow us"; and when they see a shooting star they can't even make a wish.

I wish to thank Giovanna La Varra for her precious advice, and Caterina Grimaldi for her attentive reading.

The Toy Media

Fausto Colombo

A TOY STORY

An unorthodox yet, I believe, efficient way of explaining the Italian road to invention and to the use of the media is to go beyond the serious mask that the problem often presents and, instead, to pinpoint its essence as a kind of lightness, a tendency to play.

I know that serious factors seem to dominate: we could, for example, point to the role of the daily papers and publishing in the building of a national identity, a task later undertaken by radio during Fascism and then by television after the World War Two. Or to the ability of the means of communications to allow us to experience the country's great historical events: tragedies (the Messina, Friuli, Irpinia and Aquila earthquakes for example; or the kidnapping and murder of Aldo Moro; or the small yet still great drama of Vermicino); triumphs (including sporting victories in four football world-cups, the first two broadcast on the radio, the others seen on TV); or more controversial moments (from Piazza Fontana to the massacre of Ustica, the dramatic facts of the G8 meeting in Genoa, and the underground news about social networks and movements); and then there is our historical memory and the celebration of the Italian identity by such vast online archives as that of the RAI. And I have only mentioned a few of the thousands of examples of the serious task of the media.

And yet... and yet there is the possibility of a different history – one which we might call playful – to be found in the Italian media, both from the point of view of television production and from the more varied one of consumption, whether for a niche or a mass-market. This alternative history is revealed in two ways: on the one hand there is media technology, for however little or much national industry has known or been able to propose it to the market at various times; on the other hand there is the content of the media, which can express a kind of jokiness or community playfulness, as though it were a part of the nation's heritage. This is the path I want to follow by evoking various significant episodes from the past fifty years of Italian history.

MEDIA TOYS

There are toys and then there is playing, as every child knows – and so do adults. And the latter is able to create the former, but not vice-versa. Instinct is necessary as is the wish to play, so that any kind of implement, more or less adapted to such a function, can become a toy, a tool for pleasure. And so a broomstick becomes a gun, and a box becomes Treasure Island. But let's imagine for a moment that the maker of a broomstick is a child who wants to play. Won't he shape the wooden stick like the butt of a gun? Won't he perhaps make a small hole to suggest the opening of the barrel? Well then, we really can say that certain Italian designers have produced communicative interfaces with the same philosophy. Let's take Sottsass and the Valentine he produced for Olivetti in 1968: a typewriter that, of course, fitted into the office world but which the designer evidently had designed for a different kid of writing. The body is red and the keys are black. At the time red meant something, because flags of that colour were being waved everywhere, and so you could imagine the sheets typed on the Valentine to be photocopied but also then become – after an editorial treatment far different from today's digital processes – the pages of a novel, a short story, or a manual for a dead-certain, possible, perhaps difficult, probably unlikely revolution. Generally, though, the 1960s witnessed an explosion of toy-like or serious technologies, invented by technicians who were often impeccable, but which were aimed at a mainly playful use, hinted at like a wink of the eye right from the planning stage. One obvious example is the Geloso tape-recorder, designed and assembled in Italy by the firm of the same name which was successful during the boom years

but which wound down at the beginning of the 1970s. If sound technology marked the adventures of the national culture industry (the Ricordi affair comes to mind), the Geloso tape-recorder (the mythical Gelosino that cropped up in many nostalgic places at the time) alluded to a use that was peraphs even infantile: secret diaries, daring recordings of your parents' arguments and secrets, and lots of other things. Another example: portable record-players, devices that literally swallowed a 45rpm record and automatically played the piece of music. An early example of mobile technology was the Penny (to mention a widespread model). It was brilliantly coloured (yellow and orange) and hinted at fun and pleasure. In the 1960s, the period of singer-songwriters and progressive rock, concept albums turned 45s and coloured record-players into children's objects: LPs with marvellous covers begged for attentive listening, without wild or even tame dancing, and they separated childhood from adolescence and even more from youth, once and for all. Even if, in a certain sense, those graphic and at times cartoon-like covers conveyed in turn a suggestion of fun and escape. And what can we say about radios? They were once important objects and an imposing piece of home furniture, and were reinterpreted by Brionvega with its TS502 "cube" radio, this, too, glaringly coloured, an object designed to be enjoyable and curious with its invitation to be opened and closed as well as to be turned on and off. That radios were a possible toy had also been understood by firms (such as Autovox with its Magic Drum, or Ultravox with its Quadrifoglio) that miniaturised them and made them portable, thus encouraging a new way of using them: that of Sunday afternoon walks which – in the 1960s and the early 1970s – saw men of all ages with a small loudspeaker pressed against their ear in order to listen to championship football games which were not yet broadcast on TV and which were played, sacredly, only on the Lord's day. During the

1970s, young people, often highly politicised, though more often than not simply attracted by trying something new, began to play not only with the apparatus for reception but also with that for transmitting, and with surprising ease they started off the phenomenon of free radios, launching themselves bodily against the RAI flagship, like Greenpeace dinghies smashing against Japanese whalers. Improvisation, virtually no financial backing and shaky schedules were the broadcasters' characteristics which, in fact, were more concerned with playing than with doing business: we know, as with games of chance, that it is not earning that counts but only having fun.

Deep down, though, in order to understand the toy-like side to Italian technology, it is worthwhile remembering that during the boom years nearly all the domestic appliance industries – even those targeting the serious national housewives and so not really suitable to being presented as objects for play: fridges, washing machines, dishwashers and so on – advertised through the stories presented by Carosello, a programme devoted to adverts. This was of course obligatory anyway as Sipra had a monopoly on TV advertising, but there is no doubt that the infantile and rather dreamlike aspect of this much loved evening theatre infected the use of domestic appliances. For example, Philco Italia (at the time a branch of the American firm with its factory in Brembate di Sotto) promoted its products with a famous cartoon, produced by Armando Testa, which was on the air in various series between 1966 and 1972: the stories of the planet Papalla whose immediately recognisable inhabitants, completely spherical with two huge glasses-like eyes on top and an enormous nose, also round of course, lived a kind of parallel life worthy of any Pixar film. Toys, precisely. Toys for transforming object-symbols of wellbeing for all into something more profound and beneficent, as only children's toys can be.

The theme of Carosello brings us round to the role of television. I repeat: television itself, rather than the television set which was subject to the same trends mentioned with regard to radio (Zanuso and Sapper designed the mythical Algol for Brionvega). For years it had had an undoubtedly serious aura, perhaps because it was condemned to showing black and white images. It was colour, as Gianfranco Bettetini pointed out many years ago, which, not so much marked the entry of television into the sphere of realism, as, on the contrary, to definitely classify it as belonging to the fantastic world of everyday imagery. But here the story changes because, with the start of the "coloured twenty years" (copyright by Peppino Ortoleva), the Italian industry producing domestic appliances (including those used by the media) began to lose ground, limp, and finally be pushed to the sidelines where the most it could do was to survive. The first mythical television set, indelibly identified by many a nostalgic person with the football triumphs of 1982, was the Black Triniton, a set made by Sony. This is how Davide Enia, in a funny yet sweet play, remembers it in the words of a Sicilian family on the mythical 3-2 victory of Italy over Brazil:

[...] Then just in time for the world cup, by scraping together all her cash, my mum managed to get hold of a new colour telly: a Sony Black Trinitron... lovely... a whopper... but if you can believe it: in colour!... a colour telly in the early '80s was really new and awesome in Palermo... so they all came back to my place to see the matches: friends and relatives... and in fact when the players came onto the field and got into position, in my place they all did the same thing straight away, at the same time as the players; well of course, it was us: all us fans got into our own positions.

So, in that family where they sat in front of the television in a precise order, one in which the atavistic rule of the family hierarchy coincided with the mysterious rules for warding off bad luck, we can pinpoint the Italians' ability to become players, to use the occasions offered

by technological means to transform them from serious gadgets into toy-like objects.

SERIAL PLAYERS

I have said that a child can turn a broomstick into a rifle through his imagination. Luckily the reverse is also true: the wish to play can turn even the most dangerous gun into a harmless figure, even funny one, once a moustache and a pair of glasses have been drawn on the butt. In fact, Italians have often behaved like this both in the content of the media and with their technological interfaces. In the case of the former, for example, a serial kind of content encouraging great collective rites has always been very successful. This happened with the novels by Salgari; the 1930s radio variety programme *I Quattro Moschettieri* with Nizza and Morbelli which sparked off an exciting chase after cigarette cards (and the famous hunt for the ferocious Saladin, the card which could never be found); Arbore and Boncompagni's radio show *Alto Gradimento*; from the 1970s certain "community" programmes such as Fiorello's *Viva Radio Due* or Presta and Dose's *Il Ruggito del Coniglio*. The same thing also happened with many satirical magazines, from "Bertoldo" and "Marc'Aurelio" to "Il Male", "Frigidaire", and "Cuore", as well as with the television, often with the authors as the protagonists (from *L'Amico del Giaguaro* to Arbore, once again, in *Quelli della Notte* and *Indietro Tutta*), as well as others chosen and voted in by the viewers, used perhaps to watching the television plays and variety shows in the 1960s, or the Sanremo festival where the viewers enjoyed themselves by running it down as well as trying to discover the current health of our nation's songs.

But it was in the area of the tactical and often innovative use of technology that our playful vocation for upsetting things found its most fertile terrain. It is enough to mention what happened in our country from the 1990s onwards with the spread of digital mobile phones (the GSMs that took the place of the old Etacs): at first there was a rush to get hold of the latest offers which rapidly led to the spread of "telefonini", or "little phones" which not only infected adults but also the young and children (this rush, by the way, never stopped; Italy is one of the countries that uses mobile phones the most: there are more of them than there are inhabitants). It was the very young and children – who had been given phones by their parents which, according to them, would allow them to control their youngsters – who elaborated some amazing techniques for getting round any kind of checks and putting up passive resistance. In the meantime they (like their contemporaries throughout the world) made the most of text messages which, for the phone makers and the telephone companies, ought to have been nothing other than a service for updating software and nothing more. Text messages led to a genuine new language consisting of abbreviations, a mixture of languages, graphic images that twisted letters and made use of punctuation (so-called emoticons). But where Italian boys and girls using mobile phones really broke new ground (and for some time there was nothing like it in other countries) was in their use of phone calls. They dialled the number they wanted and, after the first ring they hung up before anyone picked up. The name of the caller came up on the screen indicating who had called. This was great for letting your parents know that you had called without spending a penny. But this technique underwent interesting variations and different meanings: one ring meant something and two meant something else, and so on. This was a case where what old Simmel called sociability had the upper hand over technological and financial limits. Rather like what happens today with the social media, which the Italians are completely in love with (in December 2010, more than 16 million Italians had a Facebook ac-

count, and Italy was sixth in Mark Zuckerberg's special list of enthusiasts of social networking).

If we can draw a moral from what I have briefly reviewed, it is that the media – and above all their technological interfaces – work in Italy only when they do not take themselves too seriously and evoke the world of games, enjoyment, and the pleasures of chatting and of being in direct contact. For a long time our national industry managed extremely well to unite technology and play by proposing a very particular mixture of invention, imagination and design. But at a certain point things changed and that very ability dried up, as it were, and so much so that – to mention just one example – Olivetti never managed to produce computers with the same characteristics as its brilliant typewriters. But then, in the sphere of miniaturisation and the mobility of gadgets, Sony's Walkmans had easily superseded the old transistor radios just as Apple easily took up the successful idea of toy-like devices.

We cannot deny it: our industry has been beaten on its own ground, perhaps because it didn't completely believe in it. But then, we Italians continue to personalise and reinvent – as users – technologies, even ones not originally invented by us. I don't know if this can cheer us up but, after all, it's better than nothing.

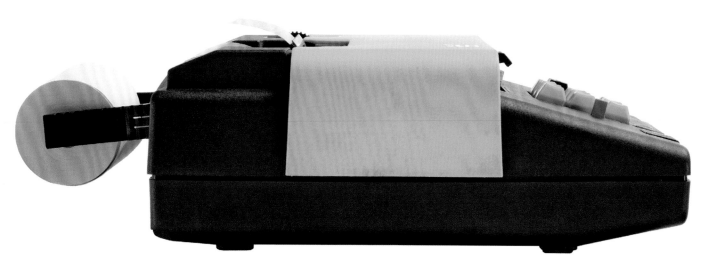

Creativity 1, 2 and 3

Claudio Giunta

Among the many things we should be celebrating this year is the fiftieth anniversary of that marvellous thing known as Battaglia's dictionary. The *Grande Dizionario della Lingua Italiana*, the Great Dictionary of the Italian Language, in fact, was first published exactly fifty years ago in 1961, after having been in preparation for about a decade: the first volume was A-BALB. The twentieth and last volume in 2002 was TOI-Z. A well-spent forty years.

In the Battaglia dictionary the noun *creativo*, creator, in the sense of "copywriter, the originator of advertising campaigns", had not been recorded. We can find *creatività*, creativity, soberly defined as "the ability, faculty, or tendency to create", with references to Croce and Pavese. Let's call the sober creativity of the Battaglia dictionary *Creativity no. 1*.

On the other hand the noun *creativo* is to be found in the Treccani dictionary which came out in 1986. And there the capacity to create, *creatività*, has this epigrammatic definition: "creative ability, the capacity to create with intelligence and imagination, [...] a dynamic intellectual process whose characterising factors are: a particular sensibility for problems, the capacity to produce ideas, to originate innovatively, the ability to create with the intellect, the ability to synthesise and analyse, the ability to define and give a structure in a new way to one's own experiences and knowledge." I will refer to the plethoric, volcanic, overwhelming creativity *creatività*, of the Treccani dictionary as *Creativity no. 2*.

Creativity no. 1 is that of writers, painters, sculptors and musicians: the art we study at school. It is the kind of art which occupied the minds of Croce, Pavese and Salvatore Battaglia.

Creativity no. 2 is the one linked to the new arts that are not studied at school, or have been only recently (cartoons, graphics, songs, video-clips, fashion) and, above all, to pseudo-cultural products and mass media entertainment.

Creativity no. 2 comes after *Creativity no. 1*, not just because poets, painters and musicians chronologically came before singers, video-makers and fashion designers, but also because the usual way of thinking (more exactly: the usual way of thinking in schools) considers that the first kind of creativity is on a higher level than the second. During the 1980s, this hierarchy stopped being taken for granted. In many cases it also stopped being true.

Creativity no. 2 was, for the most part, English or American. This had been the case in the preceding decades too, but in the 1980s the weight of its presence changed and everything began to multiply because radio and commercial TV network schedules had to be filled. Everything began to be imported and, inevitably, there was also a load of crap.

I liked a lot of Italian *Creativity no. 2* in the 1980s and I still like it and it still exists, a sign not only that I was right but also that the artists I liked really have changed the language. Highlights:

The song *Vita spericolata* by Vasco Rossi was next to last at the Sanremo festival in 1983, and my school friends and I realised *straight away*, the day after, that a mistake had been made.

In 1980, Elio e le Storie Tese started up.

In 1983, the *Zanardi e Pertini* album by Andrea Pazienza came out.

In 1979, *Colombo* by Altan was published.

Now it is obvious that this *Creativity no. 2* was in fact *Creativity no. 1*: in other words, *Creativity*. Full stop.

Before the 1980s, there was already everything: films, songs, cartoons, TV. But things changed in the 1980s. There was everything but also infinitely more of it. The only thing that there hadn't been before, the only case of *Creativity no. 2* that was wholly of the 1980s, were videogames. Space Invaders came out in 1978. Pac-Man in 1980. And this was to have consequences on public spaces. Amusement arcades began to open (cf. 883, *Jolly Blue*, 1992 [the song] and 1998 [the film: rotten]). And bars began

the sad slide down to where they are today: to extremely gloomy video-poker. And this obviously had its effect on private games in your own room, for this was the beginning of the Age of IT for everyone: a luminous writing machine with the names of star wars (Vic 20, Commodore 64) and the words *press play on tape* and *loading*, pronounced as they were written, without understanding them but understanding what was essential, i.e. that a minute later we would be playing Donkey Kong (and this Donkey Kong, raised to the power of ten, would then be the IT over the next thirty years for 99.9% of Italians, except that what was then known as "Donkey Kong" would slowly change name to become "Internet").

Creativity no. 2 has a dark side to it, because it is often accused of leading to a *Creativity no. 3* or *Mass Creativity*, which is not creative but empty. *Creativity no. 3* is what lies behind the ephemeral careers of those enrolled in the DAMS arts, music and theatre course in Bologna (DAMS originated in Bologna in 1971, but "doing DAMS" comes from the 1980s) and, today, the candidates on *X Factor*, and it is what convinces them that it is right to follow the pleasure principle ("Do what you like", "Express yourself") rather than the reality principle ("Learn a trade"). This is true, but there's nothing that can be done about it.

While *Creativity no. 1* asks for silence and the solitude of study, *Creativity no. 2* is best surrounded by noise: and it likes group work. And so the real laboratory for *Creativity no. 2* is television. *Creativity no. 2* arrived on the scene in the 1950s, took hold in the 1960s, and was firmly established in the 1970s; but *Creativity no. 1* also spread, triumphed, and broke through in the 1980s because television came into existence then.

Television from the 1950s to the 1970s was not real television. More than anything else it was an object: the *television set*. In the 1980s, *television* became a genre, a language, a business (*working in television*), and a way of seeing the world, a world that was far more varied and fun that the real world.

On television in the 1980s there was absolutely nothing to explain because everything was so obvious. No longer did you have to spend half an hour in a newspaper library taking notes.

The day I came into the world, April 7, 1971, the programmes on the national TV channel began at 12.30 p.m. with animated cartoons and then, between one news programme and another, we had: 2 p.m. *Una lingua per tutti*. Courses in French and German; 5 p.m. For the very young: *Paolino in soffitta* and *Tutti cowboys*; 5.40 p.m. Children's TV: *Sipario* and *Gli eroi di cartone*; 6.40 p.m. *La fede oggi*; 7.10 p.m. *Sapere. La società postindustriale*; 9.00 p.m. *Giallo di sera*; 10.00 p.m. *Incontro a Pasqua: Paura e libertà*.

Programmes ended after the 11 o'clock news. The second channel, on the other hand, began to transmit at 9 p.m. (the news) and ended at 10.30 p.m. with a documentary about Ella Fitzgerald. That was it. In the "Corriere della Sera" newspaper the list of radio programmes was longer than that for the television.

Five years later, April 7, 1976, it was all much the same except that now, near to the list of programmes on the two national channels, there were those of Swiss TV (9.45 p.m. *Come nasce un'università*), Capodistria (8.30 p.m. *Questo mondo non è per bambini*) and Montecarlo (9 p.m. *I due orfani* with Totò).

Five years on, April 7, 1981, the age of innocence came at an end. Radio programmes are hardly listed. Swiss TV, Capodistria and Montecarlo had been shunted into a tiny column, while Canale 5 had a column to itself and transmitted the film *Mi svegliai signora*, the programme for music for the young *Pop com*, and the series *Man from Atlantis* and *Hawaii Five-o*. The RAI hung in with a national-popular mixture: a documentary about Spanish fauna, *Intervista con la scienza*, *Spaziolibero - I programmi dell'accesso* (just the sound of the title, even after so many years, makes me yawn) and *Happy Days*.

Three years later, April 7 1984, not only was the age of innocence a distant memory but the battle was really underway, and those who know what the future held realise that it couldn't have been any different to what it is: it is like seeing a film of Hitler as a child (1983: "Stern" published the fake diaries of Hitler believing them genuine), or reading in a newspaper of the times a reference to a strange infective disease that seemed to hit those who led a disorderly life (1981: the first mention of AIDS in medical literature). The RAI tried to keep in the game with *Al Paradise*, a variety show conducted by Milva and Oreste Lionello. But the zeitgeist was heavily influencing Canale 5 where there were already the seeds of all the programmes of the next thirty years: *Il pranzo è servito*, *T.J. Hooker*, *The Jeffersons*, *Risatissima*. And in the second half of the evening on Italia 1 – after *Diff'rent Strokes*, *Knight Rider*, and *The A-Team* – there was the heavy artillery: the comedy sketch programme *Drive In*.

Drive In was one of the three matrix programmes of the 1980s; in this case matrix means "Something that does not represent the beginning of a phenomenon but expresses its quintessence and, at the same time, marks a turning point (the Phenomenon becomes a Phenomenon[2]) and a point of no return (the Phenomenon[2] inevitably become Phenomenon[3, 4, 5]...)". Nicola Lagioia remembers above all the idiocy of *Drive In* gags: "Hiiii", this thirty-year-old from Biella would say, "I'm mister Tarocò with the accent on the q! (and we laughed)" (*Riportando tutti a casa*, Turin, Einaudi, p. 25). I remember some appalling jokes too, but in *Drive In* it was the people who were more important than the gags; in other words, it was the first programme where what was important was not just to hear but to *see* these weird people, and Faletti dragged up as Vito Catozzo or Francesco Salvi camouflaged as the front-man for the *I budini molli* rock group, made me laugh. This was *Creativity no. 2*, and not of the worst kind. But of course no one watched *Drive In* for the comedians. For me, as for all the boys of my generation, *Drive In* represented above all the great times of our first wanks and the comments we made the next day at school. It was a turning point (and television *could do this*!) and a point of no return: so much so that the *Drive In* of 2011 is the newscast that goes out on the same channel: *Studio Aperto*. The second matrix programme was *Deejay Television*. This was how it went. At the beginning of 1982, Claudio Cecchetto took over the Radio Music frequency and started up Radio Deejay. At first they only broadcast music; there wasn't much advertising, apart from some jingles, because there were very few advertisers. Then that summer there arrived the first DJs, first of all Gerry Scotti. A couple of years later Cecchetto started up a collaboration with Berlusconi and the radio started a second programme on the TV: *Deejay Television*, a review of music videos which copied MTV, which had also just started up, but with radio DJs presenting it. "I launched Deejay Television thanks to Carlo Freccero who realised that if you used six video clips which had cost the record company three hundred million each for free, then you could do a half hour show that was worth 1.8 billion" (interview with Gigi Vesigna, *Famiglia cristiana*, 6.12.1998). It ended up that all Italians aged between 12 and 25 watched *Deejay Television*: just ask any forty-year-old today what he remembers about TV then and you will see, or be reminded, how we spent our afternoons after school. The videos were introduced by Linus, Albertino, Scotti, Kay Rush and, in later years, Amadeus and Jovanotti: almost all the stars of radio and television musical entertainment started here. When you have a success like that on *Deejay Television* while you are still young, the problem is to stay on top: you decline, wobble, rest on your laurels and become pathetic. They didn't. This was the via Panisperna of Italian radio and television.

The third matrix programme was not actually a programme but a television event, the first of a legion of similar events, even if none of them has ever been as appalling: the death of Alfredo Rampi at the age of six in an arte-sian well in Vermicino, near Frascati, in June 1981. The little boy took three days to die, and for almost two of them the RAI did not stop pointing its cameras at the mouth of the well. Alfredo Rampi's death was the first time that I really became a viewer of a Television Event. I have a hazy memory of the world cup in Argentina, of the finding of Aldo Moro and (even if it seems crazy to me) of the earthquake in Irpinia. But these are not memories of things, they are memories of me watching television. Instead, I can still clearly see the TG1 journalists with their microphones, the volunteers crawling headfirst down into the well, President Pertini. And, as for me as a child, I remember above all the excitement (all my family awake, my mother cleaning the floor at three in the morning with tears in her eyes) and the five-a-side football match finals played by my class the day after Alfredo's death. We won. And among the many shameful things of my adolescence there is this: when we went back to school I said to the teacher, on behalf of the entire team, "We want to dedicate our victory to Alfredino Rampi". I was ten years old but television rhetoric ("Who do you want to dedicate this victory to?") had already poisoned my blood.

This really was the Matrix Event. If *Drive In* was extensive totality (soft porn could also be seen on television) then Vermicino was intensive totality: you could also die on television. So it is not strange that the death of Alfredo Rampi remained impressed in the mind of Aldo Nove who, in 1981, was fourteen years old (cf. the excellent article *Vermicino*, in *Superwoodbinda*), and of Francesco Bianconi from the indie rock group Baustelle who was eight (cf. the excellent *Alfredo*, in the extraordinary album *Amen*).

(After which, hearing people speak about those years and reading books about the history of the 1980s that began to come out – ones that spoke above all of *Dallas* and *Dynasty*, of the New Musketeers Gardini, De Benedetti, Berlusconi and Agnelli, of drinking in Milan, of yachting holidays – books, in other words, that tell us things we already know and remember, the things that everybody at the time saw and that even then seemed strange, interesting or epoch-making. What comes to mind is the suspicion that the real *pop* masterpiece of the 1980s is to be found in this gigantic lesson of reality: to have made everyone, including today's historians, believe that that was life, that those things really counted and defined the spirit of the times, while instead all this *appearance* was, in fact, only appearance and that life was running along different lines and that another reality – a real one – was being prepared. In order to understand this I think it would be better to read the first novel of the decade, *Altri libertini* by Tondelli (1980), the story of a generation of wretches bent on escape; or else the last novel of the decade, *La grande sera* by Pontiggia, 1989, the tale of a man alone, desperately bored, and bent on escape.) And finally, having lived throughout the 1980s as a minor, means that I only experienced the reflections of the products of *Creativity no. 1* which had been passed through the filter of *Creativity no. 2*.

For example, at the time I wasn't quite certain who Aldo Busi was. Only in the following decade was I interested enough to read *Seminario sulla gioventù* (1984) and the reportages written for *Epoca* and collected together in *Altri abusi* (1989), which is one of the most beautiful Italian books of the second half of the twentieth century. But I remember Busi in *Mixer Cultura* while he ill-treated Guido Almanasi: "Three of you! Three of you were needed to translate *Alice in Wonderland*?"; or when, on the Maurizio Costanzo Show, he found himself next to Massimo Boldi, who at first joked about Busi's homosexuality and then put his arm around him so as to appear likeable. The jokes were not much, just a comedian's banter, but I have never forgotten the insult of the arm around the shoulders.

And yet. I had no idea what the Trans-avant-garde was. But I knew that the "art critic" Achille Bonito Oliva had been photographed nude on the cover of "Frigidaire", and that even Roberto D'Agostino always talked about him on *Quelli della notte*. Only years later did I nearly die laughing while reading by mistake some pages of *The Italian Trans-avant-garde / La Transavanguardia italiana*: "The work becomes a microcosm that receives and establishes art's opulent capacity to allow repossession, to get back to being possessors, of a fluid subjectivity, to the point of entering the inner folds of the private sphere which, in any case, bases its own drive on, and on nothing else, the value and motivation of its own operation. The ideology of poor-ism and the tautology of Conceptual art..." (p. 51). *The ideology of poor-ism*. Perhaps the real characteristic of the 1980s' pseudo-culture was that a load of absurd *Creativity no. 3* was passed off, with the help of all this candyfloss, as *Creativity no. 1*. Out of all the fashionable decorative and graffiti art (Zakanitch, Basquiat, Haring and, in Italy, the Fiorucci shops etc.) I was luckily only touched by tired commercial echoes in the form of Naj Oleari fabric accessory bags flaunted by the girls at school during the break. Twenty-five years later I embrace them all, one by one, in their dining-rooms.

Design, Market and Consumption

Giovanni Cutolo

What Italy has managed to achieve over the past fifty years in the practice and theory of design, particularly in the sphere of furniture, lamps and interior design in general, is highly reminiscent of what happened centuries ago with music. From the second half of the seventeenth century to the end of the eighteenth the amazing creativity of Italian composers, almost all from the Neapolitan school, left a deep mark on the history of music in virtually all European countries. Paris, the cultural centre of France and of the whole of Europe, opened its doors to Italian opera and, in 1801, even built a theatre exclusively for producing Italian operas.

The composer at the court of Louis XIV, Giovan Battista Lulli, who changed his surname to Lully to make it more French, contributed to the birth of French opera. Whether opera or symphonic and chamber music, the music that for over a century was composed and heard in the courts of all the major capital cities was Italian or in the "Italian style". Thanks to the talent of such masters as Arcangelo Corelli, Alessandro and Domenico Scarlatti, Antonio Vivaldi, Francesco Durante, Nicola Porpora, Baldassarre Galuppi, Niccolò Jommelli, Niccolò Piccinni, Giovanni Paisiello, Domenico Cimarosa and many others, amongst whom numerous composers born outside Italy, a great amount of high-quality music was composed and circulated; this helped to redefine the standards of composition, execution, and representation and deeply influenced the musical taste of the time.

This unchallenged hegemony was to define a new musical language so well-characterised and widespread as to convince the greatest German, French, Russian and English composers to use the Italian language for the librettos of their theatrical works and for writing the indications in their scores. The librettos of the greater part of the operas by Händel, Gluck, Mozart and many others were in Italian, just as were the notations that Haydn, Schumann, Schubert, Beethoven,

Chopin and many others used for marking the movements of their sonatas and symphonies.

Analogous to this, and just as extraordinary, is the creativity that lies at the heart of the phenomenal success of Italian design throughout the world. This began with the extraordinary success of Italian furniture design, which became the international ambassador and recognised benchmark of Italian good taste. This was then translated into the model for a cosmopolitan style of interior decoration inspired and backed up by constant and imaginative innovation. Today Italian design is a recognisable stylistic hallmark and by now identifies and characterises a kind of design that is no longer just Italian but international. While the French can be proud of having for centuries created and imposed on the world furnishing in Louis XIII, Louis XIV, Louis XV and Louis XVI styles, we Italians have at last manage to invent a style that is authentically and recognizable national and that we might call… Louis Design.

In paying a deserved tribute to the many designers who have made a contribution to the success of the Italian project, it should also be underlined how the definition of the style and language of our design has been matched by its increasing presence on the international scene. This has been made possible by the courage of entrepreneurs who were able to invest in research while trusting in a new culture; they created the favourable conditions for the development of design and for its promotion in all the markets of the world. It is obvious to everyone how by now furnishings designed in Italy have contributed to the level of good taste by taking everywhere the positive values of a formal and aesthetic quality that is continually being renewed, and by following the criteria of a rigorous standard of construction. A further confirmation of the prestige that Italian production has universally reached is the fact that an increasing number of people con-sider the products of Italian design as the representatives of one of the most advanced frontiers of new luxury. A new luxury which is expressed, not just by the traditional show of wealth, but through a refined capacity to incorporate in the products the immaterial values of a new and intangible quality expressed by design itself. This design is characterised and identified as cultural luxury, the distinctive mark of the new frontier of good taste. The good taste of Italian design.

For centuries luxury has been identified above all with the possession and ostentation of rare and therefore precious objects, the result of the talent and manufacturing skills of doughty craftsmen and made accessible by the sensibility of canny merchants. It has only been a few decades that luxury and industry have slowly been showing a new convergence, one made possible by the increasing role of design in the industrial production of goods.

Knowledge of design applied to industrial production has determined a change in the very idea of luxury, one which is now widely to be seen more in a knowledge of materials resulting from the conjunction of industrial quantity and the quality of design, than from the obsolete cultural parameters expressed by the richness of the materials used. Thanks to design, the consumer has grown and continues to grow by learning to move inside that artificial forest of products that modern society has slowly been constructing.

At the same time as this construction, a knowledge of materials has been being defined, one that has made available the intellectual tools for understanding and distinguishing, leading to an appreciation of the results but also to a criticism of production systems. The development of this knowledge of materials has encouraged the definition of value parameters for everything that is produced; this has come about through the protection of intellectual property, the safeguarding of the creativity of designers, and the investments of the produc-

ers, but it has also created the conditions for the control and criticism of production systems so as to correct it whenever it risks giving people and towns products made by devastating nature and insanely impoverishing the planet. A notable contribution to defining reference parameters and to continually revising them has been made by the permanent monitoring activities of the Italian association for industrial design, activities that culminate every three years with the award of the Compasso d'Oro prizes. Due to this there has been an enrichment and refinement of the knowledge of materials that is an essential tool for being able to transform every consumer into a Virtuous Hedonist, in other words a detached purchaser able to avoid the siren's call and manipulations of more or less hidden persuaders: purchasers who know what they want and where to find it, having leant to put their own needs into order and to recognise their own wishes.

A parameter for measuring the changes in consumption is given by the current transformation of what is known as the market for luxury goods. A market that, due to the impulse of the new knowledge of materials, is beginning to fragment. And so today we can refer to three different types of luxury:

- aristocratic luxury seen above all in the search for and enjoyment of such absolutely immaterial privileges as space, silence, security, tranquillity and other similar intangible values;
- democratic luxury which, instead, is characterised by the tendency to give increasing importance to the immaterial values of products, those values to be found in production inspired by design culture;
- popular luxury which remains basically tied to a deep-rooted preference for tangible values identified with the richness of the materials from which the product is made: metals, rare stones, wood and precious textiles.

However, it is a fact that in the realm of luxury there are to be found living together aristocratic enthusiasms and democratic enthusiasms, tradition and innovation, the ample time of myths and the brief one of fashion, in such a manner that there have been those who hold that it is time to allow anybody to have a kind of right to luxury. A right that would imply the overcoming of the relationship that we currently have with merchandise, a relationship that continues to be too influenced by the mentality of the economy of needs which, at least in the developed Western countries, has been replaced for some time now by the economy of desires.

Normally each person's desires are aimed at things we do not possess and, for that very reason, which we desire, while it seems almost inevitable that whoever owns something no longer desires it. But, as is well known, pleasure does not so much derive from the possession of things so much as the enjoyment offered by the fleeting moment in which they are conquered or, in other words, the moment they are bought, the moment when the satisfying of the desire for ownership gives ephemeral pleasure. The result is the paradox that whoever owns everything seems to be unsatisfied because they have by now consumed any possibility for further pleasure, having already satisfied all their desires. The fact of the matter, though, is that happiness is not to be found in possessing the things we desire but, rather, in those moments of acute pleasure that we feel each time we gratify our desire by conquering the thing we wish to have by owning it and having it in our possession.

Once again it Is obvious how the problem of consumption is a wholly psychological and, therefore, a cultural problem, and this assumes both knowing how to give meaning to the things we already own and knowing how to select those that can stimulate new desires. It is in this sense that we can consider design as a cultural luxury. To recline in an *Eames Lounge Chair* and read with the help of an *Arco* lamp,

without knowing who either Eames or Castiglioni are, does not diminish the functional pleasure resulting from the undoubted comfort of the chair or the excellent quality of the light. However, it certainly does reduce an intellectual pleasure. Because ignorance of the history of objects, the lack of knowledge of their software, diminishes that kind of added value that consists of their aura as a work of art produced in the age of their technical reproducibility. Works of art, as we know, are also such because of their functional uselessness. A work of design, instead, has a double existence: it is not just functional but also aesthetic. We sit on the chairs ranged around the dining table at the most for four hours out of twenty-four; so they have their functional life as well as a longer aesthetic life as object to be looked at. Similarly, the lamp on our desk has its function of illuminating when there is not enough natural light, in other words for some six to eight hours out of twenty-four; instead, for the most part of its life it is not judged by the quality of its light but by its positive or negative contribution to the beauty of the room's furnishings.

The Compasso d'Oro came into existence in 1954, two years after the foundation of ADI, the association for industrial design; a few years later Umberto Eco published a book about semiology called *Opera aperta*, the last chapter of which was titled *Del modo di formare come impegno sulla realtà*, Of the Way of Shaping as a Commitment to Reality. In it Eco spoke, among other things, of the unavoidable problem created by alienation by underlining how, even if it were possible to resolve the problem of the alienation Marx referred to in his writings about the economy, there would still remain unresolved and irresolvable the problem of the existence of alienation in the anthropological context in which humankind lives and acts. As Eco wrote, it remains evident that "for the very fact of living, working, producing things, and relating to others, we are alienated". Almost prophetically, for

this was in 1963, Eco considered that the negative effects of this structural and uncancellable alienation might be lessened and made more bearable by design. Eco wrote, "Industrial design seems to resolve the problem: it unites beauty and usefulness and restores to us a humanized and human-scale machinery. Liquidisers, knives and typewriters that express their possible use through a series of pleasurable relationships which invite the hand to touch and use them: it's a solution. Humanity would be harmoniously integrated with their functions and with the tool that makes them possible."

Today we can recognize Umberto Eco's prophetic abilities, but above all we must not undervalue his thoughts in which we find highlighted both the cultural and the strategic importance of design.

Now we must look more closely in order to go further ahead. Now it is necessary to pinpoint and communicate precisely the very cultural value that design products have gained due to their being the bringers of beauty, the transport vehicles of "aesthetic ingredients", however little of them there might be. This has become an increasingly important role in the light of the trend that has progressively shifted modern art away from beauty. It is not by chance that a well-known art critic has recently stated, in fact, that art's role today is no longer that of representing standards of beauty; and he underlined the fact that by now and for quite some time it is design that has had the task of carrying out this function. If it is true that the essence of art is to be found in what is not seen when looking at the work, it is also true that its revelation can only become manifest to the eyes of those who love knowledge and awareness. So we could maintain that the relationship established between the products produced by design firms and those who use them, perhaps just by contemplating them, is a relationship made possible and enhanced by the consumer's knowledge. An introductory knowledge essential for appreciating the future results of a

design that will become the reference language for undertaking increasingly sophisticated proposals for products-services, products-experiences and products-transformations.

In front of this disconcerting scenario, one that seems to forecast the disappearance of goods while allowing a glimpse of a new economy mainly based on the exchange of rarefied immaterial values without any three-dimensional consistency, we must necessarily rethink and renew those values which production and its products can be anchored to. It is almost certain that a large part of merchandise will consist of – though perhaps we should say substituted by – intangible *soft* things and objects, while there will continue to circulate social-democratically increasing quantities of *hard* things, of tangible goods whose acceptance, however, will be increasingly influenced and inspired by the intangible and soft values of design. A design able to spark off the purchaser's new involvement, one based on a kind of cultural complicity mediated by the objects; these will no longer be chosen on the basis of objective parameters, the expression of their material value, but they will be increasingly chosen on the basis of subjective criteria, the expression of their empathetic adherence to the taste of each purchaser. In this way there will gradually come about a process of cultural transformation determined by the characteristics of the merchandise, a merchandise finally able to shift the purchaser's attention from the vulgarity of values expressed by the weight of the materials used, to the refined elegance of intangible values, those that are inherent in every object of good design. A design that, as has already been indicated, and careless of the utopian socialising of the founding fathers, will increasingly become a cultural luxury indulged in with increasing discernment by an increasing number of Virtuous Hedonists, new and non-coercible consumers able to make autonomous choices about what they buy, oriented by an individual taste which is increasingly informed, detached, sophisticated and educated.

By enriching their knowledge of materials, consumers can be transformed into Virtuous Hedonists, learn to recognise beauty, and reach a more genuine kind of happiness because it will not depend exclusively on money and cannot be confused simply with the possession of things. Design must take sides and fight; it must become both aesthetic and ethical by incorporating the idea of sustainability into its projects. The planned product must be at the service of humankind and of cities but must also respect the environment and the planet's resources. Only by adhering to these principles can design allow more people to discover a new happiness, one that is in the reach of those who, living in an artificial forest, have learned to recognise beauty. Because, even if it is true that "Capitalism economically deputises for happiness, makes up for its absence, simulates it by purchasing, and pretends that it is the same for everybody and is an exchangeable benefit" (Geminello Alvi, *Il secolo americano*, Milan, Adelphi, 1996, p. 463), it is equally true that consumers who manage to transform themselves into Virtuous Hedonists escape from this simulation because of the fact that the condition acquired through their knowledge allows them to understand that beauty and happiness cannot always be bought. Virtuous Hedonists know, furthermore, that happiness cannot be stored up and that it is presumptuous to believe that it can increase as a result of the economy, just as it is false to believe that it can be reached or replaced by money. The battle for the spread of design is everyone's battle because the spread of beauty nourishes and makes plausible a promise of happiness that we all need to believe in.

Fashion and Industrial Design

Giannino Malossi

Time passes, styles and technologies change, but the invisible distance that for decades has separated the theory and practice of industrial design from the fashion milieu is still an open question. And yet clothes and accessories are industrial products made serially like all the other products in this globalised world of ours. And given that industries and markets are governed everywhere by technical laws and need rationality, at least with regard to productive processes and relationships, there is no real reason to hive off the world of fashion and textiles from the rest of the industrial production that is of interest to the industrial designer. The production of new furniture, domestic appliances, cars or electric products increasingly expresses and makes its own the styling of the moment. For some time it has been made clear that fashion and industrial design have in common the same process of economic development: both produce an immaterial kind of added value by elaborating the functional, symbolic and linguistic qualities that are part of industrial products. Furthermore, consumer culture does not distinguish between fashion and design. For the simplified language of the media they are interchangeable synonyms. So what is it that makes fashion different from and, in some ways, incompatible with design? In order to answer this question it is useful to look at the cultural production, theoretical materials, thoughts of the protagonists and stories that fashion and design have produced over the last few decades. Seen in this perspective, the difference is extremely marked and the divergences are very evident. In simple words, we are dealing with this: industrial design thinks, or at least thinks it thinks. Fashion doesn't: it does not think at all. Design, in fact, consists of the very process of the theoretical elaboration of and thinking about the practices of industrial planning. With all respect to the hordes of academicians who devote themselves to courses in Fashion Theories, fashion is a social process for elaborating semantic conventions and does not recognise processes of theoretical reflection – unless *a posteriori* – that lie outside its own sphere, and then only on condition that their outcome leaves fashion untouched. Fashion is not the result of a rational cognitive process. If possible, for the protagonists of fashion there is not even a rational cognitive process in general. This is why, for example, there is nothing like fashion criticism. For the same reason, fashion's social system is subjectively built around the rhetorical figures of the designer, the *maison* and, more recently, the brand, and has elaborated a complex ritual which is acted out with great ceremony and at six-monthly intervals in venues specifically for them and codified in the mystic rite of fashion shows. Fashion's refusal to think in some way about its own cultural dimensions – which, of course, exist – seems to be a part of its make-up, one necessary for a mentality centred on improvisation and emotive impulsiveness. The rootedness of this late romantic-bourgeois vision of *creativity*, which includes the obsessive use of this word to justify logical gaps, is the key to understanding just why in the world of fashion no time is lost studying projects. What counts is the intuition of the moment, and this is fashion theory in a nutshell. In fact, though, this logic holds up for a practical and cynical reason: fashion, since it has existed, i.e. since early industrialisation, is more an expression of the value of use than of the quality of the project. A question of distinction and of consumption rather than of technology and functionality. For the textile industry, fashion allows an industrial shortcut, one taken as soon as conventions make it possible, to arrive at the market without starting out from the fatigue of research and the uncertainties of theory. Since the media's economy of scale has allowed conventions to be determined by forking out money, fashion's cycle has acquired an uninterrupted moment of power.

Similarly to architecture, which has to contend for its space with engineering, both inside and outside industry design has existed since, at the beginning of the 20th century, there developed, not just the practice of planning anchored to theoretical and rational premises, but above all communicative dynamics of thoughts about planning. Design is made up of manifestos, academic programmes, schools, theoretical texts of analyses and reflections, and specialist journals. None of this exists for fashion. For fashion there only exist magazines for the end-users, that is for the pawn in play. However, in the 1970s and 1980s there were experiments and experiences in the relationship between fashion and design that indicated different possibilities. Among these experiences, the most significant was that of Nanni Strada.

THE CONTEXT

To understand and appreciate the work on industrial design applied to clothing by Nanni Strada – who was awarded the Compasso d'Oro prize in 1979 for a film *Il manto e la pelle* (with Clino T. Castelli as design consultant) – it is necessary to return to the cultural context of the period in which it originated. To begin with, the unusual formula of a *film* about design, a real 35mm film, is something that needs to be clarified: it is not a work of fiction. The project the film recounts is as real as it can be when dealing with design: Pantysol, the project's name, is also the official name of the industrial patent for a loom that allows a special way of manufacturing without sewing. This specific technology, developed as an integral part of the project, was the basis for the creation of a range of clothes designed by Nanni Strada. So this, then, was a film documenting a project for the technical innovation of the production process, hardware we would say today; the designer was invited to contribute to it as the originator of the new product's aesthetic forms and of the promotion (the film) aimed at presenting it and illustrating its qualities. So even in itself this film is

an example of a way of thinking about design and the economic and material processes that moulded it.

The idea of a film explaining a design project was suggested by Ettore Sottsass, curator of the 15th Milan Triennale in 1973/74 and which was the first venue for the film. Sottsass wanted to realise the whole exhibition with such experimental expressive means as films and other narrative forms using images, such as the famous *Multivision Screens*, coordinated programmes of slides projected onto a large screen and which became part of the world of design and communications of the time thanks to Charles Eames. It was all analogical and regulated by electromechanical instruments given that digital technology was still in the distant future. And already at this point it is necessary to point out that the territory of design since it has existed is one in continual movement. Twenty-first-century design is transitive according to the unavoidable definition given it at the end of the 1990s by Clino T. Castelli: just look at the present and the past, at rational logic and the emotions. Today's design is postmodern in other words, and it is inclusive, if for no other reason than for understanding how it can include such "star" designers as Lapo Elkann and Paris Hilton, designers only as a result of corporate press releases. But the sense of Pantysol cannot be understood according to today's paradigms. In the 1970s the term design was far less elastic but far more focused. It would not allow itself to be conditioned by market research and marketing. The designer was often linked by his or her role as a consultant to an industrial form, not to a private equity or an investment fund following the logic or, rather, the conventions of finance. On the other hand, in the practice of design, as in fashion, there did not exist the concept of early prototyping; according to this a work, though not completely ready, can be evaluated while it is being developed, as happens with software which is launched even though full of bugs.

The projects were analogical and their processes linear. They were finalised, if possible, by technical patents and objects produced in series. These were evaluated by the royalties with which industrial designers and even such fashion designers as Valentino and Giorgio Armani – who had had the immense luck to come into contact with Marco Rivetti's great industry, the GFT group – could become rich.

The 1970s, the years of the Pantysol project, were years with a certain tone, rigorous years when results mattered. After all, this was the part of 20th-century culture with the most positive outcome, the years of mass affluence after the reconstruction and the economic boom. Capitalism still thought it was loved by all, though it was soon to be disillusioned as is even more evident now. At the time design claimed and actually attempted to have a precise line of thought; it also had principles and only acted in the shadow of the great masters. Designers were serious. Some people, like Tom Wolfe in *From Bauhaus to Our House*, were already being ironic about their heroic principles. Today we tend to be relative, starting from production relationships. The idea going around is that only in the dynamics of the whole can there be the proof that, through what is superficially called design, there is a deep expression of the relationship between culture, its use, and the material world. Designers' recompenses no longer include royalties. Intellectual work is greatly undervalued. The value of use is now almost valueless; exchange values are condensed into a brand which, like a magic word, transforms into gold whatever it touches. And if the designer does not quickly become a star, a brand in himself, then he has no use. That's how it is.

THE OBJECT

If the Compasso d'Oro was awarded to the film that presented the project, then the project by extension was represented by a yellow

knitted dress. Defined by Nanni Strada as "the first garment in the world woven automatically, without stitching, by a circular machine", that yellow dress is today famous, exhibited in numerous shows and design museums throughout the world, but above all it was, at a global level, the first of a whole series of garments derived from *seamless* technology. But quite apart from its success, in Nanni Strada's yellow dress we can see the best example of *modern* design as it was considered at the time applied *to the potential offered to dressing by technological innovation*. In this idea of a dress as an industrial item of clothing – one that did not even take into consideration the idea of *fashion* as a language of expressive social and indentifying signs because it invented objects with a new and previously unseen semantic code – there was also industrial design's answer to the question "What shall I wear today?" A question that nowadays no one would ask of a technological device (some geek perhaps, but well...) because we are used to thinking about fashion as a repertoire of phantasmagorias and projected images, references, quotations, revivals, and all according to semantics endlessly inculcated by the media and show-business and decipherable as a catalogue of individual cultural anxieties spread throughout society. Nanni Strada's yellow dress is the conceptual outcome of research into the relationship between industrial design and fashion as it was understood from the 1960s to the late 1970s. At the time design claimed to have and to represent a clear line of thinking.

Industrial design was understood as a discipline of practical modernity, a cultural project aimed beyond itself. Design was *industrial* because it considered itself as being tied to mechanical production, *modern* because it tended to improve and renew the conditions of life and production, and, in conclusion, it was *popular,* more accessible, of higher quality, and had an impulse towards creating a more exact form for an industrial object, whether it was a chair, a transistor radio or even a garment. It tried to obtain the maximum function within an elegant and coherent expressive code with all the advantages of technical production and affluent consumers; at the same time it was not obsessed by luxury and the syndrome of social distinctions and was designed to be produced in large series through increased automation, in a few minutes, obtained with the minimum waste, easy and ready to wear, low cost but high quality, popular and fun but not shabby.

NANNI STRADA SPEAKS

NS I was awarded the 1979 Compasso d'Oro for the Pantysol project which was about research, its development, application and presentation. However, the object that represented the work was this yellow, unstitched dress. In the 1970s, I was a consultant for Calze Bloch, which was then the leading stocking and pantyhose industry, the largest Italian and, perhaps, European group of the time. You have to remember that at the end of the 1960s, with the spread of miniskirts, pantyhose had become a basic item of clothing... but this led to a notable revolution from the mechanical-textile point of view. The industry's aim was to produce more with less processing in order to lower costs, and to use mechanical technology in order to make pantyhose with the least stitching possible. This meant the production of new machinery and tubular circular knitting looms for producing stockings in a single piece. As an industrial designer, I was extremely interested in this story of stockings and pantyhose; pantyhose was the invention of the century, perhaps even more than the miniskirt: it freed girls from stockings and garters, instruments of torture. It was a great behavioural invention packaged as an industrial object. Miniskirts had been fundamental for this innovation, but pantyhose, which in a certain sense is makeup for the legs, filled the functional

gap created by miniskirts. My passion has always been for the serial production of clothing, for serial confection, design for the industrial creation of clothes. I began as a fashion designer but I hated tailoring. However, once I understood the potential of serial production, of replicating an invention, then that became my world. My vision was to cover the whole body with an industrial constructive system of clothing. The aim was not aesthetic creations but to use innovative technology for overall dressing, for covering the whole body without the restrictions dictated by conventions and symbols.

This idea was completely backed by Bloch because technical innovation of mechanics, by providing automatic machinery that supplied easily imitable low cost products, undermined high quality products. It was an attempt to use innovation to broaden the market.

GM A casebook study for an innovative and competitive economic strategy à la Schumpeter. But with two basic variants: that the deviser of the innovation was the industrial designer, a technician with humanistic and art training, and that the innovation was incorporated into a consumerist cultural dimension, the so-called world of the young: the irreverent behaviour in the face of tradition, the miniskirt and the pantyhose in question. Were you aware of this?

NS No I wasn't. Industries intuited things. With hindsight things find their place in the great scheme of things. But when you are in the middle you rely on hunches, impulse and enthusiasm. Instinct was that: it wasn't something rationalised. *Il manto e la pelle* was a meta-project into which I thrust all the concepts of my philosophy for making clothes and how to design fashion. In the first part of the film it is possible to see everything that can be done with knitted textiles on geometric principles: two-dimensional, flat, Eastern-inspired, and with the use of special weaving machines; in the other part there is this seamless tubular yellow dress. The two systems integrate into an upper and a lower one.

GM The work of the German ethnologist, illustrator and costume designer Max Tilke is often referred to as the basis of your interests.

NS That's true: the books and illustrations by Max Tilke were a source of inspiration for me at the start. But my early choices were not always quite that rational and aware. I had been trained as a dress designer. I hated tailoring because as a girl I had had to wear these horrible tailored clothes. So I wanted to do anything in life but that. When I saw Tilke's studio, apart from the beauty of seeing clothes represented flat, I became aware that the construction of these garments began with a square, an exact geometrical figure. There were no longer pleats, shoulder-pads, padding: all Western tailoring needs had disappeared. This was a revelation.

GM But fashion also has a symbolic aspect which cannot simply be reduced to an industrial, technical or geometric dimension. We confer symbolic and linguistic meanings on clothes so that it is not so much the form that conveys the message of a garment but the semantic context in which it is placed, the meaning that is constructed at a social level.

NS My approach, managed by a compulsive kind of creativity, was an attempt to apply rational design to fashion. Even in my 1971 collection for Max Mara, the square basis was originated for an industrialised concept of the garment. That was my vision. At the time there was a lot of idealisation in the air, in the period's culture; and then it is also necessary to say that for me journeys into space, the Moon Landing, influenced my generation. The idea of going beyond the limits of the known world influenced design and aesthetics.

GM In 1968, *2001 A Space Odyssey* came out, Kubrick's film about a journey beyond Jupiter and the infinite, and about the ambiguous sense of surmounting obstacles through the use of technology. This is a process that today seems to me to be highly advanced; just think

of the digital technology that is overturning the analogical world that we have known. All the final part of the film, the journey beyond physical and temporal reality, is a series of examples of photographic and visual effects; among them is the first "journey into hyperspace", kind of acceleration that we can find now in any run-of-the-mill videogame. In the film we can see a lot of the design and fashion around in that period.

NS It seemed that all materials would be synthetic, and plastic was the greatest with these clean forms and the idea of a completely rounded-off piece. For clothes, this was translated into a machine-made garment, without stitching: the thread was put into the machine, the machine started, performed articulated movements and produced a garment. It was like going to the moon: I saw with my own eyes this machine with all its bobbins and lines of threads, and then at a certain point – bang! – there came out this shapeless thing, and it was a dress!

GM Like in *Forbidden Planet*, the 1956 sci-fi film where a robot butler-cum-tailor produces in the space of a minute a dress that fits his mistress's requirements: she describes the style and Roby the robot processes the order; then you see flashing lights and twirling antennas and the dress is ready in a flash... but here we are dealing with the continuation of a feudal kind of production projected into the future. And in fact today it doesn't seem that technical innovation in the field of production has left any particular mark on fashion. For at least ten years lace and trimmings have been popular. Obviously they are showy and cost little to produce in countries with little social protection. Could this be because ours is an epoch of cynical romanticism? There are tens of thousands of machines for making clothes without stitching, seamless garments, but it seems they are only used to produce cheap knitwear.

NS For me, the basic idea was to take a technology used for making an accessory and make it capable of producing a complete garment; in other words, to shift the method for one thing over to another. For me, industrial fashion design is this: to understand the potential of something that already exists and use it to invent something that doesn't. While fashionable designers work without any interest in production processes and invent languages. These can even interest me a lot; they fascinate me at times, but they are something else. These designers do not think of a garment as having any kind of relationship with the human body. When I designed my clothes I was driven, on the one hand, by an interest in research and, on the other, by an attraction to people themselves. I have never made anything constrictive. I could never have made trousers that cling to a woman's buttocks. I have made transparent clothing because that was linked to the freedom of movement; I made a *torchon* that followed the sensual forms of the body, but I have never used adherence as provocation... I do not condemn such things, but they were the last things I had in mind. When I was very young I experienced fashion as something perverse: I find that fashion *is* something very perverse. Today there are many technologies that have a parallel life to fashion, less obvious perhaps, but they are still present. Designers have a new, fundamental role: teaching. I would never have thought of teaching, but today I find that my students are the best there are; they have potential and, if guided, they are able to come up with amazing answers: I believe that teaching, interacting, is something that has to be done; it is like research, I am interested in it... I see the students as aborigines... *digital natives*. They seem ingenuous but are actually full of potential resources.

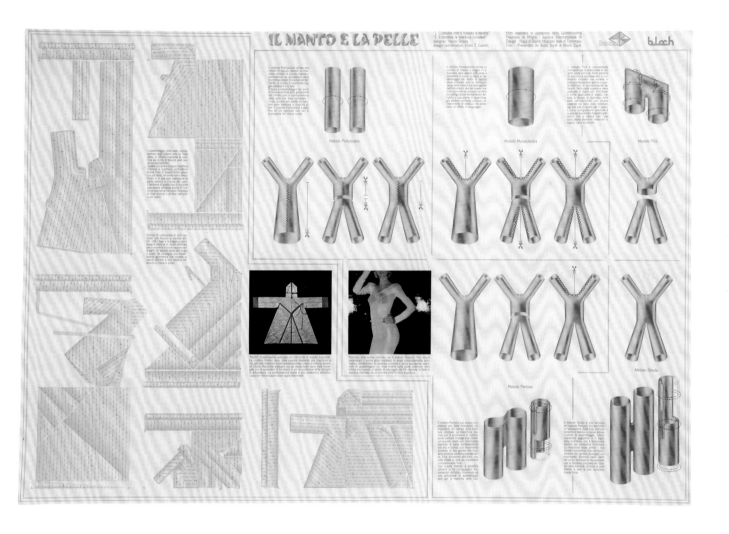

IL MANTO E LA PELLE

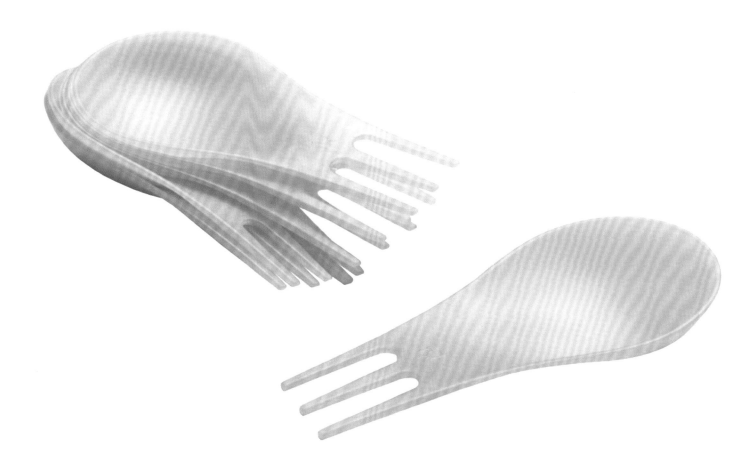

Respect for Nature as a Model for Economic Development

Luca Maroni

Everything that humanity undertakes, including life itself, is based on nature.

The first and deepest conditioner of the human state is nature.

It is impossible to renovate nature unless by respecting its times and conditions.

Awareness and knowledge of such bases have been lost.

And yet... let's consider the Italians who were able to rule the world under the Romans as a result of the unparalleled mildness of our territory and its climate.

And then think about our greatest national treasure: being internationally known and appreciated as the Bel Paese, the Beautiful Land.

And finally, as long as the climate and nature were kindly, never has mankind been able to reach such levels of wellbeing, civilisation and art.

Due to the sum of such considerations, nature should be venerated by us, even more than respected, as the precondition for every condition.

A veneration that is not static and inert, a kind of idealistic alienation, but it is and must be knowledge and application.

Knowledge, application, as well as a respect that is love: the more we respect and love nature, the more its fruit is first-class and of the highest quality. The more the system is economical, the better the producer/beneficiary organism performs.

There are infinite possibilities for illustrating the truth and immanence of such a deductive string of propositions, but here I will use the most ethereal and distinguished example that our country has recently experienced: the Italian wine-producing renaissance.

By doing and considering this, my narrative aim is not to illustrate the validity of the arguments I will mention, but to clarify the ideas of the exceptional prerogatives that derive from respecting nature as the determining beginning and end of the economic development of a system: 1. the many positive aspects of the process; 2. the process's self-generation; 3. the process's universal extensibility.

Towards the end of the 1970s, Italian wine had undergone an essential existential passage. Politics had helped and financed its production with quantity more in mind than quality. Italian vineyards were obsolete with few plants per hectare, few private producers and many new cooperatives whose architecture was notable for the appalling impact of its cement buildings. The sparse plants per hectare fruited regularly and in excess. The few grapes that matured with difficulty had scant resemblance to their congenital heredity of aroma. This was the moment of least respect for nature and for the culture and cultivation of grapes.

In the meantime wine-growing and chemical techniques had developed to the utmost their capacity to make wine sterile, impossible to ferment, antiseptic and inoxidisable so as to guarantee the product's stability by depriving it of all its natural wine-like characteristics and by substituting these with these chemical compounds that had nothing at all to do with grapes. Here too there was an example of minimum respect for nature's fruit.

So: Italian wine-in-the-glass at the end of the 1970s. Little nature and only residual traces of it; a lot of chemicals. From an olfactory point of view: highly acid, uncertain dryness, little perfume and difficult digestion.

And what was the effect on consumption? A crisis in drinking wine every day; perception of the quality of wine became incomprehensible and esoteric; a drastic rise in prices.

Since then there has been an inexorable and unstoppable process of improvement of just one all-important aspect: a respect for nature and its fruit, both from a grape-cultivation and wine-making point of view. Thanks to the private Italian producers' initiative, ability and love for nature; thanks to the veneration that the most illuminated and sophisticated foreigners have always had for Italy and its nature; and thanks to the foresight and cultural standing of such figures as Luigi Veronelli (the greatest promoter of the values of wine and food), it began to be understood that there was only one path to excellence. Respect for nature and its fruit.

Since then every kind of grape has been studied and their particular nature evaluated; each vineyard has been conceived of and realised in such a way as to allow nature the best expression of its constituents. The most beautiful hills in Italy have been planted with vines in the best qualitative arrangement and layout. The vines, the bearers of nature's fruit, are today cared for in every detail and with the greatest and most impassioned rigour: position, cultivation, pruning, fruiting, vegetation, respiration and transpiration. Few grapes hang on the vine, but they are concentrated and intensified in all their best, glycerine-soaked, aromatic alchemy. They are rigorously harvested at the acme of the process: full of juice and that magical balance between acidity and sweetness. A moment of the greatest enhancement and synthesis of their natural constituent essences.

At the same time each firm built wine-stores also constructed with the greatest, and above all aesthetic and formal, respect for the territory and the context in which they were carefully sited. Wine-stores that serve the natural and territorial values they maintain and express. Wine-stores that can hide, stand out against and harmonise with the landscape as elements that are never intrusive but are always functional and architecturally valuable: the beauty and care of buildings as a token and seal of the beauty and quality of the fruit and the place. And then there is the technique and technological infrastructure that they contain. The most sophisticated possibilities for transforming grapes into wine – though in fact only changing their state from a solid into a liquid – with the greatest respect for their original home-grown heritage. We can say that each detail of wine-stores has been conceived, developed and made workable on the principle of respect for the primary quality of the fruit. The principle of quality, we might say, has guided and mapped out each individual choice of the whole production chain, of its transformation, elaboration and confection. Overall, wine-making is both the art of respect and its highest expression.

So let's see now what the result is of this incredible enhancement and respect for nature and for its bounty and transformation.

From 1980 until now, the average consistency of the grapes harvested has increased by 50%: this is, in other words, the aroma, extracts, concentration of components, fullness, expression and potential longevity that have always marked out Italian wines and given them an increased aromatic power that is persistent, long-lasting and incisive. The acidity of the grapes and wine has been progressively reduced, as has the bitterness of their taste. On the other hand, there has been an increase of their more attractive qualities: the spontaneous and particularly grape-like taste which before had been camouflaged by an acid-bitter veil. The perfume of the wine which, until yesterday, had not always been limpid but often partially or completely covered by a mixture of various grapes due to wine-making defects or changes (sulphurous, acidic, milky, evanescent, woody, oxidising) during the fermentation process, are now marvellously integrated: naturally, spontaneously and, at last, universally appreciated as the pure liquid testimonial to the natural synthesis of the nature of grapes.

This is the miracle of nourishment: the more you respect nature and its fruit, the more its analytical composition tends to perfection and the more its most intense pleasure is shared, then the more our organism will be neither intoxicated not simply nourished.

The economic results of such a worthy process are under the eyes obvious to all of us.

There are over 5,000 wine-producing firms in all the twenty regions of Italy with international standards. The invoiced earnings of the sector are 10 billion euros; this means that it is not way off mark to say that its indirect earnings – that is, the income developed by all the outlets for selling wine (wine bars, restaurants, hotels, pubs, big distributors) – are about 10% of Italy's gross domestic product. Italian agricultural foods' financial balance (the relationship between exports and imports), not including wine, is deeply in the red; thanks to wine – the export of which has been constantly growing both in volume and value over the past ten years – it is positively moving towards solvency. Today Italy is universally appreciated as the absolute leader for quality and quantity of wine production.

It is not just the most expensive wines that have radically improved, but also the everyday wines, the producers' most economical ones. Our agricultural biodiversity's richness, with out 450 native species of grape, is unequalled in the world.

Wine, together with other agricultural products, is the only product made in Italy that invites consumers, above all foreigners, to visit the areas where it is produced: it is a primary source for agricultural tourism in our country (some 68% of foreign visitors to our country visit our countryside for reasons of agritourism).

Wine tourism is a sector in increasing expansion and in the future its diffusion and attraction will be even more remarkable. This is because foreigners are deeply in love with our country which, like no other, offers them extremely refined sensations. These are not just sensorial or technical sensations but historical, landscape, artistic, operatic and human ones. The senses of all foreigners are seduced by Italian wines, the highest expression of the naturalistic spirit and soul of this country, of this land, of its beauty and its innate art of wine producing.

There are no other sectors in which all twenty Italian regions are together similarly able to offer the same excellence in terms of the analytical value of production: a celebration of the Italian system, its overall strength, productiveness, uniquely rich variety and its particularly distinctive regional locations. Wine is the only agricultural product whose positive economic gain is almost wholly due to the producers and/or the local economic fabric (the local supply chain is some 80%).

So here are the benefits following one after the other: first taste and smell, then a naturalistic, economic and inclusive respect for nature and its bounty as a model and aim for development. These are effects and not causes and they imply new positive effects: the many-sided positivity implied by adopting respect for nature as a factor and model for developing the economic system.

And as for the ability to feed ourselves by the positive process sparked off by respecting nature... thanks to the success of the earliest, then newer and even futurist techniques of environmentally-friendly production, today we are experimenting with and diffusing biological cultivation, biodynamic agriculture and the change of the whole productive and transformer concern into a business with zero emissions and self-generated power for overall production.

Finally, with regard to the universal application of the process: there is no economic activity that does not gain from a respect for nature. On the contrary, the new frontier is precisely that of economy and industry in harmony with nature. The reconversion of structures and production – not just for agriculture but even more so for industry – from discordant ones to those in harmony with nature, is in itself an enormous boost to the economy: green economy, alternative and renewable economy, the energetic exploitation of air and marine currents.

So, a total respect for nature and an absolute empathy of mankind, its output and its consequent wellbeing: this is the most evolutionary and profitable frontier of tomorrow's world.

So, is everything already underway and is there nothing more to do? No: the spark still has to be detonated.

A cultural spark.

Because the brake on developing respect for nature, a beacon for the whole world, is today only a question of a lack of knowledge and thus of communications.

Let's return to the exemplary heart of this narrative: wine and food. How many Italians have any knowledge, awareness or perception of what has been set out above? Few. All too few.

Until today food and wine, positive emblems respecting nature as a developmental model, as we have seen, have still not been perceived by the majority of the population as such an important entity. In fact their essence and nature have not yet been explained nor have their producers been placed at the centre of the scene. It is now necessary to reveal Wine and Food Italy as a naturalistic, luminous phenomenon and display, an example of beautiful, deserving applied humanity. As a model example to be preserved, emphasised, protected and developed. However, it is necessary to pinpoint the resources and to invest them in training in order to help producers capitalise, commercialise, distribute and protect themselves against counterfeiting. It is absolutely necessary to draw up a plan at once for starting off the Agricultural and Naturalistic Cultural Renaissance of our country.

Think, for example, of the possibility of systemising the naturalistic beauty of our country's wine industry and of placing such an aim at the heart of an International Institutional Communications Campaign. The places where the best Italian wines are produced are the most beautiful and uncontaminated areas of our country: these must be appreciated and linked together in a system of naturalistic Italian wine-producing parks.

Under the aegis of the Ministry of Tourism and of that of Cultural Heritage and Activities, together with the Ministry of the Environment and the Ministry of Agriculture, it should be possible to create a system of naturalistic wine-producing parks, precisely to illustrate – above all from an environmental, landscape and naturalistic point of view – the heritage of our countryside, still completely intact precisely because of our high-quality wine production.

A kind of itinerary through, and a celebration of, the naturalistic richness and beauty of our food-farming: the territory and landscape, its edible and inimitable fruit, as an element-nourishment-monument to be appreciated, protected and made known.

Obviously, a system to communicate and create "usefulness", one that will lead to the development and generation of an added value for the territory and for Italian high-quality wine and food producers and, more generally, for the wine-tourism sector.

This is just as small example but one, however, that allows us to understand how the value and importance of one of the aspects implicit in production can favour the development of its quality through the environment.

We are speaking of cultural communication, of the perception of the importance of food and nature which can once again become an element for family training, sharing and dialoguing; one that can then begin to be transferred into schools and thus be once more a key element in individual civic education.

The greatest heritage of knowledge and value for each citizen of such a stupendous nation.

Italic Creativity and the Everyday

Alberto Abruzzese

There existed the best designers in Italy, even the best in the world, when we did not yet speak of the marvels of globalisation but only of the genius of certain individual creators able to reform our small industries in the wake of international markets. They invented various domestic articles which – because they were lamps or chairs or corkscrews or coffee machines – until then would have been described as humble, trivial or, on the other hand, as "antiques": in other words status symbols for a class of consumers who were well-off or else incapable of renewing their taste or imagery. There were also – to indicate two turning points of Italian society, the early 1970s and the late 1990s – two first-class Italian artists. One was Michelangelo Pistoletto with his *Venere degli stracci* (an extremely eloquent example of a national tradition that experiments, more than other countries, the cohabitation and the reciprocal mirroring of the authority of classicism and, with great foresight, that of rubbish, waste, the ruins of modernity and its utopias). The other is Maurizio Cattelan with his *Nona Ora* (one of the most fascinating comments of an art that leaves behind its institutional chains in order to demystify every social, and therefore religious, institution).

And this show – enriched as it is with names well-known for their fame and influence on the arts and crafts of an world which throughout the whole of Western civilisation is known for its wealthy, civilised and leisure society – is certainly a prestigious one. An extremely ambiguous word: prestige. It is divided between *truth* and *deceit* (in fact, in etymological dictionaries the semantic boundary of the word is quite slender, and so a game of prestidigitation becomes a sign of reputation and, vice-versa, of an authority that is sadly senseless, emptied of its sovereignty). By this I do not mean in any way to diminish the importance of this event. Quite the contrary: the play between enchantment and disillusionment is the quintessence of modern – philosophical and practical – existential theory. And here are to be found the combustibles and the fire at the origins of industrial civilisation and which guaranteed its development. Here the continual occurrence of – micro and macro – social processes wholly consumes its own objects of desire, burns every symbolic resource but, at the same time, produces a new cycle of enthusiasm from its own ashes. All this *at least* until now: and it seems to me right to think about this "at least until now" just before we enter, and even before we leave, the interest in national creativity imagined by the *Italian Uniqueness* exhibition and made up of images.

In just a few lines it is impossible to enter into the details of the cases and lives – the personal styles and collective customs, the media events and even the myths – of the diverse and divergent objects gathered together and thoughtfully arranged into micro-stories that are channelled into a single, unique and great affair: that of *Italic* creativity. Why do I say Italic rather than saying, as would be required by habit or by national pride, *Italian* creativity? I now have the chance to give an answer to this question, not without thanking those who have now offered me the opportunity to do so. So I can attempt to give an answer. At least I can in the few lines allowed to me by a catalogue. In fact, to do it in great style, that is with the documentation and the arguments, would need a lot more. To speak of the difference between Italics and Italians – as Piero Bassetti has been doing for years with his Globus et Locus association – is a far more complex (and far less widely accepted) task than that required of someone to write a short summary of the great flood of Italian design from the 1950s until today. Gillo Dorfles has been doing this since the period of "Civiltà delle Macchine" and, after all these years, there is the risk of repetition.

A show, by attracting crowds, also crowds the mind of the visitor, and so the visitor's catalogue – before and after, on entering and leaving – is both an explanation and a memoir, but also a kind teacher and an alert prompter: usually presumptuous but, at least on occasions, indiscrete and clarifying with respect to the live feeling of the objects on display. Objects that are as influential as they are highly seductive – as in the case of this exhibition. So mine is a suggestion to the visitor in a disturbing guise: no longer whispered but, I hope, scratchy (like sand on the skin) in order to warn of the paradoxes – real conflicts and not the prejudged ones we find in the media – which nestle in the title *Italian Uniqueness*; this is already problematic because it alludes to an important gap between the unity and uniqueness of the territory subject to the government of the state of Italy. It is even more problematic because we are dealing with a show taking place in 2011 and which, therefore, even if we don't like it, falls, precipitates, inside the inevitable celebrative framework of the 150th anniversary of the birth of our nation.

Do not consider me the hidden voice in the prompter's box but, rather, as the figure who, in an unmistakable role that also has a suggestion of the *kiss-of-Judas* or the *diabolical-tempter* about it, bends towards the ear of another: of a neighbour, the person next to you, good people, the righteous person in the village, the happy citizen, the wise man convinced he is right. Of all those people who go to exhibitions, if not to worship the Prince, certainly as a representative of a leading class or who at least think they are. My comment on the show aims at wriggling itself (everything began with a serpent) into the pleasure – into the *suggestion* (something etymologically close to *suggest*) – that takes over whoever inhabits the vision of the objects exhibited in the show and, from this sudden cohabitation, acquires the instruments for producing visitors: a space in which everything, or almost everything, is *beautiful,* or almost beautiful, in

a perfect or perfectible balance of symbolic forms of desire *embodied* in objects modelled for the use and consumption of the markets necessary for a *privileged* daily life, one that is therefore *functional* for the *ratio* that *dominates* it and *impregnates* it with itself (another relationship to suggest: that between *privilege* and *prestige*).

These consumer objects of ours are our daily life; they are extremely realistic, structured, programmatic: they tell us (communicate, share, before your very eyes) completely and wholly what they do and what they produce as social fact. This is the content of their social action – the content that searches for its medium within society – for *existing* and resulting from the consumer's spirit, from the worlds of his imagination. The same thing happens where (a vastness of whole territories or the folds and margins of territory) daily life is originated and undertaken in the sign of desperation rather than happiness (and here, instead of sign, we could cheekily say brand, now that we know the existential, cognitive and affective depths of which a brand is capable). Here – that is, where unhappiness is produced according to economic systems perfectly integrated with those that produce happiness – there dwells flesh that undergoes desperation and pain, flesh because of which the body that imagines its own spirit is a body that can only consume its own desire to consume. The human illusion of desire emerges in this territory of pain in all its violence, because there is no longer any shading between life and death, between those who, in their zero-exchange, are a medium for what is other than themselves and on their own account. I say this in order to avoid that this tragic part of my argument should only be taken as the usual criticism of consumption and of consumerist society. We cannot avoid the natural laws of life's consumption. And the life of consumption.

Once again drunk on creative cities (just think of the success of Richard Florida's book), the intellectuals of humanism and the managers of post-industrial markets state that Beauty will "save us" or, in other words, that its desirable harmony will cleanse the world of every social, economic and ethical vice. They continue to do the same thing that the Hollywood director Carl Denham has been doing for almost a century, beginning with his phantasmagorias from the 1930s; in his journey from one remake to another of the most typical 20th-century western films, he has always continued to pass the same judgement, a progressive and patronising one, in the face of the death of King Kong who, having left the fiction of the theatre, was cut down with the arms of civilisation. Denham reasons with greater socio-anthropological competence than what is said, lying just as much as he does, by the institutions and tools of modern and late-modern culture each time that they base their policies on the light of the spirit and the glossiness of merchandise. The thesis of the director (an emblematic figure for the territorial politics of images) is that who conquered the Beast of Origins, the irreducible body of Sacredness, was Beauty and not technology, not the military planes that kill in order to save and bring happiness. Beauty is the erotic mask of Force, the force of *Star Wars* which anticipated the fall of the Manhattan towers and the peace forces of globalisation. The same one as the science of exclusion that McLuhan attributed to the *languages of seeing*, to the society of writers (the marketing of passions): the cities of Emporiums and of Hollywood, great spaces for the collective subconscious that knowledge looks at and classifies without, however, feeling; in other words, without managing to include them in its own institutions.

This dallying of mine with the myths of Beauty is not impertinent, it is not a digression. Its intention is to sketch an outline for reasoning about the impact between what it might mean to refer to the *uniqueness* of Italian creators, the living testimony of excellence and prestige

in the world, and what instead it might mean to refer to the unity of the nation they belong to – a question, as we know, which is extremely problematic: for the past, for the present and for the future. A dramatic yet fortunately *open* question. I will ask again the question I asked at the start and that I have left open until now: in what sense is their success the expression of *Italic* rather than *Italian* nature? A question which contains another and crucial one: does their success depend on a strong identity, that of a collective patriotic feeling expressed by a culturally and politically unified territory (an identity derived from a Nation State, from that "regime of sense" born in 1861 as a need to resist the pressure of nations which had arisen a long time before Italy)? Or else does it depend on many localisms, each with its own *dialect*, with its own traditions and experiences of the world (the artistic qualities that have their roots in the thousand towns and the thousand "shops" of pre-unity Italy, of the many places that came to life and became a world with the Renaissance)?

I do not like the neo-renaissance rhetoric so fashionable today (yet again the bad lesson of Richard Florida who – as Aldo Bonomi warns us – overlooks, among the emerging values of creativity in the spaces of globalisation, the territory's communities, which are fairly asymmetrical with regard to urban values, to the modern ideologies of the citizens). Even less do I like anti-nationalistic polemics (which, as far as I am concerned, are legitimate but only as long as they express a full assimilation and comprehension of the historical and social needs expressed by movements for national unity: a shattered nation which has not yet been created promises nothing good and therefore needs a pluralistic way of thinking). However, this is how things stand (apart from our television that has a reason for being national because, until yesterday, that was what its programming was all about). Our designers' localism gains a reputation for the very reason that the consumer

objects they create reveal a trans-national attitude. This is because their culture is not rooted in Italian state traditions (the little Italy with its administrative, political and training institutions) but in the flows of globalisation where what is local thinks about, and measures itself against, itself as well as what is global. And it manages to do so thanks to the fact of thinking of imaginary forms that are continually *expanding* beyond the Italian historical confines and increasingly in harmony with the richness of the Italic peoples who, from Roman times, have continued to exist for centuries, have been slow to share in a single state, and who maintain originality even *after* their coerced identification with the role of citizens. Not being guaranteed as such, they became emigrants and scattered around all the nations of the world. And this they did far more as Italics than as Italians.

So this exhibition of half a century of creativity in the world invites us to believe that Beauty hides unheard-of conflicts and manages to become a Form only by expressing itself beyond the simply ideology of unity. But then, the success of creative people is far more than an expression of cosmopolitan dynamics (the sophisticated and, when possible, colonialist side of nationalism): through their work, the Italian image is dissipative far more than cohesive (and in these years the global financing of local points of high quality is one of the most evident aspects of the shattering of a link between creativity and business production which is still entrusted to their presence together on the same physical territory, as well as an administrative, trade-union, juridical and political territory). The success of creative people is realised only when they manage to dominate the market – and this means uniqueness – but only because of the coexistence in them of profound differences. However, as I take my leave from the reader, my suggestion to visitors is to push further ahead and realise – whenever you wish to avoid being caught up by the bad conscience of hu-

manists and entrepreneurs – that the nature of a culture able to affirm itself as a plurality of subjects; it is, therefore, able to break the universalist rules of patriotic feeling. It is not in itself emancipation from the violence of human relationships, a violence that national policies would like to pacify even while exercising it, and that the aesthetics and ethics of Beauty would like to exorcise by dematerialising the suffering of the flesh. This leap forward of creativity as uniqueness rather than unity is not a leap towards a freedom from the centralised and vertical practices of a nation but, rather, it is the overcoming of logics of power in a world of brands. And this is the brand in which human beings as such are immersed: the *imperialist* brand. It is another way of organising the social relationship between servants and masters. I trust that this warning can help the world-beating creativity expressed by the works exhibited in this year celebrating Italian unity to avoid being subject to ideologies and politics. Let's satisfy ourselves by admiring the forms, because this is their aim, their *place*, and because our inclination to beauty has been inculcated into us for centuries.

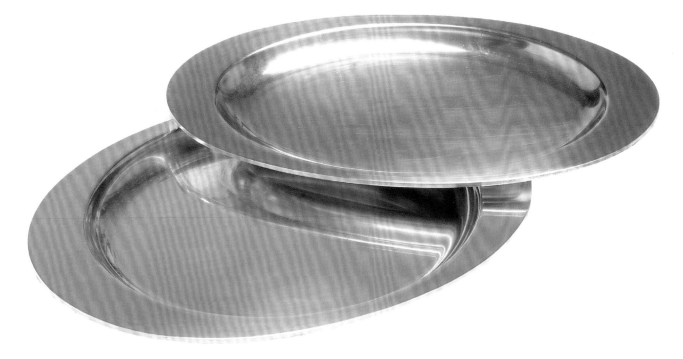

The Conservation and Restoration of Design
The methodological possibilities of the Compasso d'Oro historical collection

Sara Abram

INTRODUCTION

In 2010 a study and research programme for the Compasso d'Oro's historical collection[1] was begun. This project was in tune with the interdisciplinary character of the CCR, the Centro Conservazione e Restauro [the Conservation and Restoration Centre]. At once it became obvious that restorers, diagnosticians, historians and experts in multimedia recuperation[2] had to make observations and deep inquiries even while they were working. Teamwork was thus consolidated, above all teamwork aimed at defining and consolidating a methodological approach that could deal with the specific (and mostly unexplored) theme of restoring industrial design and creating adequate means for recording it.

There does not exist either in Italy or abroad a relevant literature about the best general principles for the conservation and restoration of design objects (whether serial, industrially produced or under the strict control of a plan). In practice, this does not mean that the sphere of restoration has never had to deal with it: by now, not only for the needs of collectors but also for those of museums, industrial design has necessarily obliged the operators in the field to face up to new and extremely diversified[3] types of material, processing and deterioration. In the meantime we have a technical kind of bibliography mainly concerned with the composition and degradation of materials and, of course, most attention is given to plastics[4].

Instead, from the theoretical point of view of restoration there has been a tendency to log design under the heading of contemporary art which, for many aspects, is quite inappropriate: if, in fact, we need to compare materials and (in part) working technologies[5], then a serial and functional product created to be "consumed" must be treated differently to an artist's unique work. Contemporary art and design undergo various contaminations[6], but in the face of the material evidence of the object, what we have to take into account above all is the function it was created to satisfy.

In discussions about design history, conservation is considered to be concerned first of all with ideas about "disposable" products and thus is linked to consumerism and concepts of duration: "Briefly stated, art and everything that has a value apart from its own historicity belong to the culture of salvaging, while to the culture of development there belong everyday artifice and everything that, aimed at comfort and, in general, to the *hic et nunc*, have above all a value for our historicity"[7]. Given the impossibility of restoring a product's original aesthetics, such elements as the designer's originality, commercial value and affective values have all been considered as reasons for potential restoration – even if partial and at times incongruous – by the beneficiary/owner. In the case in hand we are, however, faced with a "historical" collection, one about to be placed in a museum and for which we must take into consideration a greater complexity of meanings.

What are the constitutive elements of an object that is exemplary and representative of the whole Compasso d'Oro historical collection?

OBJECTS AS A RECORD

Each object belonging to this collection reveals at least two aspects: first of all it reflects the Compasso d'Oro award's role, throughout its various editions, as a promoter of industrial design in Italy; more in general, the objects the collection conserves represent from many points of view the evolution of industrial design in Italy.

For the first of these aspects, the award's aim over the years has been marked by its dynamic principles which allow us to see the individual objects in a context of intentions and stimuli that have varied throughout the course of the editions, from the first under the aegis of the large La Rinascente chain of stores, to successive ones pro-

moted by the ADI, up to the most recent developments[8]. So the conservation of the objects in the historical collection, then, must take into account the reasoning behind the award of the prizes: these are both a key to the aims of the organizers and, at the same time, a reflection of a very particular moment in Italian design.

An object such as Zanuso and Sapper's K1340 children's chair, for example, brings together these coordinates: awarded the prize in 1964 for being made completely from plastic, for its optimisation of the industrial use of the material, for its typological and aesthetic characteristics, this modular toy-furniture represented the best of the new forces of technology and thinking that the use of plastic had then managed to catalyse. In that same edition of the Compasso d'Oro three out of the six prizes were awarded for objects in which plastic was preponderant and the awards favoured products conceived with "the aim of communicating their expressive qualification and precise linguistic definition by correctly and reciprocally relating the problem to industrial processes."[9]

Objects in the collection therefore also document (and here we have arrived at the second point) a series of factors linked to the history of design: the worth and nature of the project, the characteristics of production, the materials and their manufacturing technologies, the aesthetics of the object and its link to the society of its users. Restoration must take into consideration each one of these themes and re-establish adequate conditions for the recognisability, legibility and documentation of all the elements that they represent. So design conservation seems to be undertaken according to evaluative categories similar to those of art works, in other words in a reasoned and documented dialogue between aesthetic aspects and historical ones. But it is in fact the second point that makes a huge difference: if we introduce the concept of the useful function of industrial design objects, then it follows that the restorer's choices have been presented with a precise aim.

FUNCTION AS A DISTINCTIVE CHARACTER

The function that an object answers to and, therefore, the use it has been conceived for, not only determines its scope but also represents the main stimulus for developing its design. So the evolution of a form and material answers to needs satisfied by the specific characteristics for undertaking the task and thus influences the aspect that, more than any other, differences design from works of art. It follows then that the conservation and restoration of objects is qualified and distinguished by the relationship established by the restoration of the object's useful function. The need to guarantee the complete usefulness of all the characteristics that determine the performance of furnishing, a utensil or a domestic appliance, can lead to choices for integration or renewal that would be quite unacceptable in the more traditional sectors of restoration.

The options for re-establishing functional conditions have to be given more importance than the object's purely aesthetic aspects. For example, while for the DU30 chair (Gastone Rinaldi for Rima, a 1954 Compasso d'Oro prize-winner) the traces of deterioration resulting from its use might well be acceptable[10], we cannot avoid replacing its polyurethane padding. The impossibility of restoring the specific quality of the seating of this chair (its level of comfort) would in fact deprive us of one of the object's basic characteristics. At the same time we must obviously assume it to be necessary to analyse and document all the materials that have been removed, even more so when (as in the case of foam rubber) we are dealing with materials that have had a leading role in the evolution of furnishing and that have been undergoing constant technical evolution over time.

In the same way, if it were not possible to renew the functional mechanisms of the Doney television set (Zanuso and Sapper for Brionvega, Compasso d'Oro 1962), we would lose a large part of its innovative characteristics[11], and if it were without an aerial we would be impeded from enjoying the set's portability, an aspect that decidedly underlines the distance between a television set and the idea of an item of furnishing. With regard to restoring lost functions and to the possibility of undertaking recognisable and reversible integrative actions (difficult for the eye to see and so there is even more reason for an adequate documentation) the experience garnered in recent years in our conservation and restoration centre in the field of wooden furnishings is what has allowed us to outline the methodology used for design objects[12]. In this last sector, however, restorers must acquire further information: besides coming to grips with the availability of original materials, they must be familiar with the market for modern objects and spare parts. The very concept of spare parts – their availability or otherwise, eventual market networks, and their capillarity and diffusion – is an element that is part of the history of objects and, in particular, of design.

DOCUMENTATION

The plan for intervening on the Compasso d'Oro's historical collection involves a preliminary phase for studying and pinpointing its state of conservation. Just as with the procedures necessary for intervening, we still do not have a way for sharing documentation among colleagues. So the work we undertake in Venaria has had to include the setting up of a databank for individual objects; this includes such historical, technical and conservational data as the object's dates and characteristics, its design and production (technologies and materials), its eventual setting and manner of installation: and all this so as to record the evolution or, at least, the changes of these elements over time. Particular attention is also paid to the observation of packaging systems and materials, partly in order to be able to forestall eventual interactions with the objects, and partly to be able to create a handbook of specific ways for the maintenance, transport, storage and exhibiting of each example.

The documentation sector places great importance on the reconstructions of the Imaging Laboratory which allows the visitor to explore the internal parts of the objects, understand mechanisms and construction technologies, and above all understand their context and manner of use. Particular applications of it have also been studied and experimented with for restoration interventions: for instance by previewing choices for integration or by documenting the object's original aesthetics. For certain furnished settings (such as Ugo La Pietra's Occultamento or the fitted kitchen by Augusto Magnaghi for SAFFA, awarded the prize in 1954) we can show an individual element side by side with the many possibilities for modulating, composing, or installing it.

[1] For the coordinates of the project, undertaken by the Centro per la Conservazione e il Restauro "La Venaria Reale" and by the Fondazione ADI thanks to the sponsorship of the Fondazione Amici del Centro Conservazione e Restauro and the Società Miroglio, we refer you to: La conservazione del design. La Collezione Storica del Compasso d'Oro al Centro Conservazione e Restauro, in "Kermes", n. 80, October-December 2010, p. 19.

[2] The work group, which operates under the supervision of the Laboratori di Restauro (Pinin Brambilla Barcilon) and the Laboratori Scientifici (Annamaria Giovagnoli), is composed of: Marco Demmelbauer, Roberta Genta, Anna Laganà, Paolo Luciani, Massimo Ravera, Sandra Vazquez and Bernadette Ventura (Laboratori di Restauro); Marco Nervo and Anna Piccirillo (Laboratori Scientifici); Sara Abram and Elena Bozzo (Centro di Documentazione); Elena Biondi, Alessandro Bovero and Thierry Radelet

(Laboratorio Imaging). The management of the project is assisted by Enrico Morteo and Alessandra Fontaneto for the Fondazione ADI, together with the collaboration of Giacomo Cesaro and Michele d'Innella.

[3] In the case of Italy, we must mention the creation of a restoration workshop within the Milan Triennale's museum.

[4] As an Italian example of the research into the characterisation of plastic materials, mention should be made of the work by the Fondazione Plart, Naples, together with university bodies and institutes. One of the most interesting experiences at an international level has resulted from the collaboration between Axa and the Vitra Design Museum in Weil am Rhein: the results of the project, undertaken between 2003 and 2006, were published in Plastic Art - A precarious Success Story, Cologne, Axa Art Research Grant, 2007.

[5] As was shown by the Conservation Committee of the International Council of Museums (ICOM-CC) with its joining together of "Modern Materials" and "Contemporary Art" into a single work group on the occasion of the three-yearly congress held in Rio de Janeiro in 2002.

[6] Like, for example, someone like Gaetano Pesce, the supporter of "unique works" of design and of the concept of "diversified industrial series": from this point of view the designer in contemporary society, and completely freed from the applied arts, embodies the role once claimed by artists.

[7] R. De Fusco, Storia del design, Rome-Bari, Laterza, 2002 (1st ed. 1985), p. 317.

[8] For these, reference should be made to the articles in this catalogue.

[9] Quoted in A. Pansera, Storia del disegno industriale italiano, Rome-Bari, Laterza, 1993, p. 167.

[10] For objects obtained from the market, or that have been used, wear and tear must be taken into account as indicators of the objects' vicissitudes and/or, just as a record must in any case be made of all those elements that testify to the context of their use.

[11] The first Italian television set that was completely transistorised, portable, functioning with a rechargeable battery or directly from the mains. Even if we made the television work again, it would still work only for a short time, given the evolution of television signals (which will shortly only be transmitted with digital technology).

[12] Il Restauro degli arredi lignei. L'ebanisteria piemontese: studi e ricerche, edited by C.E. Spantigati, S. De Blasi, Collana "Archivio", n. 3, Florence, Nardini Editore (in preparation).

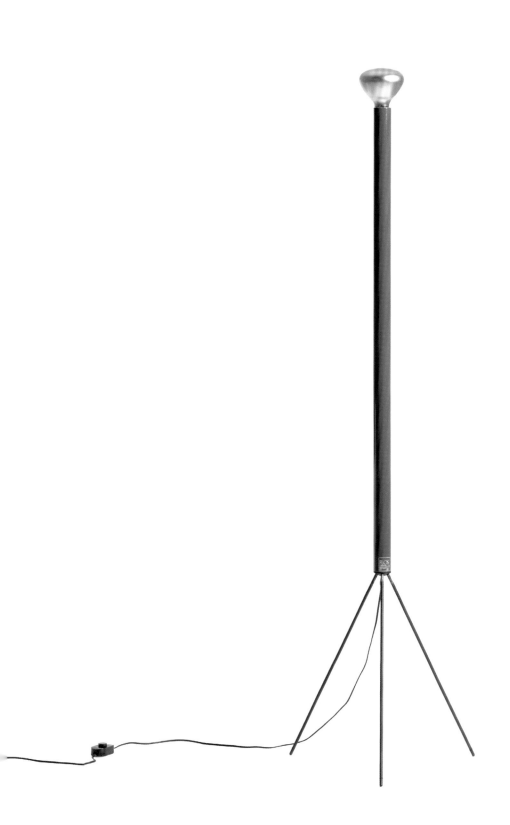

Industrial Design and Juridical Protection: the Rules, Market and Creativity Compared

Giovanni F. Casucci

Design is something that sums up a whole series of factors and values. The ICSID (International Centre for the Settlement of Investment Disputes; this is an organization responsible to the World Bank. It acts as a peacemaker or mediator in investment disputes between States and private foreign investors about bilateral agreements between the interested countries) defined it as an element for the "humanisation" of technology; a kind of necessary interface between technological opportunities and the restrictions (or peculiarities) of the first users: human beings.

In the face of such a "mission", and quite apart from whether we agree with it or not, I believe that when we speak of design we need to take into consideration that we are talking about a "result".

Design is what results from the perception (under many aspects, not just visual ones but also tactile ones, for example) of a group of characteristics aimed for and proposed by its creator.

This idea is shared by community legislators who are concerned not so much with the designer's aims as with its final effect and, above all, with the objective "impressionist" effect that it generates.

So it is possible that a designer might try to propose, unsuccessfully, a design whose overall impression does not reveal the aims it was planned for; in other words, its intended content is not perceptible.

And so it is possible that a designer might try to propose a project with an overall impression giving no sign of its inherent content and which gives us no clue as to what it is for.

This does not mean that the designer's "unperceived" contribution has no absolute value: we must look for ways of evaluation and protection different from those legally recognised by regulations for design and models.

Today we can pinpoint at least four levels of legal protection for design:
1. protection by registration (national, international and European Community);

2. protection from unfair competition and the community's non-registered design;

3. protection for authors' rights;

4. protection of three-dimensional registered trademarks (national, international and European Community).

Furthermore, these various forms of protection (which can also be invoked contemporaneously) have quite different limits and conditions of coverage from each other.

We will now examine them in detail.

PROTECTION BY REGISTRATION

The protection for design indicated in EU (98/71) and national directives (Codice di Proporietà Industriale) is, in my view, a kind of conceptual link between the following: the awarding of patents for inventions in which an inventor is given an exclusive right in exchange for their inventive lesson which, after twenty years, will become part of the public domain of knowledge; and the discipline of registered trade marks for which the protection of exclusivity is not based on any kind of concessional recognition but, rather, on the right to claim that the use of the trademark used for identifying a person or activity is protected from imitations and a conduct likely to confuse.

In fact design, like patents, after a certain maximum time limit (25 years) has to be considered as part of the public domain even though it has no claim to promoting knowledge but only an "effect".

What is more, the effect contained (and aimed for) in a design product is certainly not a semantic or identifying effect as with trademarks which lead the end user to recognise the provenance or the firm which created it.

The regulation, on the contrary, only accepts that design has the capacity of immediately characterising the "designed" product in order to make this product recognisable and distinguishable in some way from other similar products so as to attract in the eye of others for its diversity.

But who is the real interlocutor for a design product? The consumer? No, the consumer benefits from the end product but does not necessarily "dialogue" with it. He or she is the person who is "captured" by the design of a product and gives preference to one product rather than to another.

The interlocutor, instead, is the person who makes use of the design as an attraction and enticement for being bought by the consumer.

The regulation, in fact, holds that a design merits protection if in the eyes of "an informed user" it appears different from other designs in the same context. Such a difference, however, must be adequate to produce a result that makes the design recognisable.

There are those who, without entering into the reasonable business perspectives, have held that such a concept is a juridical fiction, that there does not exist a genuine figure of an informed user and that, at the most, we can speak of an attentive and curious consumer.

Those who have such an approach just cannot imagine that there can be a primary "user" for design. But contrarily to what they affirm, instead our "informed user" exists in reality and is the very person who considers design to be the best vehicle for selling a functional product: the head of strategic marketing for a firm or the manager of the acquisitions sector of a concern based on the distribution of the chosen products. Both these figures "use" design as a competitive element in order to influence the purchasing choice of the end user.

In light of these considerations it seems evident that a design merits being protected if for the "competitive" user it is suitable to attract, unlike other forms, the eye of the consumer in his or her choice of a functional product.

So my conclusion is that the regulation is aimed at protecting only one of the aspects typical of design: in other words, its competitive "eye appeal" attraction is protected by the exclusive rights of those who have invested in the characterisation of a product in the face of other products that have a "perceptive effect" unjustifiably similar to what characterises the first.

So the range of protection, then, is particularly wide and aimed at protecting the registered design, not only from identical imitations, but also from "camouflaged" variants that do not produce a different aesthetic effect from the one that has been registered.

The vulnerable element among these criteria for protection is that at the expiration of the maximum term for protection foreseen in various countries (25 years in the European Union, 20 years in the USA and only 10 years in China, for example) the design would become part of the public domain thus legitimizing a copy by whoever wanted to do so.

THE MARKET AND DESIGN: PROTECTION OF UNREGISTERED DESIGN AND UNFAIR COMPETITION

So according to this assumption, it is clear that regulations have abandoned the concept of gratifying aesthetics and of awarding what is "beautiful".

What is protected is the inherent right of a product (characterised by its design content) to maintain and defend its own difference in comparison with imitations.

On the basis of this position we can understand why in the area of the community's design institution the need has been felt for adopting the figure of "non-registered design".

Such a juridical institution aims at giving a form of protection for those who have not registered (or have not been able to register) the design characterising their own products. The logic is obvious: the fact of not having done so must not expose the creators of a design to the risk of seeing themselves unjustly and unknowingly copied by unfair competitors.

Note that the defence of unregistered design can be opposed only in cases of "copying", in the sense of the intentional copying of its characteristic elements by third parties. So the sanctions are applied in all those cases of undoubted voluntary illegality or considerable harm to the proprietor of the design.

In light of this it would seem strange to maintain that the three years foreseen by the regulation is aimed at defining a maximum general duration for the claims of the proprietor of the design thus, as a consequence, legitimating any kind of imitative behaviour such as the harmful imitation of the product after the fateful three years.

Such a reading is I believe both deviated and deviating: the imitation of the elements characterising or conferring individuality on a product is punished (in almost all up-to-date legislation) as slavish imitation or the passing off of something as one's own in the area of unfair competition.

Such protection is aimed at offering a form of competitive protection based on the interests of the market and competitors, and on the fact that fair competition cannot be undermined by confusing, imitative or parasitic conduct.

From such a viewpoint, then, the protection from unfair competition that has been agreed on is undertaken when there is a competitive relationship while the design product is still on the market (and is not considered as being generic and unspecific: commonplace, in other words).

Therefore the duration of competitive protection from imitative behaviour has no absolute limit but only a relative one: protection is given as long as there is a juridically relevant interest to be protected. The period of three years envisaged by the community only serves

to help the proprietor of the design to demonstrate this interest, which is assumed to last for three years, and that must instead be demonstrated market by market, territory by territory, in the post-three-year period.

And so as far as I am concerned it is perfectly reasonable that protection of unregistered design is a form of codification of a competitive rule with the aim of harmonising it over all the community's territory; thus it confers a presumptive concession of the proof of interest to act in favour of the proprietor for three years, allowing the proprietor of the design free to invoke protection against unfair competition only in the territories or markets in which he was effectively the first to sell the design product and in which he has a concrete and actual interest.

Competitive protection, what is more, is not particularly harmonised at a European and international level: there is only the Paris international convention that limits itself to stating generically (article 10 bis) that: "Any act of competition contrary to the honest use of industrial or commercial material constitutes an act of unfair competition."

What is often asked for in various regulations is that an imitation is also accompanied by the aim to create confusion about the origins of the merchandise, something often excluded because a slavish imitation might blatantly display a different brand mark or have a different way of being presented or priced to the public in a way that is markedly different from that of the original. Only a few regulations sanction an imitation, even if it does not create confusion but is clearly a copy of the original (such as for example the concept of the American *Trade Dress*).

In this sense an important tool is represented by ADI's self-disciplinary code, according to which:

4. Considered unfair and thus to be avoided are the imitation or abu-

sive or unreasonable exploitation of the results of other people's work. In particular we consider unfair the reproduction of another's work, without any original or innovative changes, and the exploitation of other people's labour.

5. It is necessary to avoid the imitation and systematic exploitation of the forms, lines, colours and in any case the meaningful elements of other people's industrial design objects. This principle must be applied with particular rigour when the imitative parts might fool the consumer about the provenance of the products.

According to this, simple unjustified imitation is penalised, and in the case of wilful confusion or deceit the situation is aggravated.

However, even in the best circumstances, given that we are dealing with coverage based on the protection of the market-position of the first businessman to operate (supposing him to be the legitimate possessor of the rights to the design) a coverage that is aimed at eliminating illicit copiers, such a system offers no advantages in the case in which a legitimate proprietor is late in arriving on his referential territorial market after copies have already made their first appearance. This is what happens to many businesses which, after having made their first commercial and distributive initiatives in EU countries, arrive with a certain delay on the Asian or American markets and so find themselves in a field already flooded with imitations (obviously without having registered anything first).

CAN DESIGN BECOME A SIGN?

In certain countries there is the abstract possibility of registering the actual form of the product as a three-dimensional trademark. This solution offers an extremely important advantage: that of transforming the duration of the exclusive right into periods of ten years which are renewable without limits, except for the single condition of actually

using the form as a sign uninterruptedly for more than five years.

There have been important acknowledgments of such initiatives, as in the case of the Fiat Brno Chair of the Naguchi Table in the USA. But there have also been important delusions such as in the case of the clover-shape of the Philips razor which (after almost twenty years of life as a registered mark), despite its full recognisability by the public, was declared void after the first serious case brought against an imitation made by Remington.

In fact, in the European system there is a limit to the registration as a trademark of functional forms or at least those that confer a "substantial value on the product". It is evident that because of this last (and enigmatic) definition it could be held that forms that cannot be registered might be more attractive to the consumer than a representation of the symbols of the producing firm's image.

IN SEARCH OF A DEFINITION OF "ARTISTIC VALUE"

So far we have analysed one of the characteristics of design – its capacity to attract competition – without inquiring into another characteristic: the capacity to express content.

The protection of design in Europe has seen, and still sees, various perspectives and aims opposed to each other: there are such countries as France which recognise design as an expression worthy of protection by authors' rights *tout court*, and then there are others such as Italy which seem to be afraid of giving too extensive protection.

In fact it was Italy, obliged in 2001 by EU directive 98/71 to abandon the concept of "severance" which made it difficult to apply the protection of authors' rights to industrial design, that attempted to insert a new but similar limit on such protection: "artistic value", a condition requested by the law for authors' rights only for works of industrial design.

The introduction of this requisite (which had also been proposed by other countries) obviously creates an interpretative barrier for a judge asked to evaluate if a work of design can benefit from a protection unlinked to registration rules or to a position on the market.

An indispensible assumption for attributing a certain artistic value to a particular form is represented by the definition of the concept of "art".

This is not an absolute concept, but it is necessarily linked to the historic moment in which such an evaluation has to be made. We cannot in any way limit ourselves to a "classical" concept of art: it is necessary to go further and define it in relationship to the situation in which it is destined to exist.

The modern concept of "art" has to be attributed to any work that allows a redefinition of a personal process for the redefinition of reality. On the basis of this we can consider art as being everything that results from a vision proposed by an artist, quite apart from its technical or functional aims.

There are also those who have expressed, in other contexts, substantially similar opinions, revealing, in defining the concept of art, that we are dealing with "a term which has such an enormous complexity of meanings as to be by now of indeterminate vagueness [...]. For this reason there are constantly to be found in the field of art such creative expressions as fashion, design and cinema, while the ancient muses have learned to come to grips with new means: and so we will continue to see painting, sculpture, architecture, poetry and music, but without having to take into consideration the hierarchy of 'fine' of 'applied' arts. With this double path in mind (on the one hand the evolution of the traditional 'arts' and, on the other, the widening of the concept of new creative horizons [...], we are ready to recognise the aesthetic value of a lamp, a car, or even simply of a fork or a

corkscrew: design has established itself as one of the most perceptible forms of creative activity, especially for its close interaction with the industrial production that makes it available to all" (Stefano Zuffi, *Grandi Arti Contemporanee*, Vol. 1, Milan, Mondadori, 2004).

In line with these opinions is what has been said by another authoritative expert, Fabiani, according to whom artistic value ought to be recognised each time a work is seen to possess an "autonomous representative value".

Personally, I believe that artistic value is to be found in all cases in which the design object is an occasion for communicating a social value and a cultural meaning, which is the real mission of design and designers.

Such thoughts lead us to see that two possibilities for design might be suggested in abstract: a design whose function is limited to a mere characterisation for marketing and, instead, one which incorporates a superior message (in cultural or semantic terms) which is expressed by the product.

In this sense, even if in an as yet intricate manner, certain Italian tribunals have expressed their point of view, something which allows us to hope in an increasing mental and cultural receptiveness towards this vision which represents the normal cultural views of professional designers.

The recent Flos case – with a precautionary decision by the Milan tribunal (2007) then recognised as genuinely existing and to be held in consideration also for works created before 2001 (thanks to the decision of the courts of justice on January 27 2011) – has given full recognition to the artistic value of an Arco lamp by the Castiglioni brothers on the grounds that it was an object that had already been chosen by museums as an "icon" of design.

If this remains the line followed by Italian law, then it is necessary to pose another question about the time allowed for such artistic value. Until now (in the cases of Vitra, Flos, Gio Ponti and Le Corbusier) the comparison was with works that were at least thirty or forty years old. But in what way can we estimate the artistic value of works created five or ten years ago?

In this sense a basic role for attributing such value must necessarily be expressed by entities that can help and guide national and international law in concretely establishing "artistic value", "art" (and suchlike) in relatively young works. The awarding of prizes and recognitions such as the famous Compasso d'Oro or the ADI Design Index certainly have an essential role: it is necessary for this role to be clearly recognised by the legal world, not only in Italy but abroad.

In fact, the great advantage offered by authors' rights is in recognising (thanks to the Bern international convention) without territorial boundaries (and so throughout the world) and without great formality, the protection of authorial rights for works and against unauthorized replicas. And this for seventy years after the death of the author the work is attributed to.

It is evident that historically successful works without any kind of protection could count on this last bulwark against the kind of parasitism masked as some demagogical initiative for "beauty for all".

So the mission of those (such as ADI) who recognise and indicate to the whole world the excellence of design and its icons is fundamental.

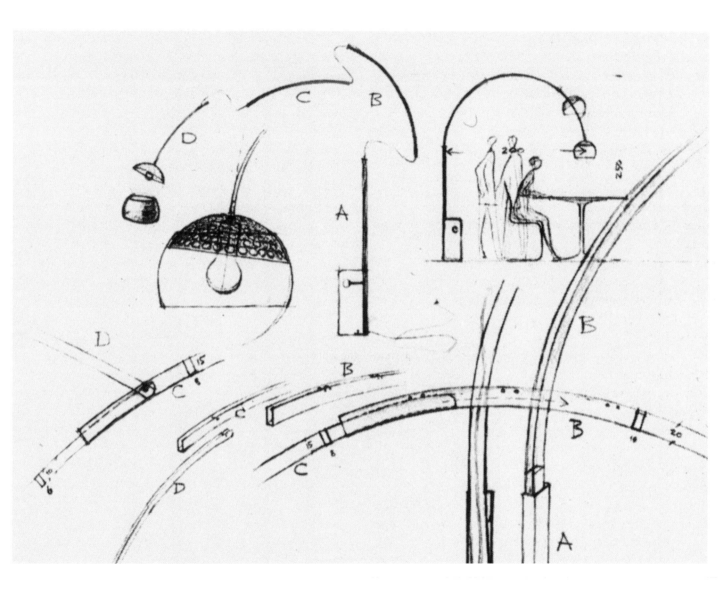

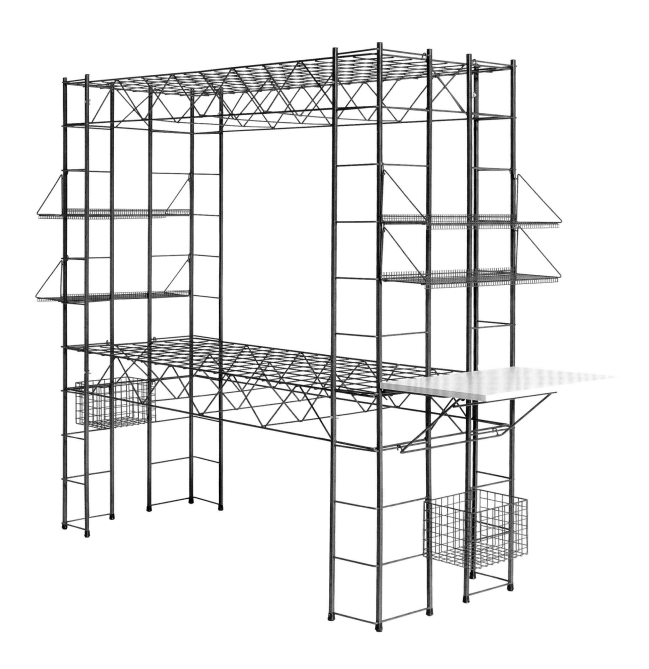

Invention and Imitation: Defending Creativity

Massimo Arlechino

We have come to the end of the *Italian Uniqueness* journey. A journey that the reader has undertaken through the pages of this catalogue and, I hope, as a visitor to the two shows that the Fondazione Valore Italia has organised in Rome in the summer of 2011 as its contribution to the festivities for the hundred and fiftieth anniversary celebrations of Italian unity.

This has been a great effort and I must thank the curator, Enrico Morteo, ADI, Enzo Eusebi the artistic director, and all the team of the Fondazione. We have, with the historical collection of the premio Compasso d'Oro, attempted to analyse the evolution of Italian-made production over the past fifty years and to see how our country has changed together with its production.

Without false modesty, what has emerged is that we Italians have had a capacity unique in the world for putting together great manufacturing ability, an inherent taste for beauty, a search for what is marvellous and sales ability: this mixture has given rise to an industrial production marked out by many small businesses, all able to produce quality of the highest level and to challenge the mighty industries of Europe and America. The four musketeers of Italian production (automation-mechanics; interior design; clothing-fashion; and food-farming) have led us to become one of the most industrialised countries in the world, despite the smallness of our territory and our complete lack of raw materials.

Our fifty-year period opens in 1961 with an Italy that, after the destruction during the war, made the most of the American Marshall Plan's financing and in the space of fifteen years had pulled itself up by its bootstraps. 1960 was probably the highpoint of the national economic boom, with the lira recognised as the most stable currency in the world. There was the will do work, enthusiasm for growth, and a great optimism for the future. The celebrations for the first hundred years of unity saw Turin become a modern metropolis, with a monorail winding like a serpent through an area designed by the greatest architects of the age; Rome, having just hosted the last Olympics to be remembered as having "a human face", now had a super-modern airport, and the whole world of show business, Hollywood included, was attracted by Cinecittà and the dolce vita. Our chemical industry led the world, under the guidance of a Nobel Prize winner who knew how to unite pure and applied research for the development of the industrial process; we also had a petrol industry that was battling on equal terms with the "Seven Sisters". Our network of infrastructures (motorways, railways, electricity system) were young and modern and able to fully satisfy the demand of the period. The banking system was happy to invest in new initiatives.

Our small businesses had, therefore, a solid base, one consisting of security, trust in the future, an excellent system of infrastructures and, all things considered, a certain political stability (despite the dizzying and at times schizophrenic changes in the make-up of the government).

In such a stable context our businesses could devote themselves to developing their real treasure: creativity.

All the Italian products of these fifty years were basically the outcome of great inventiveness. A resourcefulness that was in turn the result of a millennial culture that led the inhabitants of the Boot to be immersed in a context in which art was present everywhere. Our population absorbed beauty as though by osmosis, simply by being receptive to all the wonders that surrounded them, and then spontaneously transformed it in their craftsmanship.

The production made in Italy in the post-war period resulted from this skill: the high quality craftsmanship transfused into serial (re)production.

But the history of those fifty years also shows how the conditions present in 1961 slowly worsened, until we arrive in 2011 when our productive system finds that it has to fight in a completely different context.

I will not list here the various firsts that our country has lost in this arc of time: the reader knows very well what they are. At times we lost them due to inexperience; at times because there reappeared on the world scene countries which, after a long period of lethargy, regained the place that they deserved in the world.

But one first, however, we have held on to: our know-how.

So *Italian Uniqueness* intends to be the occasion for celebrating our country's birthday but, above all, a way for stimulating all Italians to be aware of the challenges that lie in wait for our productive system in the near future.

Culture, traditions, and know-how are the characteristics that mark out our country and our sense of belonging to it. When we say "made in Italy", we are referring to Italian culture, to Italian traditions and to Italian know-how. To defend production made in Italy means, then, to defend all these values.

Probably certain great changes provoked by globalisation are by now unstoppable: we cannot try to mop up the ocean with a dishcloth. The traditional manufacturing sectors, in which Italy excels, have shifted their barycentre eastwards, leaving Italian factories in an almost peripheral territory. The economists consider such sectors (textiles, shoemaking, furniture etc.) as "decocted" because of the high number of employees they need and because of the scarce added value they produce; many maintain that more advanced countries can no longer allow themselves to maintain these productive sectors which are incapable of facing up to Asiatic competition; they should, instead shift their industrial policies towards those sectors with a

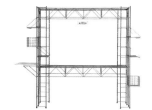

higher degree of innovation. Italy is at a crossroads: what's to be done?

I believe that it is not completely true that the traditional sectors have a low level of innovation. And I also hold that a high density of workers is not in itself a misfortune. The problem is *how* this workforce is to be applied. If we have an expert workforce which feels in its bones that it is the heir to Michelangelo and Raphael, then this high intensity workforce can only be good for Italy.

Our economic system must obviously be aimed towards the sectors of greatest innovation (precision electronics, aerospace, nanotechnology, biotechnologies etc.) but it must not forget its tradition. What we need is to find a new way of applying Italian creativity, the heritage of our tradition and culture, to new economic and technological conditions and then to know how to import the results of this process into the most typical sectors of Italian manufacture. It is obvious that we can never compete with the huge volumes of the Asian tigers' productivity, but we can continue to be those who produce objects of quality and beauty for the rest of the world, and like no one else in the world. Competition today, above all in "decocted" sectors, is carried out on mainly immaterial factors; it is real and perceived quality that leads to victory on the global market, from aesthetics to the importance of the brand and to the capacity to use new materials and technologies: these are the driving forces with which fashion, design and mechanics fight their battles every day.

For the Italy of the future there will, above all, prevail the immaterial part of the productive process, so what will be fundamental for maintaining competitiveness is knowing how to protect it adequately. And today this protection is obtained by caring for one's own rights to intellectual and industrial property.

Brands, models and patents must increasingly become familiar concepts for our productive system: only they can allow us to activate a real and material protective strategy for a process which is, instead, immaterial in itself. These are acts of law that permit, in a material form, the possession of an immaterial paternity: the paternity for an idea, for a creative process.

The imitation of a product really is a theft of other people's creativity. If it is true that our country is based, and was based for the past fifty years, on our creativity to the point of being identified with it, then the conclusion is obvious: an imitation of an Italian product is a theft of Italy itself!

If an Italian undertaking does not register its own brand or design, how can it then act against imitations and fakes? So we can understand the importance for the next few years of developing an *awareness of industrial property* among our businesses and consumers.

For years Italian institutions have been developing an important reform of the patenting system, in the attempt to make it easier for businesses and research centres to register intellectual and industrial property: from information about the procedures to the lessening of taxes; an intense promotion of information throughout the territory; the training of specialised personnel in chambers of commerce; and the setting up of anti-counterfeiting centres in various foreign markets. In recent years this work has been accompanied by in increase in deterrents against counterfeiters, the institution of special anti-counterfeiting sections in tribunals for infringing property or industrial rights, and a process of coordination between the various public administrations engaged in the fight against fakes which culminated in the recent setting up of a national anti-counterfeiting council.

The Fondazione Valore Italia wants to make its own contribution to this and aims at doing so mainly through educating the consumers. It is important that the end user is able to distinguish, not just the

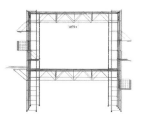

original product from the fake one but, above all, to discern the greater – and not just economic – value given to an original product precisely because of the creative idea that is at its heart. The exhibition part of *Italian Uniqueness* aims at reaching this objective: to allow the visitor to understand the value of the creative and design idea from which Italian products start out, not just the most exclusive models, but also those of daily use. It was not by chance that the historical collection of the premio Compasso d'Oro does not contain a Ferrari but lemon-squeezers and vacuum cleaners.

Our hope is that *Italian Uniqueness* might be remembered as a beautiful show about Italian productive excellence and, above all, as a moment in which we all became aware of our responsibility to protect and hand down such an important heritage, a heritage that Italy must increase because it has become a determining factor for our national identity. A heritage which in Rome will soon have a new and prestigious venue in the Palazzo della Civiltà Italiana: the *Esposizione Permanente del Made in Italy e del Design Italiano*.

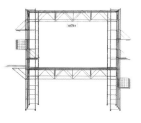

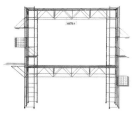

The Compasso d'Oro Juries

1954
Aldo Borletti, Cesare Brustio, Gio Ponti,
Alberto Rosselli, Marco Zanuso

1955
Aldo Borletti, Cesare Brustio, Ernesto N. Rogers,
Alberto Rosselli, Marco Zanuso
INTERNATIONAL COMMISSION FOR THE MAIN PRIZES
Ivan Matteo Lombardo, Tommaso Gallarati Scotti,
Umberto Brustio, Herbert Read, Gio Ponti

1956
Aldo Borletti, Cesare Brustio, Franco Albini,
Pier Giacomo Castiglioni, Alberto Rosselli
INTERNATIONAL COMMISSION FOR THE MAIN PRIZES
Ivan Matteo Lombardo, Tommaso Gallarati Scotti,
Umberto Brustio, Johannes Itten, Ludwig Gröte,
Giulio Carlo Argan, Franco Albini

1957
Aldo Borletti, Cesare Brustio, Franco Albini,
Pier Giacomo Castiglioni, Ignazio Gardella
INTERNATIONAL COMMISSION FOR THE MAIN PRIZES
Ivan Matteo Lombardo, Tommaso Gallarati Scotti,
Aldo Borletti, Johannes Itten, Misha Black,
Giulio Carlo Argan, Mario Labò

1959
Bruno Alfieri, Vico Magistretti, Giulio Minoletti,
Augusto Morello, Giovanni Romano
INTERNATIONAL COMMISSION FOR THE MAIN PRIZES
Franco Albini, Giulio Carlo Argan, Aldo Borletti,
Silvio Coggi, Ivan Matteo Lombardo, Tomás Maldonado,
Pierre Vago

1960
Lodovico Belgiojoso, Vico Magistretti,
Augusto Magnaghi, Augusto Morello, Marco Zanuso
INTERNATIONAL COMMISSION FOR THE MAIN PRIZES
Franco Albini, Aldo Borletti, Silvio Coggi, Hans Curiel,
Kaj Franck, Ivan Matteo Lombardo, Marcello Nizzoli

1961
INTERNATIONAL COMMISSION FOR THE MAIN PRIZES
Franco Albini, Cesare Brustio, Kaj Franck,
Tomás Maldonado, Nikolaus Pevsner

1962
Giulio Castelli, Franco Momigliano, Augusto Morello,
Bruno Munari, Gian Battista Pininfarina

1964
Dante Giacosa, Vittorio Gregotti, Augusto Morello,
Bruno Munari, Gino Valle

1967
Aldo Bassetti, Felice Dessì, Gillo Dorfles,
Tomás Maldonado, Edoardo Vittoria
SELECTION COMMITTEE FOR THE MAIN PRIZES
Aldo Bassetti, Giulio Castelli, Enzo Frateili, Pio Manzù,
Eduardo Vittoria

1970
Franco Albini, Jean Baudrillard, Achille Castiglioni,
Federico Correa, Vittorio Gregotti, Roberto Guiducci,
Albe Steiner

1979
Angelo Cortesi, Gillo Dorfles, Augusto Morello,
Arthur Pulos, Yuri Soloviev

1981
François Barré, Cesare De Seta, Martin Kelm,
Ugo La Pietra, Pierluigi Spadolini

1984
Cini Boeri, Douglas Kelley, Antti Nurmesniemi,
Giotto Stoppino, Bruno Zevi

1987
Angelo Cortesi, Rodolfo Bonetto, Marino Marini,
Cara McCarty, Philippe Starck

1989
Pierluigi Molinari, Fredrik Wildhagen,
Hans Wichmann, Cesare Stevan, Tomás Maldonado

1991
Silvio Ceccato, Marcello Inghilesi, Victor Margolin,
Pierluigi Molinari, Antti Nurmesniemi

1994
Dante Giacosa, Vittoriano Viganò, Giovanni Anceschi,
Paola Antonelli, Uta Brandes, Jacob Gantenbein,
Marja Heemskerk, Vittorio Magnago Lampugnani,
Marco Migliari, Gian Emilio Monti, Mario Trimarchi

1998
Achille Castiglioni, Giuseppe De Rita,
Marianne Frandsen, Fritz Frenkler, Sadik Karamustafa,
Tomás Maldonado, Marco Zanuso

2001
Marie-Laure Jousset, Filippo Alison,
François Burkhardt, Omar Calabrese, Francisco Jarauta,
Maurizio Morgantini, Erik Spiekermann

2004
Gillo Dorfles, Fulya Erdemci, Robert Fitzpatrick,
Pietro Petraroia, Richard Sapper, Angela Schönberger,
Tomáš Vlček

2008
Mario Bellini, Moh-Jin Chew, Lieven Daenes,
Carla Di Francesco, Carlo Forcolini, Norbert Linke,
Emanuele Pirella, Richard R. Whitaker

cover, graphic project,
editing and layout
Sergio Brugiolo, Chiara Romanelli
Studio Polo 1116, Venezia

first edition
May 2011
ISBN 978-88-317-1021

www.marsilioeditori.it

colour separation
Fotolito Veneta, San Martino Buonalbergo (VR)

printed by
Gruppo Editoriale Zanardi s.r.l., Maniago (PN)
for
Marsilio Editori® s.p.a., Venezia

edition

10 9 8 7 6 5 4 3 2 1

year

2011   2012   2013   2014   2015